THE JUSTIFICATION
OF INDUCTION

Edited by

RICHARD SWINBURNE

OXFORD UNIVERSITY PRESS

1974

CONTENTS

INTRODUCTION[1]

AN argument or inference proceeds from one or more premises to a conclusion. An argument is a valid deductive argument if all that it does is to reach a conclusion tacitly contained in the premises, that is a conclusion such that it would be self-contradictory to assert the premises but to deny the conclusion. In such a case we say that the conclusion follows deductively from the premises. Arguments which purport to be deductively valid are assessed as valid or invalid. An argument is valid if the conclusion does indeed follow deductively from the premises, invalid if it does not. An example of a valid deductive argument is:

Premise 1:   John, James, and Gerald are the only men in that room.
Premise 2:   At least one man in that room has red hair.
Premise 3:   John and James do not have red hair.
Conclusion: Gerald has red hair.

If we admit the premises we have to admit the conclusion on pain of self-contradiction.

However, most of the inferences which we make in common life are not valid deductive ones, nor are many of the inferences which scientists make professionally. When I argue from the premises that the 8.30 a.m. bus to town has seldom been late in the past, and that the time is now 8.35 a.m., to the conclusion that today's bus has gone, my argument is not deductive. I do not contradict myself if I admit the premises but deny the conclusion. Maybe today the bus has been held up at an earlier stage of its journey, and so is late. Or maybe the driver is on strike today and the bus will not run at all. Nevertheless it would generally be supposed that in the absence of further evidence the first premise shows that these latter are unjustified suppositions. (It shows that the bus is not usually held up or its driver usually on strike.) We judge that the premises make it reasonable for us to accept the conclusion, even though no contradiction is involved in asserting the premises but denying the conclusion.

Arguments which, it is claimed, are in some sense good arguments, which in some sense make it reasonable for us to accept the conclusion, while not

[1] I am most grateful to Mr. G. J. Warnock, the Series editor, for his helpful comments on an earlier version of this introduction.

being valid deductive arguments, are often termed inductive arguments. But unfortunately there is no precise agreed use for the expression 'inductive argument', nor any pair of adjectives similar to 'valid' and 'invalid' for assessing inductive arguments. I shall remedy the latter defect by using the terms 'correct' and 'incorrect' with this function. I shall say that an inductive argument is an argument which is not deductively valid but one in which, it is claimed, the premisses 'make it reasonable' for us to accept the conclusion. I shall say that a correct inductive argument is one which in the premisses do 'make it reasonable' for us to accept the conclusion, as claimed; and that an incorrect one is one in which they do not, but it is falsely claimed that they do. For the sake of consistent use, I shall henceforward use the expression 'deductive argument' (which I have not hitherto defined—I have only defined 'valid deductive argument') in a similar way and say that a deductive argument is an argument which, it is claimed, is deductively valid; if it is valid the conclusion does follow deductively from the premisses, if it is invalid it does not. (Often others have used the expression 'deductive argument' in such a way that necessarily a deductive argument is a valid argument.)

With these distinctions in mind, we must go on to inquire in what sense in a correct inductive argument the premisses 'make it reasonable' for us to 'accept' the conclusion. It would generally be agreed that such arguments as the one about the bus, from premisses reporting particular matters of fact to a conclusion reporting another particular matter of fact, are inductive. Into this group come the inferences of the scientist or ordinary man from what has happened in the past to what will happen in the future. For example:

Premiss 1:   Always within human memory the sun has risen in London at intervals of approximately twenty-four hours.
Premiss 2:   The sun rose in London this morning at 8.00 a.m.
Conclusion: The sun will rise in London at approximately 8.00 a.m. tomorrow.

It is also agreed that the arguments of the scientist from what has been observed in the past to what are the true laws of nature are inductive. When, for example, Kepler argued from the many observations of the past positions of the planets made by his predecessor Tycho Brahe to the claim that the planets (always) move in ellipses with the sun at one focus, his argument was inductive. The conclusion goes beyond the premisses. It claims more—that the planets moved in ellipses when Tycho was not observing them and will continue to do so. Yet the premisses, it is claimed, make it reasonable for us to accept the conclusion.

What these examples indicate is that in a correct inductive inference the premisses make it reasonable for us to accept the conclusion in the sense, very roughly, that they report evidence favouring the truth of the conclusion, making it rational to believe the conclusion, making it likely or adding to the likelihood of its truth. The premisses must bear a favourable evidential relation to the conclusion. For an argument to be classed as inductive it must be claimed for it that such a relation holds. An argument would not be called inductive merely because, it was claimed, the premisses made it reasonable for us to act on the conclusion, or submit it to further examination. Thus in the move from

(x) This underground cavern has only one exit
to (y) That exit leads to the surface

x certainly provides grounds for acting on y or assuming that y is true, but hardly grounds which, it could be claimed, make y likely to be true or more likely to be true than it was. For that reason it cannot be called an inductive argument. Philosophers of science often discuss the question of the grounds for 'accepting' scientific theories, but they often use 'accept' in very different senses. For Popper for example we often 'accept' a scientific theory, 'but only in the sense that we select it as worthy to be subjected to further criticism, and to the severest tests we can design' ([7], p. 419).[2] So Popper's account of what makes scientific theories acceptable is not an account of induction. Indeed Popper accepts Hume's claim, which I shall shortly discuss, that inductive inference is not reasonable (i.e. there are no correct inductive inferences), and attempts to give an account of theoretical science which exhibits it as accepting and rejecting theories on grounds other than the likelihood of their truth. However, in ordinary life we are continually relying on scientific theories or particular predictions because we believe them to some extent likely to be true. Popper holds such beliefs to be unjustified.

In a correct inductive argument, then, the premisses have to have a favourable evidential relation to the conclusion. But what favourable evidential relation? There is in the literature a certain lack of clarity in the use of the term 'inductive argument'. Some writers claim that in a correct inductive argument the premisses have to make the conclusion probable. And

---

[2] Arabic numbers in square brackets refer to works listed in the bibliography. Roman numerals, e.g. 'III', refer to papers published in this collection.

in some arguments termed inductive it may reasonably be claimed that they do just that. For example:

Premiss 1:   On 506 occasions out of 520 when this coin has been tossed it has landed heads.
Premiss 2:   It will be tossed again and will land.
Conclusion: It will land heads next time.

But in the case of many arguments which men claim to be correct inductive arguments, it is not very plausible to say that the premisses make the conclusion probable. For 'probable' means 'more probable than not'. Arguments from many particular observations to scientific laws, or theories (bodies of scientific laws), such as Kepler's argument cited earlier, are normally termed inductive. Yet it can hardly be maintained that a large number of particular facts observed by men on earth make it more probable than not that some grandiose scientific theory is true. For to say that the scientific theory is true is to say that it holds at all points of space and all moments of time, past and future. It seems implausible to suppose that observations from a very limited spatio-temporal region can make it more probable than not that a scientific theory holds of all regions of (possibly infinite) space and time. What the observations do is, we would more naturally claim, either add to the probability of the scientific theory (i.e. make it more likely than it was without them) or make the theory more likely to be true (more probable) than any equally detailed rival.

I am inclined to the view that (despite what they often say about the conclusion of a correct inductive argument being probable) most writers who use the term 'inductive' in fact think of an argument as a correct inductive argument if its premisses make its conclusion more likely to be true than any equally detailed rival (while not being a deductively valid argument). The various observations which formed the evidence for Newton's theory of gravitation made it, scientists would generally agree, more probable that all masses attracted each other with forces proportional to $\frac{mm^1}{r^2}$ than that all masses attracted each other with forces proportional to $\frac{mm^1}{r^{2\cdot15}}$, or that all masses attracted each other with forces proportional to $\frac{mm^1}{r^2} + \frac{mm^1}{r^4}$, etc. They made Newton's theory more probable than any nameable such rival, but surely not more probable than the disjunction of all such rivals (i.e. the claim that one of the rivals is true). I shall for the rest of this introduction suppose that an inductive argument is one for which, it is claimed, the premisses make the conclusion more probable than any equally detailed rival, although the argument is not deductively valid; and a correct inductive argument is one in which the premisses do make the conclusion more probable than any equally detailed rival, although the argument is not deductively valid. However, even if the expression 'inductive inference' is so used that an inductive inference is one for which, it is claimed, the premisses make the conclusion probable, or alternatively, one for which, it is claimed, the premisses add to the probability of the conclusion, a problem of justification arises similar to that which I will outline for the selected sense.

It is important to distinguish the sense in which I am using 'inductive argument' (and the other senses just distinguished) from a much narrower sense in which it used to be customary to use the expression. In the narrower sense an argument was inductive if the premisses reported of various objects of one kind that they all had some property, and the conclusion claimed that all objects (or some further object) of that kind had that property. The following argument is inductive in the narrow sense:

Premiss 1:   Swan No. 1 is white.
Premiss 2:   Swan No. 2 is white.
Premiss 3:   Swan No. 3 is white.
Conclusion: All swans are white.

Induction in the narrow sense is sometimes called enumerative induction or induction by simple enumeration. Now even if all arguments which are enumerative or inductive in the narrow sense were ordinarily judged to be in our sense correct inductive arguments (and we shall shortly see reason to suppose that they are not), the converse appears not to hold. There seem to be perfectly correct arguments to scientific theories which do not merely generalize the premisses. Newton argued to his theory of gravitation (that all bodies attract each other with forces proportional to $\frac{mm^1}{r^2}$) from propositions reporting observations, but not observations that this, that, and the other body attracted all other bodies with forces proportional to $\frac{mm^1}{r^2}$; rather, observations of the positions of planets and moons, and the rates at which bodies rolled down inclined planes. There is more to most scientific theorizing than merely generalizing observations.

When we talk about the premisses of a correct inductive argument making its conclusion probable or more probable than any equally detailed rival, we are using 'probable' in the sense of 'epistemically probable'. Epistemic probability is a relation between propositions or the states or events which they claim to hold. p makes q epistemically probable when p states evidence which makes it likely that q is true. There is no suggestion that p is in any way responsible for bringing q about (p may report a state of affairs later in time than the state alleged by q). Nor, in talking about events being probable or likely, do I take for granted that the probability or likelihood conforms to the mathematical axioms of probability. (See [1] or any other book on probability or confirmation theory for these.)

Arguments are of use for extending our knowledge. If an argument is a valid deductive one, then, if the premisses are true, the conclusion must be. If we know the premisses to be true, and see that the argument is a valid deductive one, then the argument gives us knowledge of the conclusion. With an inductive argument there are two differences. First, of course, if we know the premisses to be true and see that the argument is a correct inductive one, all that we can conclude is something about the probability of the conclusion—that it is probable or more probable than any equally detailed rival. A correct inductive argument yields only probable knowledge or reasonable belief. But, secondly, the argument will only yield probable knowledge if we know nothing else which affects the probability of the conclusion, apart from what is stated by the premisses. What is meant by this can be seen as follows. Given our ordinary understanding of correctness, this is surely a correct inductive argument:

Premiss 1:   Jones lives in Soho Street.
Premiss 2:   Ninety per cent inhabitants of Soho Street are Catholics.
Conclusion: Jones is a Catholic.

The premisses certainly make it more probable that Jones is a Catholic than that any equally detailed rival conclusion is true (e.g. that Jones is a Protestant). We would say that they give a 0·9 probability to the conclusion. If I know what is stated by the two premisses and nothing else relevant to to whether or not Jones is a Catholic, then I can infer inductively that he is. But suppose that I know in addition what is contained in these two further premisses:

Premiss 3: Jones attended the Congregational Church last Sunday.
Premiss 4: Catholics hardly ever attend Congregational churches.

I cannot now infer the original conclusion. So the addition of new knowledge to the old knowledge may mean that I cannot make the same inductive inferences from the old knowledge. Hence I can only use an inductive argument to give me probable knowledge or reasonable belief, if the premises contain all my relevant knowledge. There is a difference here between deductive and inductive inference. In a correct inductive inference in which the premises are known to be true, I can only call the conclusion probable *simpliciter* (as opposed to 'probable relative to the premises') if the premises include my total relevant knowledge. Deductive inferences extend knowledge, given that the premises are known to be true—whatever else is known to be true. Not so with inductive inferences.

CRITERIA OF CORRECTNESS IN INDUCTIVE ARGUMENTS

Ordinary people and scientists use inductive arguments all the time, and in general men agree about when an inductive argument is correct; when evidence makes a conclusion probable or more probable than some rival. We claim to recognize when some historian or detective has produced flimsy evidence for his claims, and when he has produced strong evidence. And, at any rate with some knowledge of the subject matter, we claim to recognize when a scientist has or has not produced good evidence for his theories or predictions. But it remains a difficult matter to state the precise criteria which we use for judging inductive arguments.

It used to be thought that inductive arguments were ordinarily judged correct if and only if they were enumerative. Consider inductive arguments which have as their premises reports of particular observations and as their conclusions universal generalizations. It used to be thought that an inductive argument of this kind was judged correct if its premises had the form 'this A is B', 'that A is B', etc., and the conclusion had the form 'All A's are B'. But this is neither a necessary nor a sufficient condition for an argument of the stated kind to be judged correct. It is not a necessary condition because men judge that there are correct inductive arguments which reach conclusions of the form 'All A's are B' from premises reporting particular observations, which do not have the form 'this A is B', 'that A is B', etc. We have already noted an example of this. Here is another one. Consider Boyle studying the relation between the pressure and volume of a gas at a constant temperature. He records the pressure (p) of a certain block of gas for different values of its volume (v), and then concludes that always $pv = $ constant. The premises of the argument have the form 'For volume v_n, the pressure of the gas was p_n'; the conclusion is 'pressure $\times$ volume is always constant'. An inference of this form (given certain values of v_n and p_n) would generally be admitted as a correct inductive inference, yet it does not conform to the enumerative pattern. Nor is conformity to the enumerative pattern a sufficient condition for us to judge an inference of the stated kind correct. This was pointed out by Nelson Goodman when he introduced the famous 'new riddle of induction'.[3] Suppose that all emeralds observed so far have been green. We can conclude by an inductive inference that all emeralds (future as well as past) are green. But now we introduce a new term 'grue', which is defined as follows. An object at a time t is grue if (and only if) it is green and t is before A.D. 2000, or it is blue and t is after A.D. 2000. We now, living before A.D. 2000, record our observations using this new predicate. All the emeralds which we have observed so far have been grue. So if all arguments of the enumerative pattern were correct inductive arguments, we could conclude that all emeralds (future as well as past) are grue. But this means that emeralds existing after A.D. 2000 will be blue, for to be grue after A.D. 2000 is to be blue. We do not, however, think the conclusion warranted (and indeed it contradicts the conclusion reached by the previous inductive argument).

So we do not judge that all enumerative arguments are correct inductive arguments. Nevertheless enumerative arguments which generalize fairly ordinary and familiar predicates (e.g. 'green' rather than 'grue') are no doubt in general judged correct. Likewise enumerative arguments which argue from all of a number of observed objects of some type having some property described by some ordinary and familiar predicate to a further object of that type having that property are also in general judged correct. The assumption that in certain respects (e.g. greenness as opposed to grueness) things outside the spatio-temporal region which we have observed continue to behave as they have been observed to behave within that region is basic to inductive inference. Philosophers are devoting much attention to such problems as which predicates men judge to be generalizable, and generally to the problem of laying down the criteria which we ordinarily use for judging inductive inferences correct. The problems which they face are difficult, but by no means insoluble. To solve them the philosopher has to reflect on when we would and when we would not say that an inductive inference was correct, or one hypothesis more probable than some other one. (See [1] for an account of recent philosophical work in elucidating what are the criteria which we use in evaluating inductive arguments.) One difficulty is that men's judgements of what makes what probable or more probable than something else do to some small extent vary. But the extent is a very small one, and by and large men agree about what makes what probable or more probable than something else. They agree, that is, on the criteria which they use for assessing inductive inferences. The issue which

[3] Nelson Goodman, *Fact, Fiction and Forecast* (first edition), London 1955. I have amended Goodman's example very slightly in a now traditional way.

is the subject of this volume is what justification, if any, do men have for using the criteria which they do use rather than any other criteria and for judging that inferences which satisfy those criteria are in fact correct.

THE JUSTIFICATION OF INDUCTION

This issue was first brought to prominence by Hume and has remained a disturbing one for philosophers ever since. Hume seems to assume that inductive argument is simply enumerative argument, and thus ignores the complications which we have just noted. Yet it is easy enough to phrase his basic point in a way which allows for these. Hume wrote:

In reality all arguments from experience are founded on the similarity which we discover among natural objects, and by which we are induced to expect effects similar to those which we have found to follow from such objects . . . [Experience] shows us a number of uniform effects, resulting from certain objects, and teaches us that those particular objects, at that particular time, were endowed with such powers and forces. When a new object endowed with similar sensible qualities, is produced, we expect similar powers and forces, and look for a like effect. From a body of like colour and consistence with bread we expect like nourishment and support. But this surely is a step or progress of the mind which wants to be explained.[4]

When we seek to provide some justification for our inference, Hume claims, we cannot do so.

You must confess that the inference is not intuitive; neither is it demonstrative: of what nature is it, then? To say it is experimental, is begging the question. For all inferences from experience suppose, as their foundation, that the future will resemble the past, and that similar powers will be conjoined with similar sensible qualities. If there be any suspicion that the course of nature may change, and that the past may be no rule for the future, all experience becomes useless, and can give rise to no inference or conclusion. It is impossible, therefore, that any arguments from experience can prove this resemblance of the past to the future; since all these arguments are founded on the supposition of that resemblance.[5]

Things do not always behave as we expect.

Why may [this] not happen always, and with regard to all objects? What logic, what process of argument secures you against this supposition?[6]

Hume's answer is that we have no justification for believing that things will continue to behave as they have behaved. We do believe this and act on this supposition as a matter of animal habit, but there is no justification for our doing so.

[4] David Hume, *An Enquiry Concerning Human Understanding* (first published 1751), Oxford 1902 (ed. L. A. Selby-Bigge), pp. 36 f.
[5] Op. cit., pp. 37 f.   [6] Op. cit., p. 38.

We have seen that inductive inference is a somewhat more complicated matter than Hume supposed, but it is easy enough to phrase Hume's problem in a way which allows for this. We use certain criteria by which we judge purported inductive arguments correct. What justifies us in using these criteria rather than any others and so making the particular inductive inferences which we do? What grounds have we got for supposing that a conclusion reached by the criteria which in practice we use is in fact true? This question is put clearly by Russell in the first item in this collection. Russell does not provide a justification for our using the inductive criteria which we do, but other philosophers have sought to provide such a justification, and justifications of three types have been provided in recent years. I shall call these respectively the analytic, inductive, and pragmatic justifications. This volume contains examples of each type of justification, and of counter-arguments to each. The alternative to such a justification seems to be either to hold that we just 'see' that use of our current inductive criteria is justified (as Kyburg holds in his contribution to the third item in this collection) or to hold, as Hume did, that we have no justification for using our current inductive criteria.

The analytic justification of induction proceeds as follows. It claims that what we *mean* by an inference being a correct inductive inference, its conclusion being more probable than any rival (or alternatively by the conclusion being probable), just *is* that it is a conclusion reached by our current inductive procedures, using the criteria which we do use for judging inductive arguments correct. What justifies us in using those criteria is that, in so far as those criteria pronounce some claim probable, then (of logical necessity) it is probable. If we have observed a large number of ravens in various environments and found them all to be black, then it is more probable that the next raven we observe will be black than that it will be of any other specifiable colour, and that is because of what we mean by 'probable'. Further, in these circumstances, it is rational to believe that the next raven will be black, and that is because what we mean by the 'rational' thing to believe is that which is rendered probable or more probable than any alternative by our current inductive criteria. As in other writing on induction, there tends to be a certain unclarity in expositions of the analytic justification as to exactly what are the analytic relationships involved. Is a rational belief one which is probable, or more probable than any equally detailed rival, or what? But the basic thesis is that inductive inference is rational or justified, and that this is an analytic truth which holds because of what we mean by 'rational' or 'justified'.

The normal argument in favour of this justification is that we come to understand what is meant by 'correct inductive inference' and 'rational belief' by being shown standard examples of such inferences and beliefs. Hence, the argument claims, when we subsequently call other inductive inferences correct and other beliefs rational, what we are doing is saying that they are like the standard examples. Similarly, for example, we come to learn what 'green' means by being shown standard examples of green objects—grass, leaves in spring, runner beans, etc. When thereafter we describe other objects as green what we are saying is that they are like the standard examples. Because of this, it makes no sense to question whether the standard green objects really are green. Similarly we cannot sensibly question whether the examples of purportedly correct inductive inferences by which we have been taught the meaning of 'correct inductive inference' really are correct. This is because to say of an inductive inference that it is correct is just to say that it has a form similar to that of the standard examples. This must be, the analytic justification claims, because we are taught what 'correct inductive inference' means by being shown such standard cases as examples.

The article in this collection by Paul Edwards is representative of the analytic approach. He is only one of many writers who have expounded an analytic justification in recent years. A selected list of such expositions, including a very well-known one by P. F. Strawson [15], is included in the bibliography. Stephen Barker also develops an analytic justification in his contribution to the symposium, which forms the third item in this collection. Wesley Salmon in his two contributions to that symposium and J. O. Urmson in his article oppose the analytic justification. Urmson claims that to call a deductive inference 'valid' or an action 'good' is not or not merely to classify the inference or action as similar to standard examples; it is at least in part to evaluate, appraise, and signify a certain kind of approval (whereas to call an object 'green' is not to evaluate it in any way). So although we may have learnt the meanings of 'valid' and 'good', at any rate in part, by being shown examples of inferences said to be 'valid' and actions said to be 'good, we can subsequently question whether some or all of the actions normally called 'good' or inferences called 'valid' really are so. The same, Urmson claims, applies to what I have called 'correct' inductive inference. To call an inference 'correct' is not, or not merely, to classify the inference as similar to standard examples; it is at least in part to signify a certain kind of approval of it. We learn the meaning in part of a 'correct' inductive inference ('probable' conclusion, 'rational' belief, etc.) by being shown examples of inductive inferences said to be 'correct' (conclusions said to be 'probable', beliefs said to be 'rational' etc.). But since 'correct', like 'valid' and 'good', is an evaluative term, having learnt the meaning of the word, we can then inquire whether inferences called 'correct' are really worthy of the positive evaluation contained in the term. Salmon, like Urmson, claims that it is one thing to describe the inductive criteria which we currently use, another thing to investigate whether there are any good reasons for using those criteria.

Now it is certainly the case, as Salmon points out, that we can come to question whether actions which our parents have told us are 'good' really are so. Hence we cannot mean by a 'good' act merely an act similar to certain standard 'good' acts. And in fact the process of learning ethical terms is not merely a matter of being shown examples of 'good' and 'bad' actions. It is also a matter of learning that certain responses (e.g. praise) are appropriate to good actions, and that certain other responses (e.g. blame) are appropriate to bad actions. This other process provides us with another element in the meaning of 'good' which allows us to question whether some (or perhaps all) acts currently called 'good' really are so. Now it is also the case, as Urmson emphasizes, that the process of learning the meaning of 'rational', 'justified', 'probable', etc., is not merely a matter of being shown examples of propositions and inferences standardly so characterized. It is also a matter of being shown the connection with action of the probable proposition or rational belief. We learn that, if p is probable, it is to be expected, it would be surprising if p did not occur; that anyone who can afford to bet and is interested in making money ought, if the odds are even, to place his bet on p rather than $not\text{-}p$. Those who act on what is judged probable rather than on what is judged improbable by current inductive standards (in circumstances where what they stand to lose or gain by their actions are of similar value to them) are given a certain kind of approval in the community. (They are said to be 'sensible', 'cautious', 'scientific'.) Since all this is involved in learning the meanings of 'probable', 'justified', 'rational', etc., it would not be surprising if we derived thereby an understanding of probability which allowed us sensibly to question whether some or perhaps all the conclusions called 'probable' and beliefs called 'rational' really are so. Maybe through these learning processes we have come to understand by a proposition being probable that the proposition is one towards which a certain attitude is appropriate, the attitude that what the proposition states can be expected to happen, and that we can sensibly take for granted that it will. If we have this sort of understanding of 'probable' and related terms, then we can indeed question whether the conclusions of inductive inferences of the type which we normally make really are correct. Hume's question can be asked.

A second type of justification of induction is the inductive (or 'prediction-ist') justification. According to this the justification for our belief that our inferences using normal inductive criteria reach conclusions which are probably true is that in the past our inferences using those criteria have often reached true (or largely true) conclusions, e.g. correct predictions. By and large things have behaved in the past as use of our normal induc-tive criteria led us to suppose that they would. That is good reason on this account to suppose that those criteria will be successful in future. This 'justification' of induction is called the inductive justification because it claims that a past regularity (the success of induction) is evidence for the regularity holding in future which—for certain kinds of regularity—is what our normal inductive criteria assume. Now Hume claimed that an inductive justification of induction is circular, that is that it provides a justification of induction only if you already assume that the use of normal inductive criteria is justified. And superficially that seems right. The justifi-cation assumes that the argument from 'induction has worked in the past' to 'induction will work in the future' is a correct inductive inference. But it appears that the only reason which can be provided to substantiate this assumption is that it satisfies our current inductive criteria. But what is at stake in this whole business is whether we are justified in supposing that an inference which satisfies our current inductive criteria is correct. The in-ductive justification of induction thus seems to assume this to be so in order to prove it to be so, and is in consequence circular.

However two powerful recent writers, R. B. Braithwaite and Max Black, have both championed the inductive justification of induction. Papers VII and VIII(1) contain examples of their contributions to the debate. Both claim that inductive justifications of induction are not circular in the ordin-ary sense that the conclusion of an inductive justification of induction is one of the premises from which the conclusion is derived. Rather, an inductive justification is circular in the sense (roughly) that the conclusion asserts the correctness (or reliability on the next occasion of its use) of the rule of inference by which it is reached. They claim that circularity of this kind (rule-circularity, or, in Braithwaite's terminology, 'effective circu-larity') is not vicious, does not spoil the cogency of an argument. Achin-stein attacks this claim of Black's in paper VIII(2). Black defends his claim in VIII(3) and Achinstein develops his attack further in VIII(4).

A third type of justification is the pragmatic (or practicalist) kind. The originator of this kind of justification was Hans Reichenbach (see [23] and [24]). It has been developed in recent years in many writings of Wesley Salmon, one of whose expositions has been included in this collection as paper V. The pragmatist thinks of the main task of the scientist as finding the true laws of nature, if there are any such to be found. He thinks of these as either universal or statistical in character (that is, either of the form 'all A's are B' or 'no A's are B' *or* of the form '*n* per cent A's are B', where *n* is not 100 or 0; for example 'all iron dissolves in hydrochloric acid' or '90 per cent pieces of iron dissolve in hydrochloric acid'). He is concerned mainly with inductive inferences which proceed from particular observations of objects of some kind, say A's ,which have some further property, e.g. are B's, to universal or statistical laws correlating A-ness and B-ness, such as 'all A's are B' or '90 per cent A's are B' or 'no A's are B'. Normally we suppose in such a case, if our premisses report only what proportion of A's have been observed to be B's, that the correct inductive inference is that which concludes that the same proportion holds among A's, observed and unobserved, as among observed A's. That is to say, the correct inductive inference goes from '*n* per cent observed A's have been B' to '*n* per cent A's are B'. To take a simple case, the correct inductive inference from 'all observed A's are B' is to 'all A's are B' rather than to '50 per cent A's are B'. This rule of 'positing' that the same proportions hold in a whole population as in an observed sample is known as Reichenbach's 'straight rule' (in V Salmon calls it 'The rule of induction by enumeration'— using this expression in a more general sense than I have used it). The pragmatist attempts to provide a 'justification' for the use of the straight rule. The justification consists, not in showing that the conclusions yielded by it are probably true, but in showing that if there are true laws of nature, statistical or universal, to be found, continued use of the straight rule will eventually produce them, and that there is no guarantee that continued use of any other rule will do so. The justification provided by the pragmatist for use of the straight rule consists in showing that it is in a certain respect a better rule than alternatives. Some of the complexities and qualifications involved in this 'justification' are developed in Salmon's article. For example, clearly use of the straight rule must be limited to predicates of certain types (e.g. to predicates such as 'green' as opposed to predicates such as 'grue').

I must make one point here in clarification of Salmon's paper. Like Reichenbach, Salmon regards laws of nature as statements about 'limiting frequencies' in classes (sometimes called 'probabilities' 'in the frequency sense'). They will have, as stated, the form '*n* per cent A's are B'. This, according to Salmon, means that as we study more and more A's we shall eventually come to a point where the percentage gets ever closer to *n*. Salmon gives a more technical definition in V. So if there is a natural law such as '50 per cent atoms of carbon-14 disintegrate within 5,600 years', this is a claim, not about the proportion of atoms within any finite collection of atoms which disintegrate, but about the 'limiting frequency' of the ratio of atoms disintegrating within 5,600 years to the total number of atoms as more and more atoms are considered. It is a consequence of this point that there may be on Salmon's view, no true law of the form 'n per cent A's are B'. For it may be the case, as you go on considering A's, that the proportion of A's which are B continues to oscillate significantly and does not settle down to a stable value. In that case according to Salmon there would be no true law of nature correlating A's and B's, and so neither the straight rule nor any other rule would find one.

Many objections have been made to the pragmatist justification, and some of them are contained in the article by John Lenz included as VI in this volume. He points out that although continued use of the straight rule will eventually yield the true scientific law (if there is one), so will continued use of any other of a large class of 'asymptotic' rules. Further, although continued use of the straight rule will eventually yield the true law (if there is one), no one would ever know when it had been found. Also, Lenz points out, science is often interested in making short-run predictions, e.g. about whether the next carbon-14 atom will disintegrate within 5,600 years, or the sun rise tomorrow, and the pragmatist cannot, Lenz claims, justify such inferences. In V Salmon tries to meet some of such objections to his theory.

The article IX, by Keith Campbell, claims that there is a certain incoherence involved in a sceptic's claim that 'no inductive generalization is justifiable'. This arises because the use of all general terms for describing objects involves some assumptions about how those objects have behaved or will behave. For me to describe an object as a desk commits me to the view that that object did not suddenly appear two seconds ago, and (perhaps) will not disintegrate when sat on, etc. Campbell claims that use of the general term 'inductively established generalization' itself presupposes the truth of at least one inductive generalization. So, claims Campbell, complete scepticism about all induction is unutterable.

This is connected with the interesting point made in the final article in the collection by Nicholas Maxwell. As I have characterized them, inductive arguments are necessarily non-deductive. For them to yield a justified conclusion they must start from premises reporting what is known. I assumed that we could not start from premises reporting general laws, or future states of affairs or events; that we must start from premises which report particular past or present states or events, which have been observed. This follows from the basic empiricist assumption that knowledge begins with what has been observed together with the assumption that only particular past or present states or events can be observed. I also assumed that from propositions reporting past or present states and events one cannot deduce propositions reporting future states or events. This latter I will call the A-assumption. Given the A-assumption, we need induction to infer scientific laws and particular future propositions. On the whole the A-assumption seems justified. Propositions about the present do carry some very vague deductive implications about how objects change and so about the immediate future. From a claim that an object is now inflammable or soluble or elastic we can deduce how it will behave in the immediate future, e.g. that it will burn if ignited immediately etc. But the implications are somewhat vague—for what temperature and pressure must it be the case that the object will burn? And they are also very short-term. We cannot deduce from an object being now inflammable that it will burn if ignited tomorrow. However, Maxwell suggests that physics might develop in such a way that it ascribed to objects properties the possession of which by an object carried precise implications about its behaviour in the distant future. For example, this physics might use the word 'mass' in such a sense that from the present masses of two bodies you could deduce what forces they would exert on each other in the distant future. If they did not exert those forces in future that would show that their present 'masses' were not as supposed. If the physics were well confirmed by evidence, that would justify us in attributing to objects the properties such as 'mass' the existence of which it postulated. In that case we would often not need induction to infer the future behaviour of objects; deduction would suffice.

An objector to Maxwell's postulated physics may protest that to say that an object has at some instant a 'property' such as his 'mass' is not really to attribute it to a property possessed at that instant. But why is it not? It is plausible, as we have seen, to suppose that almost all attributions of what are normally termed 'properties' carry some implications, albeit very vague ones, about immediate future behaviour. To say that something is solid or hot or fluid does seem to carry implications about its future behaviour. And if attributions to an object of what are normally called properties do carry some implications about its future behaviour, why should not the implications be precise ones about the distant future?

But if you get rid of Hume's sceptical question at one point, a similar question tends to reappear at another point. Maybe an inference from the present state of an object S_1 to a future state S_2 can be deductive. But then can we really know that an object is in state S_1? As we ordinarily use the word 'know', we can be said to know that objects have the ordinary properties of fluidity, solidity, inflammability, greenness, etc., that they have. Maybe there is still the possibility of our being mistaken about *any* judgement about a matter of empirical fact. Maybe, when I judge that some object is green or solid, I am the victim of an illusion or dreaming. It is for this reason that Hume and others have doubted whether we are rightly said to *know* even which ordinary properties some object has at present, e.g. whether an object is green or solid or square. But if attributing a property to an object is to carry very precise long-term implications about its behaviour, the danger of our being mistaken in our judgements about which properties objects have is surely very much greater. Something that happens in a thousand years' time could show that we were wrong in some claim about the present. The grounds for sceptical doubt about whether we really know anything about the present are enormously increased. It looks as though, if we do not need induction to get to the future, we shall not even be able to have knowledge of the present. Paradoxically, it is the fact that we need the shaky inductive step to pass from knowledge of the present to reasonable belief about the future that means that we can have any knowledge of the present at all.

I

ON INDUCTION

BERTRAND RUSSELL

In almost all our previous discussions we have been concerned in the attempt to get clear as to our data in the way of knowledge of existence. What things are there in the universe whose existence is known to us owing to our being acquainted with them? So far, our answer has been that we are acquainted with our sense-data, and, probably, with ourselves. These we know to exist. And past sense-data which are remembered are known to have existed in the past. This knowledge supplies our data.

But if we are to be able to draw inferences from these data—if we are to know of the existence of matter, of other people, of the past before our individual memory begins, or of the future, we must know general principles of some kind by means of which such inferences can be drawn. It must be known to us that the existence of some one sort of thing, A, is a sign of the existence of some other sort of thing, B, either at the same time as A or at some earlier or later time, as, for example, thunder is a sign of the earlier existence of lightning. If this were not known to us, we could never extend our knowledge beyond the sphere of our private experience; and this sphere, as we have seen, is exceedingly limited. The question we have now to consider is whether such an extension is possible, and if so, how it is effected.

Let us take as an illustration a matter about which none of us, in fact, feel the slightest doubt. We are all convinced that the sun will rise tomorrow. Why? Is this belief a mere blind outcome of past experience, or can it be justified as a reasonable belief? It is not easy to find a test by which to judge whether a belief of this kind is reasonable or not, but we can at least ascertain what sort of general beliefs would suffice, if true, to justify the judgement that the sun will rise tomorrow, and the many other similar judgements upon which our actions are based.

It is obvious that if we are asked why we believe that the sun will rise tomorrow, we shall naturally answer, 'Because it always has risen every day.' We have a firm belief that it will rise in the future, because it has

From *The Problems of Philosophy* by Bertrand Russell (1912; OPUS edn., Oxford University Press, 1967), Chapter 6. Reprinted by permission of The Clarendon Press, Oxford.

risen in the past. If we are challenged as to why we believe that it will continue to rise as heretofore, we may appeal to the laws of motion: the earth, we shall say, is a freely rotating body, and such bodies do not cease to rotate unless something interferes from outside, and there is nothing outside to interfere with the earth between now and tomorrow. Of course it might be doubted whether we are quite certain that there is nothing outside to interfere, but this is not the interesting doubt. The interesting doubt is as to whether the laws of motion will remain in operation until tomorrow. If this doubt is raised, we find ourselves in the same position as when the doubt about the sunrise was first raised.

The *only* reason for believing that the laws of motion will remain in operation is that they have operated hitherto, so far as our knowledge of the past enables us to judge. It is true that we have a greater body of evidence from the past in favour of the laws of motion than we have in favour of the sunrise, because the sunrise is merely a particular case of fulfilment of the laws of motion, and there are countless other particular cases. But the real question is: Do *any* number of cases of a law being fulfilled in the past afford evidence that it will be fulfilled in the future? If not, it becomes plain that we have no ground whatever for expecting the sun to rise tomorrow, or for expecting the bread we shall eat at our next meal not to poison us, or for any of the other scarcely conscious expectations that control our daily lives. It is to be observed that all such expectations are only *probable*; thus we have not to seek for a proof that they *must* be fulfilled, but only for some reason in favour of the view that they are *likely* to be fulfilled.

Now in dealing with this question we must, to begin with, make an important distinction, without which we should soon become involved in hopeless confusions. Experience has shown us that, hitherto, the frequent repetition of some uniform succession or coexistence has been a *cause* of our expecting the same succession or coexistence on the next occasion. Food that has a certain appearance generally has a certain taste, and it is a severe shock to our expectations when the familiar appearance is found to be associated with an unusual taste. Things which we see become associated, by habit, with certain tactile sensations which we expect if we touch them; one of the horrors of a ghost (in many ghost-stories) is that it fails to give us any sensations of touch. Uneducated people who go abroad for the first time are so surprised as to be incredulous when they find their native language not understood.

And this kind of association is not confined to men; in animals also it is very strong. A horse which has been often driven along a certain road resists the attempt to drive him in a different direction. Domestic animals expect food when they see the person who usually feeds them. We know that all these rather crude expectations of uniformity are liable to be misleading. The man who has fed the chicken every day throughout its life at last wrings its neck instead, showing that more refined views as to the uniformity of nature would have been useful to the chicken.

But in spite of the misleadingness of such expectations, they nevertheless exist. The mere fact that something has happened a certain number of times causes animals and men to expect that it will happen again. Thus our instincts certainly cause us to believe that the sun will rise tomorrow, but we may be in no better a position than the chicken which unexpectedly has its neck wrung. We have therefore to distinguish the fact that past uniformities *cause* expectations as to the future, from the question whether there is any reasonable ground for giving weight to such expectations after the question of their validity has been raised.

The problem we have to discuss is whether there is any reason for believing in what is called 'the uniformity of nature'. The belief in the uniformity of nature is the belief that everything that has happened or will happen is an instance of some general law to which there are *no* exceptions. The crude expectations which we have been considering are all subject to exceptions, and therefore liable to disappoint those who entertain them. But science habitually assumes, at least as a working hypothesis, that general rules which have exceptions can be replaced by general rules which have no exceptions. 'Unsupported bodies in air fall' is a general rule to which balloons and aeroplanes are exceptions. But the laws of motion and the law of gravitation, which account for the fact that most bodies fall, also account for the fact that balloons and aeroplanes can rise; thus the laws of motion and the law of gravitation are not subject to these exceptions.

The belief that the sun will rise tomorrow might be falsified if the earth came suddenly into contact with a large body which destroyed its rotation; but the laws of motion and the law of gravitation would not be infringed by such an event. The business of science is to find uniformities, such as the laws of motion and the law of gravitation, to which, so far as our experience extends, there are no exceptions. In this search science has been remarkably successful, and it may be conceded that such uniformities have held hitherto. This brings us back to the question: Have we any reason, assuming that they have always held in the past, to suppose that they will hold in the future?

It has been argued that we have reason to know that the future will resemble the past, because what was the future has constantly become the past, and has always been found to resemble the past, so that we really have experience of the future, namely of times which were formerly future, which we may call past futures. But such an argument really begs the very question at issue. We have experience of past futures, but not of future futures, and the question is: Will future futures resemble past futures? This question is not to be answered by an argument which starts from past futures alone. We have therefore still to seek for some principle which shall enable us to know that the future will follow the same laws as the past.

The reference to the future in this question is not essential. The same question arises when we apply the laws that work in our experience to past things of which we have no experience—as, for example, in geology, or in theories as to the origin of the Solar System. The question we really have to ask is: 'When two things have been found to be often associated, and no instance is known of the one occurring without the other, does the occurrence of one of the two, in a fresh instance, give any good ground for expecting the other?' On our answer to this question must depend the validity of the whole of our expectations as to the future, the whole of the results obtained by induction, and in fact practically all the beliefs upon which our daily life is based.

It must be conceded, to begin with, that the fact that two things have been found often together and never apart does not, by itself, suffice to *prove* demonstratively that they will be found together in the next case we examine. The most we can hope is that the oftener things are found together, the more probable it becomes that they will be found together another time, and that, if they have been found together often enough, the probability will amount *almost* to certainty. It can never quite reach certainty, because we know that in spite of frequent repetitions there sometimes is a failure at the last, as in the case of the chicken whose neck is wrung. Thus probability is all we ought to seek.

It might be urged, as against the view we are advocating, that we know all natural phenomena to be subject to the reign of law, and that sometimes, on the basis of observation, we can see that only one law can possibly fit the facts of the case. Now to this view there are two answers. The first is that, even if *some* law which has no exceptions applies to our case, we can never, in practice, be sure that we have discovered that law and not one to which there are exceptions. The second is that the reign of law would seem to be itself only probable, and that our belief that it will hold in the future, or in unexamined cases in the past, is itself based upon the very principle we are examining.

The principle we are examining may be called the *principle of induction*, and its two parts may be stated as follows:

(*a*) When a thing of a certain sort A has been found to be associated with a thing of a certain other sort B, and has never been found dissociated from a thing of the sort B, the greater the number of cases in which A and B have been associated, the greater is the probability that they will be associated in a fresh case in which one of them is known to be present.

(*b*) Under the same circumstances, a sufficient number of cases of association will make the probability of a fresh association nearly a certainty, and will make it approach certainty without limit.

As just stated, the principle applies only to the verification of our expectation in a single fresh instance. But we want also to know that there is a probability in favour of the general law that things of the sort A are *always* associated with things of the sort B, provided a sufficient number of cases of association are known, and no cases of failure of association are known. The probability of the general law is obviously less than the probability of the particular case, since if the general law is true, the particular case must also be true, whereas the particular case may be true without the general law being true. Nevertheless the probability of the general law is increased by repetitions, just as the probability of the particular case is. We may therefore repeat the two parts of our principle as regards the general law, thus:

(*a*) The greater the number of cases in which a thing of the sort A has been found associated with a thing of the sort B, the more probable it is (if no cases of failure of association are known) that A is always associated with B.

(*b*) Under the same circumstances, a sufficient number of cases of the association of A with B will make it nearly certain that A is always associated with B, and will make this general law approach certainty without limit.

It should be noted that probability is always relative to certain data. In our case, the data are merely the known cases of coexistence of A and B. There may be other data, which *might* be taken into account, which would gravely alter the probability. For example, a man who had seen a great many white swans might argue, by our principle, that on the data it was *probable* that all swans were white, and this might be a perfectly sound argument. The argument is not disproved by the fact that some swans are black, because a thing may very well happen in spite of the fact that some data render it improbable. In the case of the swans, a man might know that colour is a very variable characteristic in many species of animals, and that, therefore, an induction as to colour is peculiarly liable to error. But this knowledge would be a fresh datum, by no means proving that the probability relatively to our previous data had been wrongly estimated. The fact, therefore, that things often fail to fulfil our expectations is no evidence that our expectations will not *probably* be fulfilled in a given case or a given class of cases. Thus our inductive principle is at any rate not capable of being *disproved* by an appeal to experience.

The inductive principle, however, is equally incapable of being *proved* by an appeal to experience. Experience might conceivably confirm the inductive principle as regards the cases that have been already examined; but as regards unexamined cases, it is the inductive principle alone that can justify any inference from what has been examined to what has not been examined. All arguments which, on the basis of experience, argue as to the future or the unexperienced parts of the past or present, assume the inductive principle; hence we can never use experience to prove the inductive principle without begging the question. Thus we must either accept the inductive principle on the ground of its intrinsic evidence, or forgo all justification of our expectations about the future. If the principle is unsound, we have no reason to expect the sun to rise tomorrow, to expect bread to be more nourishing than a stone, or to expect that if we throw ourselves off the roof we shall fall. When we see what looks like our best friend approaching us, we shall have no reason to suppose that his body is not inhabited by the mind of our worst enemy or of some total stranger. All our conduct is based upon associations which have worked in the past, and which we therefore regard as likely to work in the future; and this likelihood is dependent for its validity upon the inductive principle.

The general principles of science, such as the belief in the reign of law, and the belief that every eve nt must have a cause, are as completely dependent upon the inductive principle as are the beliefs of daily life. All such general principles are believed because mankind have found innumerable instances of their truth and no instances of their falsehood. But this affords no evidence for their truth in the future, unless the inductive principle is assumed.

Thus all knowledge which, on a basis of experience, tells us something about what is not experienced, is based upon a belief which experience can neither confirm nor confute, yet which, at least in its more concrete applications, appears to be as firmly rooted in us as many of the facts of experience. The existence and justification of such beliefs—for the inductive principle, as we shall see, is not the only example—raises some of the most difficult and most debated problems of philosophy.

RUSSELL'S DOUBTS ABOUT INDUCTION

PAUL EDWARDS

I

A. In the celebrated chapter on induction in his *Problems of Philosophy*,[1] Bertrand Russell asks the question: 'Have we any reason, assuming that they [laws like the law of gravitation] have always held in the past, to suppose that these laws will hold in the future?'[2] Earlier in the same chapter he raises the more specific question: 'Do *any* number of cases of a law being fulfilled in the past afford evidence that it will be fulfilled in the future?'[3] We may reformulate these questions in a way which lends itself more easily to critical discussion as follows:

(1) Assuming that we possess *n* positive instances of a phenomenon, observed in extensively varied circumstances, and that we have not observed a single negative instance (where *n* is a large number), have we any reason to suppose that the *n* + 1st instance will also be positive?

(2) Is there any number *n* of observed positive instances of a phenomenon which affords evidence that the *n* + 1st instance will also be positive?

It is clear that Russell uses 'reason' synonymously with 'good reason' and 'evidence' with 'sufficient evidence'. I shall follow the same procedure throughout this article.

Russell asserts that unless we appeal to a non-empirical principle which he calls the 'principle of induction', both of his questions must be answered in the negative. 'Those who emphasized the scope of induction,' he writes, 'wished to maintain that all logic is empirical, and therefore could not be expected to realize that induction itself, their own darling, required a logical principle which obviously could not be proved inductively, and must therefore be *a priori* if it could be known at all.'[4] 'We must either

From *Mind*, Vol. 68 (1949), pp. 141–63. Reprinted by permission of the author and Basil Blackwell.

[1] [Reprinted above, pp. 19–25. Page references below are to the OPUS edition, apart from those in square brackets, which are to the corresponding pages in this book.—Ed.]
[2] p. 35 [p. 21].   [3] p. 34 [p. 20].
[4] *Our Knowledge of the External World* (2nd edn.), p. 226.

accept the inductive principle on the ground of its intrinsic evidence or forgo all justification of our expectations about the future.'[5]

In conjunction with the inductive principle, on the other hand, question (1) at least, he contends, can be answered in the affirmative. 'Whether inferences from past to future are valid depends wholly, if our discussion has been sound, upon the inductive principle: if it is true, such inferences are valid.'[6] Unfortunately Russell does not make it clear whether in his opinion the same is true about question (2).

As against Russell, I shall try to show in this article that question (1) can be answered in the affirmative without in any way appealing to a non-empirical principle. I shall also attempt to show that, without in any way invoking a non-empirical principle, numbers of observed positive instances do frequently afford us evidence that unobserved instances of the same phenomenon are also positive. At the outset, I shall concentrate on question (1) since this is the more general question. Once we have answered question (1) it will require little further effort to answer question (2).

I want to emphasize here that, to keep this paper within manageable bounds, I shall refrain from discussing, at any rate explicitly, the questions 'Are any inductive conclusions probable?' and 'Are any inductive conclusions certain?' I hope to fill in this gap on another occasion.

It will be well to conduct our discussion in terms of a concrete example. Supposing a man jumps from a window on the fiftieth floor of the Empire State Building. Is there any reason to suppose that his body will move in the direction of the street rather than say in the direction of the sky or in a flat plane? There can be no doubt that any ordinary person and any philosophically unsophisticated scientist would answer this question in the affirmative without in any way appealing to a non-empirical principle. He would say that there is an excellent reason to suppose that the man's body will move towards the street. This excellent reason, he would say, consists in the fact that whenever in the past a human being jumped out of a window of the Empire State Building his body moved in a downward direction; that whenever any human being anywhere jumped out of a house he moved in the direction of the ground; that, more generally, whenever a human body jumped or was thrown off an elevated locality in the neighbourhood of the earth, it moved downwards and not either upwards or at an angle of 180°; that the only objects which have been observed to be capable of moving upwards by themselves possess certain

[5] *Problems of Philosophy*, p. 38 [p. 24]; also *Outline of Philosophy*, p. 286.
[6] *External World*, p. 226.

special characteristics which human beings lack; and finally in all the other observed confirmations of the theory of gravitation.

B. The philosophers who reject commonsense answers like the one just described, have relied mainly on three arguments. Russell himself explicitly employs two of them and some of his remarks make it clear that he also approves of the third. These three arguments are as follows: (*a*) Defenders of commonsense point to the fact that many inferences to unobserved events were subsequently, by means of direct observation, found to have resulted in true conclusions. However, any such appeal to observed results of inductive inferences is irrelevant. For the question at stake is: Have we ever a reason, assuming that all the large number of observed instances of a phenomenon are positive, to suppose that an instance which is still unobserved is also positive? The question is not: Have we ever a reason for supposing that instances which have by now been observed but were at one time unobserved are positive? In Russell's own words: 'We have experience of past futures, but not of future futures, and the question is: Will future futures resemble past futures? This question is not to be answered by an argument which starts from past futures alone.'[7]

(*b*) Cases are known where at a certain time a large number of positive instances and not a single negative instance had been observed and where the next instance nevertheless turned out to be negative. 'We know that in spite of frequent repetitions there sometimes is a failure at the last.'[8] The man, for instance, 'who has fed the chicken every day throughout its life at last wrings its neck instead'.[9] Even in the case of the human being who is jumping out of the Empire State Building, 'we may be in no better position than the chicken which unexpectedly has its neck wrung'.[10]

(*c*) The number of positive and negative necessary conditions for the occurrence of any event is infinite or at any rate too large to be directly observed by a human being or indeed by all human beings put together. None of us, for example, has explored every corner of the universe to make sure that there nowhere exists a malicious but powerful individual who controls the movements of the sun by means of wires which are too fine to be detected by any of our microscopes. None of us can be sure that there is no such Controller who, in order to play a joke with the human race, will prevent the sun from rising tomorrow. Equally, none of us can be sure that there is nowhere a powerful individual who can, if he wishes, regulate the movement of human bodies by means of ropes which are too thin to be detected by any of our present instruments. None of us therefore can be

[7] *Problems of Philosophy*, p. 36 [p. 22].   [8] Loc. cit., p. 36 [p. 22].
[9] Loc. cit., p. 35 [p. 21].   [10] Ibid.

sure that when a man jumps out of the Empire State Building he will not be drawn skyward by the Controller of Motion. Hence we have no reason to suppose that the man's body will move in the direction of the street and not in the direction of the sky.

In connection with the last of these three arguments attention ought to be drawn to a distinction which Russell makes between what he calls the 'interesting' and the 'uninteresting' doubt about induction.[11] The uninteresting doubt is doubt about the occurrence of a given event on the ground that not all the conditions which are known to be necessary are in fact known to be present. What Russell calls the interesting doubt is the doubt whether an event will take place although all the conditions known to be necessary are known to obtain. Russell's 'interesting doubt', if I am not mistaken, is identical with Donald Williams's 'tragic problem of induction'.[12]

II

As I indicated above, it is my object in this article to defend the common-sense answers to both of Russell's questions. I propose to show, in other words, that, without in any way calling upon a non-empirical principle for assistance, we often have a reason for supposing that a generalization will be confirmed in the future as it has been confirmed in the past. I also propose to show that numbers 'of cases of a law being fulfilled in the past' do often afford evidence that it will be fulfilled in the future.

However, what I have to say in support of these answers is so exceedingly simple that I am afraid it will not impress the philosophers who are looking for elaborate and complicated theories to answer these questions. But I think I can make my case appear plausible even in the eyes of some of these philosophers if I describe at some length the general method of resolving philosophical puzzles which I shall apply to the problem of induction.

Let us consider a simple statement like 'there are several thousand physicians in New York'. We may call this a statement of commonsense, meaning thereby no more than that anybody above a certain very moderate level of instruction and intelligence would confidently give his assent to it.

The word 'physician', as ordinarily used, is not entirely free from ambiguity. At times it simply means 'person who possesses a medical degree from a recognized academic institution'. At other times, though less often, it means the same as 'person who possesses what is by ordinary standards a

---

[11] Loc. cit., p. 34 [p. 20].
[12] 'Induction and the Future', (*Mind*, 1948), p. 227.

considerable skill in curing diseases'. On yet other occasions when people say about somebody that he is a physician they mean both that he has a medical degree and that he possesses a skill in curing diseases which considerably exceeds that of the average layman.

Let us suppose that in the commonsense statement 'there are several thousand physicians in New York' the word 'physician' is used exclusively in the last-mentioned sense. This assumption will simplify our discussion, but it is not at all essential to any of the points I am about to make. It is essential, however, to realize that when somebody asserts in ordinary life that there are several thousand physicians in New York, he is using the word 'physician' in one or other of the ordinary senses just listed. By 'physician' he does not mean for example 'person who can speedily repair bicycles' or 'person who can cure any conceivable illness in less than two minutes'.

Now, supposing somebody were to say 'Really, there are no physicians at all in New York', in the belief that he was contradicting and refuting commonsense. Supposing that on investigation it turns out that by 'physician' he does not mean 'person who has a medical degree and who has considerably more skill in curing disease than the average layman'. It turns out that by 'physician' he means 'person who has a medical degree and who can cure any conceivable illness in less than two minutes'.

What would be an adequate reply to such an 'enemy of commonsense'? Clearly it would be along the following lines: 'What you say is true. There are no physicians in New York—in *your* sense of the word. There are no persons in New York who can cure any conceivable disease in less than two minutes. But this in no way contradicts the commonsense view expressed by "there are several thousand physicians in New York". For the latter asserts no more than that there are several thousand people in New York who have a medical degree and who possess a skill in curing disease which considerably exceeds that of the average layman. You are guilty of *ignoratio elenchi* since the proposition you refute is different from the proposition you set out to refute.'

Our discussion from here on will be greatly simplified by introducing a few technical terms. Let us, firstly, call '*ignoratio elenchi* by *redefinition*' any instance of *ignoratio elenchi* in which (i) the same sentence expresses both the proposition which ought to be proved and the proposition which is confused with it and where (ii) in the latter employment of the sentence one or more of its parts are used in a sense which is different from their ordinary sense or senses. Secondly, let us refer to any redefinition of a word which includes all that the ordinary definition of the word includes but which includes something else as well as a '*high* redefinition'; and to the sense which is defined by a high redefinition we shall refer as a high sense of the word. Thus 'person who has a medical degree and who is capable of curing any conceivable disease in less than two minutes' is a high redefinition of 'physician' and anybody using the word in that fashion is using it in a high sense. Thirdly, we shall refer to a redefinition of a word which includes something but not all of what the ordinary definition includes and which includes nothing else as a '*low* redefinition'; and the sense which is defined by a low redefinition we shall call a low sense of the word. 'Person capable of giving first aid' or 'person who knows means of alleviating pain' would be low redefinitions of 'physician'. Finally, it will be convenient to call a statement in which a word is used in a high or in a low sense a *redefinitional statement*. If the word is used in a high sense we shall speak of a highdefinitional statement; if it is used in a low sense we shall speak of a lowdefinitional statement.

A short while ago, I pointed out that the man who says 'there are no physicians in New York', meaning that there are no people in New York who have a medical degree and who can cure any conceivable illness in less than two minutes, is not really contradicting the commonsense view that there are physicians in New York. I pointed out that he would be guilty of what in our technical language is called an *ignoratio elenchi* by redefinition. Now, it seems to me that the relation between the assertion of various philosophers that past experience never constitutes a reason for prediction or generalization except perhaps in conjunction with a non-empirical principle and the commonsense view that past experience does often by itself constitute a reason for inferences to unobserved events has some striking resemblances to the relation between the redefinitional statement about physicians in New York and the commonsense view which this redefinitional statement fails to refute. And more generally, it strongly seems to me that almost all the bizarre pronouncements of philosophers— their 'paradoxes', their 'silly' theories—are in certain respects strikingly like the statement that there are no physicians in New York, made by one who means to assert that there are no people in New York who have medical degrees and who are capable of curing any conceivable disease in less than two minutes.

In making the last statement I do not mean to deny that there are also important differences between philosophical paradoxes and the high-definitional statement about physicians. There are three differences in particular which have to be mentioned if my subsequent remarks are not seriously misleading. Firstly, many of the philosophical paradoxes are not without some point; they do often draw attention to likenesses and differences which ordinary usage obscures. Secondly, the redefinitions which are implicit in philosophical paradoxes do quite often, though by no means always, receive a certain backing from ordinary usage. Frequently, that is to say, there is a secondary sense or trend in ordinary usage which corresponds to the philosophical redefinition, the 'real' sense of the word.[13] Thirdly, philosophical paradoxes are invariably ambiguous in a sense in which the highdefinitional statement about the physicians is not ambiguous.[14]

Now, while fully admitting all these (and other) differences, I wish to insist on the great likenesses between philosophical paradoxes and the redefinitional statement about the physicians. And in this article I am mainly concerned with the likenesses, not with the differences. My main object of course is to point out the likenesses between the highdefinitional statement 'there are no physicians in New York' and the statement that past experience never by itself affords a reason for making inferences to unobserved events. However, my points there will be clearer if I first make them in connection with another celebrated paradox.

Following Plato, Berkeley[15] argued in favour of the view that heat and cold are not really 'in the object'. Ordinary people would unhesitatingly say that water of, e.g. 50° Centigrade is hot. Against this, Plato and Berkeley would point out that to a man who a moment before had held his hands in a jug of water with a temperature of 80° C. the water of 50° C. would appear cold. Similarly, to a race of individuals whose body-temperature was say 75° C., water of 50° would regularly appear cold. But the percepts of those to whom the water of 50° appears cold are just as genuine as the percepts of people to whom the water appears hot. Now, since it would be wrong to say that the water of 50° is really cold simply because of these genuine percepts of cold, it cannot any more rationally be said to be hot. The cold has 'just as good a right to be considered real' as the hot; and therefore, 'to avoid favouritism, we are compelled to deny that in itself'[16] the water is either hot or cold.

It is not difficult to show that this argument is a case of *ignoratio elenchi* by redefinition. When an ordinary person says that water of 50° C. is hot all he means is that human beings, with their body-temperature being what it is, would in *all ordinary circumstances* have sense-impressions of heat on

---

[13] Prominent instances of this phenomenon are 'real certainty', 'real knowledge', 'real sameness', 'real freedom', and 'really contemporaneous events'.

[14] The last of these points seems to me to be of enormous importance for understanding the phenomenon of philosophical paradoxes.

[15] *Three Dialogues between Hylas and Philonous*, p. 208 (Everyman edn.).

[16] The phrases are Russell's, used in a very similar context (*Problems*, p. 14).

coming into contact with such water. In saying that water of 50° is hot, is *really* hot, an ordinary person in no way denies that under certain *special* conditions a human being would have genuine sense-impressions of cold. He also in no way denies that to a race of individuals whose body-temperature is 75° the water would genuinely appear cold. Pointing to these facts does therefore not refute the ordinary man. Berkeley is clearly guilty of a high redefinition of 'hot' or 'really hot'. To him something is hot only if, in addition to appearing hot to human beings in ordinary circumstances, it also appears hot to them under special circumstances and if it appears hot to beings with a body-temperature which is much greater than the actual body-temperature of human beings.

However, this is not quite accurate since, like most other philosophical paradoxes, the paradox about heat and cold has a double meaning. It would be inaccurate simply to say that Berkeley is guilty of *ignoratio elenchi* by redefinition. On the other hand, without in any way being inaccurate, it can be said that Berkeley and Plato have laid themselves open to the following dilemma: 'Either you mean by "hot" what is ordinarily meant by it—if you do, then what you say is plainly false; or else you are using "hot" in a high sense—if so what you say is true, but in that case you are guilty of *ignoratio elenchi* by redefinition. In either event you have failed to refute commonsense.' Very similar answers can also be made to Berkeley's and Russell's arguments concerning colours, shapes, and the other qualities which commonsense believes to exist independently of being perceived.

At the same time it must be admitted that Berkeley's arguments have a certain value. In ordinary speech we make a fairly rigid distinction between 'real' and 'unreal' data. Among the unreal data we lump together both the percepts which we have under special conditions (and percepts which do and would appear to beings differently constituted from ourselves) and what we experience e.g., in dreams and hallucinations. 'Real' we call only those percepts which a normal observer has under certain standard conditions.

A classification of this sort obscures the many likenesses between the 'real' percepts and percepts appearing under special conditions, while also hiding the many differences between the latter and data which are experienced in dreams and hallucinations.

The situation becomes quite clear if we divide data into three and not merely into two groups, as follows:

the R-data: percepts appearing to a normal observer under standard conditions, the A-data: percepts appearing to a normal observer under special conditions or to an abnormal observer in certain normal or special circumstances, and

the D-data: data appearing in dreams, hallucinations, etc.

It is unnecessary for our purposes to discuss exactly what are the likenesses between the R-data and the A-data. It is unnecessary, too, to discuss what exactly are the differences between the A-data and the D-data. It is sufficient to point out that while Berkeley is wrong in believing or suggesting that there are no differences between the R-data and the A-data, he is right in insisting that the differences between the R-data and the A-data are not nearly as great as ordinary speech suggests. In the case of colours, Berkeley's argument has the further merit of bringing out the fact that the expression 'X's real colour' has *two* perfectly proper senses. His argument helps one to realize that 'X's real colours' may mean 'the colour which X exhibits to a normal observer under certain standard conditions' *as well as* 'the colour which X exhibits to a normal observer under a finer instrument than the human eye, e.g. a microscope'.

III

A. Supposing a man, let us call him M, said to us, 'I have not yet found any physicians in New York.' Suppose we take him to Park Avenue and introduce him to Brown, a man who has a medical degree and who has cured many people suffering from diseases of the ear. Brown admits, however, that he has not been able to cure *all* the patients who ever consulted him. He also admits that many of his cures took a long time, some as long as eight years. On hearing this, M says, 'Brown certainly isn't a physician.'

Supposing we next take M to meet Black who has a medical degree and who can prove to M's and to our satisfaction that he has cured every patient who ever consulted him. Moreover, none of Black's cures took more than three years. However, on hearing that some of Black's cures took as long as two years and ten months, M says, 'Black certainly isn't a physician either.'

Finally we introduce M to White who has a medical degree and who has cured every one of his patients in less than six months. When M hears that some of White's cures took as long as five and a half months, he is adamant and exclaims, 'White—what a ridiculous error to call him a physician!'

At this stage, if not much sooner, all of us would impatiently ask M: What on earth do you mean by 'physician'? And we would plainly be justified in adding: Whatever you may mean by 'physician', in any sense in which we ever use the word, Black and Brown and White are physicians and very excellent ones at that.

Let us return now to Russell's doubt about the sun's rising tomorrow or about what would happen to a man who jumps out of the Empire State Building. Let us consider what Russell would say in reply to the following question: Supposing that the observed confirmatory instances for the theory of gravitation were a million or ten million times as extensive as they now are and that they were drawn from a very much wider field; would we then have a reason to suppose that the man will fall into the street and not move up into the sky? It is obvious that Russell and anybody taking his view would say 'No'. He would reply that though our *expectation* that the man's body will move in the direction of the street would be even stronger then than it is at present, we would still be without a *reason*.

Next, let us imagine ourselves to be putting the following question to Russell: Supposing the world were such that no accumulation of more than five hundred observed positive instances of a phenomenon has ever been found to be followed by a negative instance; supposing, for instance, that all the chickens who have ever been fed by the same man for 501 days in succession or more are still alive and that all the men too are still alive feeding the chickens every day—would the observed confirmations of the law of gravity in that case be a reason to suppose that the man jumping out of the Empire State Building will move in the direction of the street and not in the direction of the sky? I am not quite sure what Russell would say in reply to this question. Let us assume he would once again answer: 'No—past experience would not even then ever be a *reason*.'

Thirdly and finally, we have to consider what Russell would say to the following question: Supposing we had explored every corner of the universe with instruments millions of times as fine and accurate as any we now possess and that we had yet failed to discover any Controller of the movements of human bodies—would we then in our predictions about the man jumping out of the Empire State Building be in a better position than the chicken is in predicting its meals? Would our past observations then be a reason for our prediction? Whatever Russell would in fact say to this, it is clear that his remarks concerning the 'interesting' doubt about induction require him to answer our question in the negative. He would have to say something like this: 'Our *expectation* that the man's body will move in a downward direction will be even stronger than it is now. However, without invoking a non-empirical principle, we shall not *really* be in a better position than the chicken. We should still fail to possess a *reason*.'

As in the case of the man who refused to say that Brown, Black, and White were doctors, our natural response to all this will be to turn to Russell and say: What do you mean by 'being in a better position'? What on earth do you mean by 'a reason'? And, furthermore, why should anybody be interested in a reason in your sense of the word?

Russell's remarks about the need for a general principle like his principle of induction to serve as major premiss in every inductive argument make it clear what he means by a reason: like the Rationalists and Hume (in most places), he means by 'reason' a *logically conclusive* reason and by 'evidence' *deductively conclusive* evidence. When 'reason' is used in this sense, it must be admitted that past observations can never by themselves be a reason for any prediction whatsoever. But 'reason' is not used in this sense when, in science or in ordinary life, people claim to have a reason for a prediction.

So far as I can see, there are three different trends in the ordinary usage of 'reason for an inductive conclusion' and according to none of them does the word mean 'logically conclusive reason'. Among the three trends one is much more prominent than the others. It may fitly be called the main sense of the word. According to this main sense, what we mean when we claim that we have a reason for a prediction is that the past observations of this phenomenon or of analogical phenomena are of a certain kind: they are exclusively or predominantly positive, the number of the positive observations is at least fairly large, and they come from extensively varied sets of circumstances. This is of course a very crude formulation. But for the purposes of this article it is, I think, sufficient.[17]

Next, there is a number of trends according to which we mean very much less than this. Occasionally, for instance, we simply mean that it is *reasonable* to infer the inductive conclusion. And clearly it may be reasonable to infer an inductive conclusion for which we have no reason in the main sense. Thus let us suppose I know that Parker will meet Schroeder in a game in the near future and that it is imperative for me not to suspend my judgement but to come to a conclusion as to who will win. Supposing I know nothing about their present form and nothing also about the type of court on which the match is to be played. All I know is that Parker and Schroeder have in the previous two seasons met six times, Parker scoring four victories to Schroeder's two. In these circumstances it would be reasonable for me to predict that Parker will win and unreasonable to predict

---

[17] I have so far left out one important element in the main sense of 'reason for an inductive conclusion'. I shall come to that in Section IV. In the meantime this omission will not affect any of my points.

that Schroeder will win. Clearly however, in the main sense of the word I have no reason for either prediction.

Again there is a trend according to which any positive instance of a phenomenon is *a* reason for concluding that the next instance of the phenomenon will be positive. Thus in the circumstances described in the preceding paragraph, it would be quite proper to say we have *more reason* for supposing that Parker will win than for predicting Schroeder's victory. It would be quite proper also to say that we have *some reason* for supposing that Schroeder will win. It would be proper to say this even if Schroeder had won only one of the six matches. To all these and similar trends in the ordinary usage of 'reason for an inductive conclusion' I shall from now on refer as the second ordinary sense of the word.

There can be no doubt that, in both these ordinary senses of the word, we frequently have a reason for an inductive conclusion. In these senses we have an excellent reason for supposing that the man jumping out of the Empire State Building will move in the direction of the street, that the sun will rise tomorrow and that Stalin will die before the year 2000. The answer to question (1) is therefore a firm and clear 'Yes': in many domains we have a multitude of exclusively positive instances coming from extensively different circumstances.

The same is true if 'reason' is used in the third ordinary sense. However, I propose to reserve our discussion of that sense for Section V below. For the time being it will be convenient and, I think, not at all misleading to speak as if what I have called the main sense is the *only* ordinary sense of 'reason for an inductive conclusion'.

It should now be clear that, when Russell says that observed instances are never by themselves a reason for an inductive conclusion, he is guilty of an *ignoratio elenchi* by redefinition. His assertion that the premises of an inductive argument never by themselves constitute a *logically conclusive* reason for an inductive conclusion in no way contradicts the commonsense assertion that they frequently constitute a reason *in the ordinary sense of the word*. Russell's definition of 'reason' is indeed in one respect not a redefinition since in certain contexts we do use 'reason' to mean 'deductively conclusive reason'. However, it is a redefinition in that we never in ordinary life use 'reason' in Russell's sense when we are talking about inductive arguments.

Moreover, if 'reason' means 'deductively conclusive reason', Russell's questions are no more genuinely questions than, e.g., the sentence 'Is a father a female parent?' For, since part of the definition of 'inductive inference' is inference from something observed to something unobserved, it is a *contradiction* to say that an inference is both inductive and at the same time in the same respect deductively conclusive. Russell's 'interesting' doubt, then, is no more sensible or interesting than the 'doubt' whether we shall ever see something invisible or find an object which is a father and also female or an object which is a man but not a human being.

In a similar fashion, Russell's remarks about the future future which we quoted in Section 1B constitute an *ignoratio elenchi* by redefinition.[18] If the word 'future' is used in its ordinary sense in the statement 'the future will resemble the past and the present in certain respects', then we have plenty of evidence to support it. For in the ordinary sense of the word, 'future' simply means 'period which has to the past and the present the relation of happening after it'. In its ordinary sense, 'future' does *not* mean 'period which has to the past and the present the relation of happening after it *and* which can never itself be experienced *as a present*'. The period which is referred to by 'future' in its ordinary sense may very well one day be experienced as a present.

In the ordinary sense of the word 'future' therefore, what Russell calls past futures *are* futures. They are futures in relation to certain other periods which preceded them. Now, the appeal to the fact that past futures resembled past pasts and past presents constitutes excellent inductive evidence for the conclusion that the future will resemble the past and the present. Stated fully, the argument is as follows: a period which has to the past and present the relation of happening after it will resemble the past and the present in certain respects because in the past periods which stood in the same temporal relation to other periods were found to resemble those periods in these respects.

It should be emphasized that in the conclusion of this argument 'future' means 'future future', as that phrase would normally be understood. It refers to a period which by the time at which the statement is made has not yet been experienced, i.e. has not yet become a present or a past.

The appeal to the resemblance between past futures and past pasts and presents is not to the point only if in the sentence 'the future will resemble the past and the present' the word 'future' means 'period which has to the present the relation of occurring after it *and* which can never be experienced as a present'. In that case, of course, past futures are not really futures. For, when they were experienced they were experienced as presents. However, anybody who in ordinary life or in science says or implies that the future will resemble the past and the present does not use 'future' in this

---

[18] The paragraphs which follow are a summary in my own words of the main point of F. L. Will's delightful article 'Will the Future be like the Past?' (*Mind,* 1947).

sense. He means to assert something about a future which may one day be experienced as a present.

B. If Russell had answered in the affirmative any of the three questions which we imagined ourselves to be addressing to him, his question (1) would be a genuine question in the sense that it could then not be disposed of by an examination of definitions alone. But even then Russell would have been guilty of *ignoratio elenchi* by high redefinition. For in order to have a reason, in the ordinary sense of the word, for inferring that the next instance of a certain phenomenon is positive it is not necessary to observe all the positive and negative necessary conditions for the occurrence of this instance. Nor is it necessary that the collection of positive observed instances should be larger or taken from more extensively different circumstances than many we actually have. Nor, finally, is it necessary that breakdowns should never have occurred in *any* domain. All that is necessary in this connection is that there should have been no breakdowns in the same domain. Or if any did occur in the same domain they must have proved capable of correlation with certain special features which are known not to be present in the subject of the prediction.

Anybody who takes the trouble to observe the ordinary usage of the word 'reason' in connection with inductive arguments can easily check up on these claims.

It may be interesting to return for a moment to the case of the chicken which finally had its neck wrung. If we had explored every corner of the universe with wonderfully fine instruments and failed to discover a Controller of human movements, then in any ordinary sense of 'being in a better position' we should undoubtedly be in a better position in the case of the man jumping out of the Empire State Building than the chicken in regard to its meals. If Russell even then denied that we are in a better position he is surely using the phrase 'being in a better position' in a strange sense. Or else he is asserting a very plain falsehood. For to say that possession of one set of observed facts, say P, puts one in a better position with regard to a certain inductive conclusion, say *c*, than possession of another set of observed facts, say Q, simply means that P is a reason for *c* while Q is not, or that P is a better reason than Q.

Moreover, even without having explored every corner of the universe, we *are* in a very much better position in the case of predicting the sun's rising or the movement of a man jumping from the Empire State Building than the chicken is regarding its meals. The truth is that Russell's analogy, although it is not wholly pointless, is very weak indeed. Its only merit consists in bringing out the fact that neither we nor the chicken have explored every corner of the universe. On the other hand, there are two important differences which Russell obscures when he says that even in the case of our most trusted scientific theories we may be in no better a position than the chicken. Firstly, the number of observed instances supporting our prediction in a case like the man's jumping from the Empire State Building is obviously much greater than the number of positive instances observed by the chicken. And secondly, although we cannot definitely say that there is nowhere a Controller of human motions, we certainly have no reason whatsoever to suppose that one exists. We have no reason whatsoever to suppose that a living individual, in any ordinary sense of 'control', controls the movements of human beings who jump out of a house. The chicken, on the other hand, if it knows anything, knows that it depends for its meals on another living object.

C. Let us now turn to question (2): Is there any number, n, of observed positive instances of a phenomenon which affords evidence that the $n + 1$st instance will also be positive? I have already mentioned the familiar fact that scientists as well as ordinary people of a certain level of intelligence do not rely for their inductive conclusions on the number of observed positive instances exclusively. However, it will be easier to discuss the question before us if we proceed on the assumption that according to commonsense the strength of past experience as evidence depends on the number of observed positive instances and on nothing else. All important points can be made more easily if we proceed on this assumption.

Now, in two senses the answer to question (2) must be admitted to be a clear 'No'. Firstly, even if there were in every domain or in some domains a number of observed positive instances which constitutes the dividing line between evidence and non-evidence or, as it is more commonly expressed, between sufficient and insufficient evidence, there is no reason whatsoever to suppose that the number would be the same for different domains. There is no reason to suppose that in the domain of animal learning, for example, the number is the same as in the domain of the movements of the heavenly bodies. But, secondly, there is no such number in *any* domain. For we are here clearly faced with a case of what is sometimes called 'continuous variation'. There is no more *a* number dividing sufficient from insufficient evidence than there is a number dividing bald people from those who are not bald or poor people from people who are not poor.

These facts, however, imply nothing against commonsense. For, from the fact that there is no rigid division between sufficient and insufficient evidence, it does not follow that there are no cases of sufficient evidence.

From the fact that there is no number which constitutes the borderline between adequate collections of positive instances and those which are not adequate it does not follow that no number of positive instances is adequate. Although we cannot point to a number which divides bald people from people who are not bald, we can without any hesitation say that a man without a single hair on his head is bald while one with a million hairs on his head is not bald.

Furthermore, just as we can say about many people that they are bald and about many others that they are not bald although we have not counted the number of hairs on their heads and just as we can say that Rockefeller is rich although we cannot even approximately say what is the dollar-equivalent of his total possessions, so we can very often say *that* a number of observed instances constitutes sufficient evidence although we cannot say *what* this number is. The number of instances supporting the theory of gravitation which human beings have observed is for example more than sufficient evidence—in any ordinary sense of the word—for supposing that the man jumping out of the Empire State Building will move in a downward direction. But nobody knows what this number is. Human beings simply do not bother to keep records of all instances which confirm the law of gravity.

IV

A few words must now be said about the claim, made by Russell, Ewing, and others, that empiricism cannot provide a justification of induction since any inductive or empirical justification of induction would necessarily beg the question. If the principle of induction 'is not true', to use Russell's words, 'every attempt to arrive at general scientific laws from particular observations is fallacious, and Hume's scepticism is inescapable for an empiricist'. But 'the principle itself cannot, without circularity, be inferred from observed uniformities, since it is required to justify any such inference'.[19]

In the light of our remarks about redefinitions it is easy to see that all claims of this nature are either mistaken or else cases of *ignoratio elenchi* by redefinition. Before showing this, it will be well to restate the principle of induction in a form which is less confusing than that which Russell uses. Let us try the following formulation:

The greater the number of positive instances of a phenomenon which have been observed, assuming that no or none except easily explicable negative instances

[19] *History of Western Philosophy*, p. 699.

have been found, *and* the greater the number of kinds from which the positive instances are drawn, the less often does it happen that a new instance of the phenomenon turns out to be negative.[20]

I admit that this statement is rather vague and I also admit that, unless one qualifies it so as to deprive it of all factual significance, one can find exceptions to it.

At the same time, it seems plain that the principle as here stated is very much closer to the truth than its contrary. Furthermore, whether or not it would be correct to regard the inductive principle as a *premiss* of all inductive arguments, it does seem to me part of the *reason* for every inductive conclusion. I mean by this that we would not apply 'reason' to a large number of positive and widely varied instances if the contrary of the inductive principle were true or nearer the truth than the inductive principle. Supposing, for example, it had been found in all domains that after 10,000 instances had been observed, all of them positive and gathered from very varied circumstances, chaos was found among the rest. After the 10,000th instance, in other words, predictions always became thoroughly unreliable. Supposing that in these circumstances we discover a new species of animal —let us call them grats. We want to find how long it takes the grats to solve a certain puzzle and find that all our first 10,000 subjects can solve it in less than an hour. Would we say, knowing what happened in all the many observed domains after the 10,000th instance, we had a reason for supposing that the 10,001st grat would also solve the puzzle in less than an hour? It seems clear that most of us would refuse to say this.

It is now apparent that my analysis in Section III of the main sense and also of the second ordinary sense of 'reason for an inductive conclusion' was incomplete. It will be sufficient here to indicate how my analysis requires to be supplemented in the case of the main sense. To say that *p* is a reason for an inductive conclusion, in the main sense of 'reason', is to say firstly that part of *p* asserts what I earlier claimed the whole of *p* to assert *and* secondly that the rest of *p* asserts the inductive principle. Part of *p* asserts the inductive principle at least in the sense of asserting that it is much closer to the truth than its contrary.

Miss Ambrose, in her splendid article on induction, has tried to meet the charge of *petitio principii* by contending that the principle of induction is not a premiss of inductive arguments, but a principle of inference or substitution *according* to which 'inductive inferences are made'.[21] But this

---

[20] Cf. Ernest Nagel, *Principles of the Theory of Probability*, p. 72.

[21] 'The Problem of Justifying Inductive Inference', *Journal of Philosophy*, 1947, pp. 260 ff. Miss Ambrose's point is not actually made in order to answer the charge of *petitio principii*. However, if what she says were true of all possible forms of the inductive principle, the charge would have been implicitly disposed of.

seems to me an inadequate reply to the charge. For the enemies of com-monsense might admit that what Miss Ambrose says is true of the principle as Russell is in the habit of formulating it. But they might then proceed to restate it in some such way as I have done, maintaining that in this sense it does form part of the reason for every inductive conclusion. At this stage they would undoubtedly renew their charge that the inductive argument cannot be supported by an inductive argument without begging the question.

And I want to show now that my admission that the inductive principle is part of the reason for every inductive conclusion implies nothing against commonsense or against empiricism. For this purpose it is necessary to distinguish two possible senses of any statement of the form 'All S are P'. Such a statement may either mean 'All *observed* S are P'; or it may mean 'All S *whatsoever* are P'. I propose to refer to statements of the first class as 'universal premisses' and to statements of the second class as 'universal conclusions'. Now, the charge of *petitio principii* could be sustained only if the inductive principle were meant as a universal *conclusion* when form-ing part of the evidence of inductive conclusions. But it is clear that when it forms part of the evidence of inductive conclusions, the inductive principle is or requires to be meant only as a universal *premiss*. We would refuse to regard a large collection of exclusively positive and widely varied instances of a phenomenon as a good reason for predicting that the next instance will also be positive if in all or most previous cases large collections of exclusively positive and widely varied instances turned out to be a thorough-ly unreliable basis for prediction. However, given a large collection of exclusively positive and widely varied instances of a phenomenon, it would be sufficient for a correct application of 'reason' that in all or most *observed* cases large collections of exclusively positive and widely varied instances turned out to be a reliable basis for prediction. Any opinion to the contrary rests on the belief, exploded in the previous section, that according to ordinary usage 'reason for an inductive conclusion' means 'deductively conclusive reason for the inductive conclusion'.

V

I can well imagine that some people will not be moved by what I have said. Even if Russell himself were convinced, there are undoubtedly other philos-ophers who would take me to task for evading what they would declare to be the real issue. 'You may have shown,' it would be said, 'that in the ordinary sense of "reason" and "evidence" past observations do often constitute a good reason and sufficient evidence. But how do you know that what is a reason in the ordinary sense is *really* a *reason*? The fact that the sun has risen every day so far is admittedly a reason, in the ordinary sense, for supposing that it will again rise tomorrow. For to say this is simply to say that it has always risen in the past. But *can you predict* that the sun will again rise tomorrow simply because it has always risen in the past? The question, the interesting doubt about induction in this instance is not: Have we any reason in the ordinary sense for supposing that the sun will rise tomorrow? To this, we agree, the answer is "Yes". The real question is: Having a reason, in the ordinary sense, for believing that the sun will rise tomorrow, can we infer from this with any reliability that the sun will again rise tomorrow?'

Before I take up this objection I should like to fill in a gap in my analysis of the ordinary usage of the phrase 'reason for an inductive conclusion'. It will be remembered that in Section III I distinguished between three trends in the ordinary usage of this phrase. Firstly there is what I called the main sense of the word; secondly there is a set of trends which I grouped together as the second sense of the word; and finally there is a trend or sense to which I alluded but which I have so far not attempted to analyse. According to both senses I analysed, '*p* constitutes a reason for *c*' (where *c* stands for some inductive conclusion) asserts the existence of *observed* events exclusively. Its truths need not at all be affected by the discovery that *c* is false.

Now, the third sense which I have not yet analysed is much less prominent than the main sense but, so far as I can see, much more prominent than the trends which I have grouped together as the second sense. When 'reason' is used in this third sense the observed facts referred to by 'reason' in the main sense are part of its referent, but they are not the whole of it. It is not indeed a necessary condition for the application of 'reason' (in this sense) to a set of propositions, say *p*, that the prediction based on *p* be *true*. But, where the prediction refers to a multitude of events, it is a necessary condition that it be considerably nearer the truth than its contrary. Where the prediction explicitly refers to a single event only, it is a necessary condition that a considerable majority of instantial predictions having the same relation to *p* be true. Thus, according to the third sense, we would have had a reason for believing that the man jumping out of the Empire State Building will move in a downward direction although subsequent observation shows him to move into the sky—provided that in most other cases, as yet unobserved at the time of making our prediction, human bodies did in similar circumstances move downwards. With our large collection of exclusively positive and widely varied past instances, we would have had a reason for believing that all men who will jump out of houses are going to move in a downward direction even if a few of them disappeared in the sky so long as *most* of them moved as we predicted. We would have had no reason in this third sense if in the case of a large proportion of subsequent jumps—approaching half the total number of new jumps—bodies failed to move in a downward direction.

It will be helpful to use different signs to distinguish between a reason in the main and a reason in the third sense. Let us use the sign 'reason m' to stand for reasons in the main sense and the sign 'reason f' to signify reasons in the third sense. Using this terminology, we may restate the objection outlined at the beginning of the present section as follows: 'You have shown that frequently people have reasons m for believing in inductive conclusions. However, the real question is whether, without appealing to a non-empirical principle, they ever have reasons f; and this you have not shown.' I could have stated this charge more easily by using the words 'probable' and 'certain'. But, as I explained earlier, an explicit discussion of the questions 'Are any inductive conclusions probable?' and 'Are any inductive conclusions certain?' is beyond my scope.

In reply to this charge, I wish to make two comments. The first of these is as follows: it simply is a fact that, given certain sets of observations, human beings can make true predictions. It simply is a fact that given reasons in the sense of reason m we very often also have reasons in the sense of reason f. This is a fact just as it is a fact that human beings can make genuine observations and just as it is a fact that certain objects have certain spatial relations to one another and that some events happen after other events. It is logically and also I think factually possible to have feelings of doubt and anxiety concerning the outcome of any prediction whatsoever. But it is also possible to have such doubts about the genuineness of observations at the present moment and about the reality of spatial and temporal relations. The possibility or the actual existence of such feelings no more implies that human beings cannot in certain circumstances make true predictions than it implies that they never make genuine observations or that there are no real relations in space and time.

Secondly, it seems to me that a person who has all the information which ordinary mortals have but who nevertheless asks, with an air of infinite puzzlement 'How can we now predict something which is not yet?' is tacitly confusing the statement 'c is true' with the statement 'c has been or is being directly verified'[22]. '*c* can now be correctly predicted' does indeed imply '*c* is true', but it does not imply '*c* has been directly verified'. To say that we have a reason *f* for *c* does imply that *c* is at least probable. It does not imply that *c* has already been directly tested. Now, if 'correctly predict' is used in any ordinary sense, then the question 'How can we now predict an event which is not yet?' produces no cramps and can easily be answered by referring to the truth of past predictions in certain circumstances. Questions like 'How can we now predict something which is not yet?' give rise to headaches only if '*c* can now be correctly predicted' is used in such a way as to imply '*c* has been directly verified'. Sentences like this then produce cramps and headaches because they are not really questions at all. They are like rhetorical questions. The sentence 'How can we now predict something which is not yet?' is then another way of *asserting* the *necessary* proposition that in the high sense of 'predict' in which '*c* can now be correctly predicted' implies '*c* has been directly verified', it is impossible ever to predict a future event. But this of course does not at all contradict the commonsense view that in the ordinary sense of 'predict' we can frequently predict future events. This objection, too, is therefore an *ignoratio elenchi* by redefinition.

To be more precise: the sentence 'How can we now predict something which is not yet?' produces a cramp if one believes oneself to be asking the (easy) question which the sentence expresses with every word in it used in its ordinary sense when one is in fact *asserting* the necessary proposition that in a certain high sense of 'predict' we can never predict anything at all.

Following Moore, Mr. J. N. Findlay has forcibly drawn attention to the queerness of the philosopher's doubt when he utters sentences like 'But how can any one set of facts furnish a valid basis for an inference concerning another set of facts?',[23] 'How do you know that one thing ever happens after another?' or 'How do you know that one thing is ever to the left of another?' Findlay suggests that we take a specific instance—e.g. what we would normally describe as a pencil lying to the left of a pen—point it out to the doubting philosopher, and say, 'This is how.'[24] In the case of predictions we could take a piece of chalk and call out, 'I now predict that when I release this piece of chalk it will move in a downward direction.'

---

[22] This distinction is brought out very lucidly by Sydney Hook in his *John Dewey*, p. 79.

[23] Williams, op. cit., p. 227.

[24] 'Time: A Treatment of Some Puzzles', *Australasian Journal of Psychology and Philosophy*, 1941, p. 217; cf. also Friedrich Waismann's introduction to Schlick's *Gesammelte Aufsätze*, pp. xxi ff.

We would then release it, and, as it falls in a downward direction, we would point to it and say, 'This is how we can know in advance.' Since the philosopher is just as familiar with these facts as we are and since he does not, in one important sense at least, query any of them, it is apparent that, without realizing it, he is using one or more of his words in a strange sense.

III

SYMPOSIUM ON INDUCTIVE EVIDENCE

(1) The Concept of Inductive Evidence

WESLEY C. SALMON*

I

HUME, it is often said,[1] tried to find a way of proving that inductive inferences with true premises would have *true* conclusions. He properly failed to find any such justification precisely because it is the function of *deduction* to prove the truth of conclusions on the basis of true premises. Induction has a different function. Given true premises, the inductive inference establishes its conclusions as *probable*. Small wonder that Hume failed to find a justification of induction. He was trying to make induction into deduction, and he really succeeded only in proving the platitude that induction is not deduction.

Arguments along this line are appealing, and they have given rise to widely accepted attempts to dissolve the problem of induction. To understand and evaluate them we must, however, take account of ambiguities of the term 'probable'.

One important type of probability concept identifies probability with

From *American Philosophical Quarterly*, vol. 2 (1965), pp. 265–80. Reprinted by permission of the authors and Editor of *American Philosophical Quarterly*.

* This paper and the following comments were presented, with minor modifications, as a Symposium on Induction and Probability at the meetings of the American Philosophical Association, Western Division, Milwaukee, Wisconsin, 30 April–2 May, 1964. The author wishes to express his gratitude to the National Science Foundation for its support of his research on probability and induction.

[1] The view outlined and criticized in this section is a composite drawn from various sources and is not to be attributed to any single author. Among those who subscribe to some such view I would include A. J. Ayer, *Language, Truth and Logic* (Dover Publications, New York, 1952); Paul Edwards, 'Russell's Doubts about Induction', *Mind*, vol. 58 (1949), pp. 141–63 [pp. 26–47 of the present volume. Ed.]; Asher Moore, 'The Principle of Induction', *Journal of Philosophy*, vol. 49 (1952), pp. 741–58; Arthur Pap, *Elements of Analytic Philosophy* (Macmillan, New York, 1949) and *An Introduction to the Philosophy of Science* (The Free Press of Glencoe, New York, 1962); P. F. Strawson, *Introduction to Logical Theory* (Methuen, London, 1952).

relative frequency. If we were to claim that inductive conclusions are probable in this sense, we would be claiming that inductive inferences with true premises often have true conclusions, though perhaps not always. Unfortunately, Hume's argument shows directly that this claim cannot be substantiated. It was recognized long before Hume that inductive inferences cannot be expected *always* to lead to the truth. The suggestion that Hume merely showed the fallibility of induction is a mistake.[2] Hume's argument shows not only that we cannot justify the claim that *every* inductive inference with true premises will have a true conclusion, but further that we cannot prove that *any* inductive inference with true premises will have a true conclusion. We can show neither that inductive inferences establish their conclusions as true, nor that they establish their conclusions as probable in the frequency sense. The introduction of the frequency concept of probability gives no help whatever in circumventing the problem of induction, but this is no surprise, for we should not have expected it to be suitable for this purpose.

A more promising probability concept identifies probability with degree of rational belief. To say that a statement is probable in this sense means that one would be rationally justified in believing it; degree of probability is the degree of assent a person would be rationally justified in giving. Probability is a logical relationship objectively determined by the available evidence. To say that a statement is probable in this sense means that it is supported by evidence. But, if a statement is the conclusion of an inductive inference it *is* supported by evidence—by inductive evidence—this is what it *means* in this context to be supported by evidence. Trivially, then, the conclusion of an inductive inference is probable under this concept of probability. To ask, with Hume, if we should accept inductive conclusions is tantamount to asking if we should fashion our beliefs in terms of the evidence, and this, in turn, is tantamount to asking whether we should be rational. In this way we arrive at an 'ordinary language dissolution' of the problem of induction. Once we understand clearly the meanings of such key terms as 'rational', 'probable', and 'evidence' we see that the problem arose out of linguistic confusion and evaporates into the question of whether it is rational to be rational. Such tautological questions, if meaningful at all, demand affirmative answers.

Unfortunately, the dissolution is not satisfactory. Its inadequacy can be exhibited by focusing upon the concept of inductive evidence and seeing

---

[2] See, for example, Jerrold Katz, *The Problem of Induction and Its Solution* (University of Chicago Press, Chicago, 1962), p. 115.

how it figures in the foregoing argument.[3] The fundamental difficulty arises from the fact that the very notion of inductive evidence is determined by the rules of inductive inference. If a conclusion is to be supported by inductive evidence it is necessary that it be the conclusion of a correct inductive inference with true premises. Whether the inductive inference is correct depends upon whether the rule governing that inference is correct. The relation of inductive evidential support is, therefore, inseparably bound to the correctness of rules of inductive inference. In order to be able to say whether a given statement is supported by inductive evidence we must be able to say which inductive rules are correct.

For example, suppose that a die has been thrown a large number of times and we have observed that the side two came up in one-sixth of the tosses. This is our 'evidence' *e*. Let *h* be the conclusion that, 'in the long run', side two will come up one-sixth of the times. Consider the following three rules:

(1) (Induction by enumeration) Given m/n of observed *A* are *B*, to infer that the 'long run' relative frequency of *B* among *A* is m/n.

(2) (*A priori* rule) Regardless of observed frequencies, to infer that the 'long run' relative frequency of *B* among *A* is $1/k$, where *k* is the number of possible outcomes—six in the case of the die.

(3) (Counter-inductive rule) Given m/n of observed *A* are *B*, to infer that the 'long run' relative frequency of *B* among *A* is $(n - m)/n$.

Under rule (1), *e* is positive evidence for *h*; under rule (2). *e* is irrelevant to *h*; and under rule (3), *e* is negative evidence for *h*. To determine which conclusions are supported by what evidence, it is necessary to arrive at a decision as to what inductive rules are acceptable. If rule (1) is correct, the evidence *e* supports the conclusion *h*. If rule (2) is correct, we are justified in drawing the conclusion *h*, but this is entirely independent of the observational evidence *e*; the same conclusions would have been sanctioned by rule (2) regardless of observational evidence. If rule (3) is correct, we are not only prohibited from drawing the conclusion *h*, but also we are permitted to draw a conclusion h^1, which is logically incompatible with *h*. Whether a given conclusion is *supported by evidence*—whether it would be *rational to believe* it on the basis of given evidence—whether

---

[3] Wesley C. Salmon, 'Should We Attempt to Justify Induction?' *Philosophical Studies*, vol. 8 (1957), pp. 33–48, contains a similar criticism of this type of argument. In that discussion I focused upon the concept of rationality; here the main emphasis is upon the concept of inductive evidence. Barker and Kyburg, in their comments on the present paper, bring the concept of rationality to the forefront again.

it is *made probable* by virtue of its relation to given evidence—depends upon selection of the correct rule or rules from among the infinitely many rules we might conceivably adopt.

The problem of induction can now be reformulated as a problem about evidence. What rules ought we to adopt to determine the nature of inductive evidence? What rules provide suitable concepts of inductive evidence? If we take the customary inductive rules to define the concept of inductive evidence, have we adopted a proper concept of evidence? Would the adoption of some alternative inductive rules provide a more suitable concept of evidence? These are genuine questions which need to be answered.

We find, moreover, that what appeared earlier as a pointless question now becomes significant and difficult. If we take the customary rules of inductive inference to provide a suitable definition of the relation of inductive evidential support, it makes considerable sense to ask whether it is rational to believe on the basis of evidence as thus defined rather than to believe on the basis of evidence as defined according to other rules. For instance, I believe that the *a priori* rule and the counter-inductive rule mentioned above are demonstrably unsatisfactory, and hence, they demonstrably fail to provide a suitable concept of inductive evidence.[4] The important point is that something concerning the selection from among possible rules needs demonstration and is amenable to demonstration.

There is danger that we may be taken in by an easy equivocation. One meaning we may assign to the concept of inductive evidence is, roughly, the basis on which we ought to fashion our beliefs. Another meaning results from the relation of evidential support determined by whatever rule of inductive inference we adopt. It is only by supposing that these two concepts are the same that we suppose the problem of induction to have vanished. The problem of induction is still there; it is the problem of providing adequate grounds for the selection of inductive rules. We want the relation of evidential support determined by these rules to yield a concept of inductive evidence which is, in fact, the basis on which we ought to fashion our beliefs.

The foregoing problem is not circumvented by replacing rules of induction by confirmation functions. Confirmation functions determine evidential relations. Carnap's presentation of a continuum of inductive

[4] See Wesley C. Salmon, 'Regular Rules of Induction', *Philosophical Review*, vol. 65 (1956), pp. 385–8, and 'Inductive Inference' in *Philosophy of Science: The Delaware Seminar*, vol. II, ed. Bernard H. Baumrin (John Wiley, New York, 1963) [pp. 85–97 of the present volume are an extract from the latter paper—Ed.].

methods drives this point home. The problem is precisely the same. How are we to decide which confirmation function from among this super-denumerable infinity of confirmation functions provides a suitable concept of inductive evidence?

We began this initially promising approach to the problem of the justification of induction by introducing the notion of probability, but we end with a dilemma. If we take 'probability' in the frequency sense, it is easy to see why it is advisable to accept probable conclusions in preference to improbable ones. In so doing we shall be right more often. Unfortunately, we cannot show that inferences conducted according to any particular rule establish conclusions that are probable in this sense. If we take 'probability' in a non–frequency sense it may be easy to show that inferences which conform to our accepted inductive rules establish their conclusions as probable. Unfortunately, we can find no reason to prefer conclusions which are probable in this sense to those which are improbable. As Hume has shown, we have no reason to suppose that probable conclusions will often be true and improbable ones will seldom be true. This dilemma is Hume's problem of induction all over again. We have been led to an interesting reformulation, but it is only a reformulation and not a solution.

II

In view of the multiplicity of possible inductive rules and the extreme difficulty in providing any sort of justification for the selection of one rather than another, it is tempting to hunt for still other ways of avoiding the task. One frequent theme begins by citing the ultimacy of the principles for which a justification is sought. It is impossible, we are told, to justify all principles, for in the absence of principles which can be used for purposes of carrying out the justification there is no conceivable means for achieving it. We are reminded that it is impossible to provide a justification of deduction, for, as we have learned from Lewis Carroll's 'What the Tortoise said to Achilles',[5] the attempt will come to grief in a circle or an infinite regress. If we insist upon a justification for induction while we are content to omit the requirement for deduction, we are showing unseemly prejudice against one kind of inference. The fact that induction is not deduction does not mean that induction is inferior to deduction, or that induction stands in special need of justification.[6]

[5] *The Complete Works of Lewis Carroll* (The Modern Library, New York, 1936), pp. 1225 ff.
[6] Again, the argument sketched is a composite. Among those who contribute to this standpoint are A. J. Ayer, *The Problem of Knowledge* (Penguin Books, London,

The first step in evaluating this kind of argument consists in becoming clear on the lesson to be learned from the colloquy between Achilles and the tortoise. This lesson, very simply, is that no supply of tautologies or logical truths can sanction the drawing of a conclusion from premises unless there is a rule of inference whose function is to sanction inferences. *Modus ponens*, for instance, is a rule; the fact that there is a corresponding tautology in the propositional calculus does not make the rule dispensable. If there is any problem of justification here, it is the problem of justifying the adoption of a rule, which is neither true nor false, rather than a problem of establishing the truth of a statement. If Achilles had had the wit to point out that his need was not for additional premises, but rather for a rule of inference, the conversation might have taken a different and more constructive turn. The tortoise, it might be noted, was not reticent about accepting the pronouncements of logic; he was not questioning the legitimacy of accepting certain statements as *truths*.

The sole ground, it seems to me, for accepting or rejecting rules is in terms of the aims that will or will not be achieved by conforming to them. The aim of deductive logic, I take it, is to be able to draw true conclusions from true premises. To achieve this aim we endeavour to adopt as rules of deductive inference only those rules which are truth-preserving. We accept *modus ponens* as a rule of deductive inference because we believe it will never sanction drawing a false conclusion from true premises. But can we justify *modus ponens* as a rule of deductive logic by proving that it is truth-preserving? We can, of course, prove a metatheorem to the effect that *modus ponens* in the object language is truth-preserving. The metaproof, however, requires inference in the metalanguage, and this in turn requires that the metalanguage have *modus ponens* or some other rule of inference which is at least as suspect. To prove that a kind of rule is truth-preserving, it is necessary to have and use rules of deduction in that very proof. Hence, we cannot prove, without either circularity or vicious regress, that *modus ponens* is truth-preserving—that is to say, we cannot justify deduction.

1956); Stephen Barker, *Induction and Hypothesis* (Cornell University Press, Ithaca, 1957); Max Black, *Language and Philosophy* (Cornell University Press, Ithaca, 1949), and *Problems of Analysis* (Cornell University Press, Ithaca, 1954); Rudolf Carnap, 'The Aim of Inductive Logic', *Logic, Methodology and Philosophy of Science*, eds. Ernest Nagel, Patrick Suppes, and Alfred Tarski (Stanford University Press, Stanford, 1962), and 'Replies and Systematic Expositions', § 26, *The Philosophy of Rudolf Carnap*, ed. Paul Arthur Schilpp (The Open Court Publishing Co., LaSalle, 1963); Nelson Goodman, *Fact, Fiction, and Forecast* (Harvard University Press, Cambridge, Mass., 1955); Katz, op. cit.; Henry E. Kyburg, Jr., *Probability and the Logic of Rational Belief* (Wesleyan University Press, Middletown, Conn., 1961); Strawson, op. cit.

In view of this situation, it is sometimes said that we must utilize a kind of deductive intuition or logical common sense to 'see' that *modus ponens* is a correct and legitimate form of inference. Then, the argument continues, if we are willing to allow the necessity of deductive intuition and common sense as the ultimate appeals in justifying deductive logic, why should we not allow a similar role to inductive intuition and inductive common sense? If an individual is so deductively blind that he cannot see the legitimacy of concluding *q* from *p* and *if p then q*, then there is nothing we can do with or for him. He simply does not belong to the community of sane and rational individuals. Communication, in any form, with such a person is impossible. The task of deductive logic is not to try to justify such rules as *modus ponens* but rather to present systematically the acceptable rules of deductive inference.

Similarly, the argument continues, if a person is so inductively blind that he cannot see the superiority of induction by enumeration, i.e. rule (1), over the *a priori* rule (2) and the counter-inductive rule (3) there is nothing to be done. We can no more logically compel a person lacking in inductive common sense to accept acceptable rules than we can in the case of deduction. The task of inductive philosophy is not the justification of induction, but the formulation in systematic fashion of our inductive intuitions. This formulation may be no easy task, incidentally, for our intuitions may lie deeply hidden and may be in apparent conflict with one another, but sufficient critical reflection should enable us to straighten them out. In any case, the ultimate appeal for the justification of inductive rules is our intuitive sense for the concept of inductive evidence.

Persuasive as the foregoing analogy may seem, I think it is fundamentally misleading and unsound. The reason is simple. In the case of *modus ponens* I may reflect upon the rule very carefully and think of all sorts of instances of its application. Try as I will, I cannot conceive the possibility of any situation in which its use would lead from true premises to a false conclusion. So deeply ingrained is this conviction that I am inclined to declare that any alleged counter-example to *modus ponens* would *ipso facto* have to involve an equivocation or a misuse of the conditional form of statement. Part of what we mean by a conditional statement is that it shall be the valid major premiss of *modus ponens*. However, there is no need to dogmatize in advance. We cannot prove, without circularity, that no counter-example to *modus ponens* will ever be found. If an apparent counter-example is discovered it will receive the most careful scrutiny. Although we cannot now conceive the possibility of a genuine counter-example, future developments might make us change our minds. For the present, however, we can find no grounds whatever for withholding the judgement that *modus ponens* is truth-preserving.

The situation with induction is quite different. After a small dose of Hume's *Enquiry* we can, without difficulty, imagine all sorts of states of affairs in which practically all—if not absolutely all—of our future inductive inferences with true premises turn out to have false conclusions. We can, furthermore, construct perverse kinds of inductive rules (as judged in the light of our inductive intuitions) and describe possible worlds in which these rules would be very successful indeed. We cannot provide, without circularity, any reason for supposing that we do not, in fact, live in some such world. A Cartesian demon could addle our brains and throw us into linguistic confusion, but we cannot conceive of anything he could do to make *modus ponens* not literally truth-preserving. He would, however, have no trouble in completely subverting any inductive rule we can set forth. It is one thing to appeal to logical intuition concerning the acceptability of rules which, to the best of our most critical reflection, must be truth-preserving in all possible worlds. It is quite another to make such an appeal to our (inductive) logical intuition for the acceptability of inductive rules when critical reflection reveals that they may turn our to be entirely unsatisfactory in our actual world and distinctly less successful than others we can formulate. There are live options in the case of inductive rules quite unlike any which exist in the case of rules of deduction.[7]

There is a close connection between the argument just discussed and that taken up in the first section of this essay. Our usage of terms like 'rational', 'probable', and 'evidence' is closely linked to our inductive intuitions and our common sense of the inductive evidential relation. All were learned at mother's knee, and all are second nature to us. We can, nevertheless, state alternative and conflicting inductive rules, we can describe different linguistic usage, and we can imagine radically different inductive behaviour. The problem is: Can we give adequate reasons for preferring our usage, intuitions, and behaviour to the alternatives? If we can, that is a justification of induction. If we cannot, then we cannot justify induction. It is not, however, an adequate answer to say that we prefer them just because they are ours. Yet it seems to me that this is precisely what we are saying if we say that the generally accepted inductive rules stand in no need of justification, or if we say that our inductive intuition

---

[7] The choice between a two-valued and a three-valued logic is not at all the same sort of thing. Two-valued logic is a specialization of three-valued logic. No such relation exists in the case of inductive rules; here there is genuine conflict. The choice between *modus ponens* and affirming the consequent would be more to the point.

and our ordinary usage are the ultimate standards in terms of which we must justify. To say these things is to rule out the alternatives without a hearing, and to reject them simply because they fail to conform to what we already accept. Such an approach bespeaks a regrettable unwillingness to apply critical standards to cherished principles.

It may be objected that I am forgetting the ultimacy of the principles or rules under discussion, and the consequent impossibility of furnishing any kind of justification for them. In making precisely this point, Ayer remarks, 'When it is understood that there logically could be no court of superior jurisdiction, it hardly seems troubling that inductive reasoning should be left, as it were, to act as judge in its own cause.'[8] The difficulty is, to pursue the metaphor, that there are too many courts of equal jurisdiction. Vicious circularity manifests itself; if each type of reasoning is left 'to act as judge in its own cause', there are many conflicting judgements. For instance, in the court of affirming the consequent, the following argument would seem to lead conclusively to a verdict:

> If affirming the consequent is valid,
> then $2 + 2 = 4$.
> $2 + 2 = 4$.
> _____
> $\therefore$ Affirming the consequent is valid.

This argument has true premises, it conforms to the form of affirming the consequent, and it asserts the validity of this form.[9] If we allow customary inductive methods to act as judge in their own behalf, we do so by ignoring all other judges and listening only to the judgement in the particular court we happen to be in.

Strawson also has seen fit to make a legal reference in dealing with the same point: 'But it makes no sense to inquire in general whether the law of the land, the legal system as a whole, is or is not legal. For to what legal standards are we appealing?'[10] This analogy is a useful one. It is, indeed, pointless to ask whether the legal system as a whole is legal, but this does not mean that the legal system is exempt from criticism and stands in no need of justification. What does make sense is to ask whether adherence to this legal system will achieve ends we seek to realize, and whether some

[8] Ayer, *The Problem of Knowledge*, ed. cit., p. 75.
[9] Salmon, 'Should We Attempt to Justify Induction', op. cit., presents inductive examples.
[10] Strawson, op. cit., p. 257.

other legal system would achieve these ends more efficiently. Similarly, although we cannot justify inductive rules by reference to other inductive rules, we can try to show that there are reasons for preferring one inductive rule to others. This is precisely what proponents of pragmatic justification or vindication of induction have attempted to do. Realizing fully the impossibility of showing that any particular rule will yield true inductive conclusions from true premises, theorists of this persuasion have still tried to give deductive grounds for the selection of appropriate inductive rules. Instead of allowing inductive intuition, common sense, or ordinary usage to provide the ultimate criteria for the concept of inductive evidence, these 'practicalists' (as Max Black has called them) attempt to provide a stronger grounding for inductive rules, and consequently a deeper understanding of the concept of inductive evidence.

(2) Is There a Problem of Induction?

STEPHEN F. BARKER

WITTGENSTEIN, Strawson, and others have held that the traditional problem of induction is a pseudo-problem, resulting from conceptual confusion; a puzzle to be dissolved, not a problem to be solved in its own terms. Professor Salmon disagrees and tries to rescue the grand old problem from dissolution; or perhaps I ought rather to say that he tries to resurrect that grand old corpse of a problem which many of us had hoped would now be allowed to moulder in peace.

What is this problem of induction, as Salmon sees it? It involves a contrast between deduction and induction. As I understand him, Salmon admits that our practice of reasoning deductively—our practice of preferring *modus ponens* to affirming the consequent, and so on—is a practice which, considered as a whole, is something we cannot justify. Salmon thinks that any attempt at justification would itself employ deductive reasoning, and therefore would fail through begging the question. Nevertheless, Salmon does not feel that this makes deduction an irrational practice. He does not doubt that the practice of deductive reasoning is suitable, satisfactory, proper, adequately grounded, and a practice we ought to adhere to. For it seems to him that when we reflect upon any one of our specific rules of deduction—for instance, *modus ponens*—we find it is inconceivable that the rule could lead us from true premises to a false conclusion.

What sort of inconceivability is involved here? Salmon expresses himself cryptically. But surely the sense in which it is inconceivable that *modus ponens* could be unreliable is not like the sense in which it is inconceivable that a man now living could be 100 billion years old. People with more flexible and more versatile imaginations than ours might well be able to conceive of a man's being 100 billion years old, but even they could not conceive of *modus ponens* as being unreliable. No, the sense in which it is inconceivable that *modus ponens* could be unreliable must be like the sense in which it is inconceivable that there could be spherical pyramids. With shapes, being a sphere necessarily precludes being a pyramid, and with arguments, being in the form *modus ponens* necessarily precludes being unreliable. Reflection upon the senses we attach to these terms enables us to see that this is necessarily so.

But now for induction. Our practice of reasoning inductively can very crudely be described as the practice of attributing to unobserved phenomena the simplest regularities that we have detected in observed phenomena; or, still more crudely, it can be described as the practice of obeying the so-called rule of induction by simple enumeration. With regard to this practice, Salmon feels qualms not felt about deduction. He maintains that there is a crucial difference between the status of induction and that of deduction. Deduction is safe, since it is inconceivable that it could go wrong; but induction may be unsafe, according to Salmon, for we can conceive of its going wrong.

What would it be like for the practice of induction to go wrong? Well, now, we can conceive of people who made it their practice to reason in some anti-inductive manner—they always attribute to the unobserved something other than the simplest regularity detectable in the observed. To suppose that induction could go wrong, according to Salmon, is to suppose that the long-run relative frequency with which people who follow the practice of reasoning inductively get true conclusions from true premisses is less than the long-run relative frequency with which people who follow the practice of reasoning in some anti-inductive manner do so. Perhaps the world is under the governance of a malicious Cartesian demon who makes it his sport to see to it that people who reason inductively will usually reach false conclusions even when their premisses are true, and who sees to it that people who reason in some anti-inductive manner usually get true conclusions when their premisses are true. In such a world induction would not pay. Now, how do we know that our actual world is not like this? We can conceive that induction might not be effective as a means of leading us to truth. Thus induction may be unsafe in a way in which deduction cannot be. This is what leads Salmon to believe that we need a justification of induction, a justification of a sort not called for in connection with deduction. We need some account of why it is rational to adopt the practice of inductive reasoning rather than some anti-inductive practice. We need some grounds for believing that induction is a suitable, satisfactory, proper practice, adequately grounded, that we ought to pursue. (These words 'rational', 'suitable', 'satisfactory', etc., are the terms Salmon uses.)

So far, I have been summarizing what I think Salmon is saying. Now I have several criticisms. My first and main objection to Salmon's way of trying to build up a problem here is that he neglects or underrates a most important certainty that we do possess regarding induction. I fully agree with him that it is conceivable that induction might be less successful than some other way of reasoning about the world; this is conceivable, and it is a logical possibility. But it is not probable. We know for an absolute certainty that it is not probable that any anti-inductive practice will be as successful in the long run as induction will be. Here of course I am using the term 'probable' in the sense of rational credibility, not in the relative frequency sense. Built into this normal sense of the word 'probable' is a commitment to the practice of induction. To be sure, we do not know with certainty that people who practise induction will be more successful in reaching true conclusions than will those who practise some form of anti-induction; but what we do know with certainty is that those who practise induction will probably be more successful—that is, that it is reasonable to believe that they will be more successful. That this is so reflects an aspect of what the word 'probable' means in its normal sense. Just as it is inconceivable that *modus ponens* should *be* unreliable, so it is inconceivable that inductive inferences should not *probably* be the most successful kind in the long run. But to grant this to grant that we do have good reason for regarding induction as reliable. This means that there is no problem of induction, in Salmon's sense. There is no more of an over-all problem about the reliability of induction than there is an over-all problem about the reliability of deduction.

Salmon will reject what I have just said, for he thinks of it as a shuffling evasion. He will reply that even if induction is probably reliable, even if this is necessarily true in virtue of the normal meaning of the word 'probable', still there remains a serious problem of induction. The problem is: Why is the fact that induction is probably reliable any real reason for relying upon induction? Why should we prefer probable conclusions to improbable ones?

But I am afraid this won't do. The question 'Why should we believe probable conclusions?' still is not a successful way of posing a problem of induction. For the question 'Why believe probable conclusions?' is too much like the questions 'Why is the beauty of a thing a reason for admiring it?', 'Why is the immorality of an action a reason for refraining from it?' and 'Why is the goodness of a thing a reason for desiring it?' All these questions, when asked earnestly and tenaciously, arise from conceptual confusions. It is a mistake to search earnestly for some deep proof that the beauty of a thing constitutes a real reason for admiring it; this is a mistake because when I say that a thing is beautiful I am not merely describing it: also an essential part of what I am doing is taking a stand in favour of admiring it. It is mistaken to search earnestly for a proof that immoral actions are to be avoided, since to say that an action is immoral is not merely to describe it: also an essential part of what one is doing is taking a stand against performing it. It is mistaken to ask earnestly for proof that the good is to be desired, since in saying that a thing is good I am not merely describing it: also an essential part of what I am doing is taking my stand is favour of desiring it. Similarly, it is mistaken to ask earnestly whether probable conclusions are to be preferred, since in saying that a conclusion is probable one is not merely describing it: also an essential part of what one is doing is taking one's stand in favour of believing it. Thus it is inconsistent (in a broad sense) to deny that probable conclusions are to be preferred.

Salmon advocates a radical questioning of induction; he wants to question whether the whole practice of induction is not perhaps mistaken, root and branch. What I am arguing is that he has not succeeded in framing a coherent question. Moreover, I am suggesting that there is no coherent radical question needing to be asked here, for the general practice of induction is justified simply by the fact that its conclusions are probable, and it is inconsistent to deny the preferability of probable beliefs. Of course this does not mean that we are necessarily bound blindly to accept all conventional inductive practices, any more than we are bound to accept all conventional moral practices. Of course it can be coherent to question and to criticize particular inductive procedures, just as it can be coherent to question and to criticize particular prevailing practices. But we do this by contrasting the given practice with other accepted practices, trying to show that it does not gibe with them. Such internal criticism of induction aims at a harmonious reconciliation of conflicting tendencies that may be present in our inductive practices. But this is very unlike the radical external criticism of induction advocated by Salmon.

As Salmon frames his problem, it is the question whether induction is more 'rational', 'suitable', 'satisfactory', and 'proper' than are anti-inductive methods. It is important to notice that these words are inadequate to carry the load Salmon imposes upon them. Already built into the normal sense of the word 'rational' is a reference to inductive standards; in the normal sense of the word 'rational', a rational man is necessarily one who, among other things, reasons inductively rather than anti-inductively. The man who expects for the future the opposite of what he has observed in the past is a paradigm case of irrationality: we point to him when we teach children the meaning of the term 'irrational'. The words 'proper', 'suitable', and 'satisfactory' are no better for Salmon's purposes, for what can they mean in this context except rational, or probably reliable? The point is that the senses of this whole family of words are permeated by commitment to the practice of induction, a practice which shapes our entire form of life. Salmon wants to call into question the legitimacy of this form of life; yet such a question cannot be coherently formulated in our language, or in any language, spoken by persons like ourselves. Salmon would like us radically to question the practice of induction which shapes our whole form of life, but words fail. We cannot express such a question. We reach one of those points at which, as Wittgenstein says, one feels like uttering an inarticulate cry. And I say that the question which cannot be put, far from revealing the essence of man (as the darker philosophers would have it), actually reveals itself not to be a question.

One final comment. I think Professor Salmon tends to be slightly unfair when he in several places intimates that to regard the problem of induction as deserving dissolution rather than solution is to regard it as trivial. That is not so. One can regard the problem of induction as a conceptual confusion and yet still regard it as a deep and important confusion. There is nothing shallow or trivial about the problem as it appears in Hume's thought, and it is greatly to Hume's credit that he had the intellectual penetration without which he could not have fallen into his conceptual difficulties about induction. We do not necessarily denigrate a philosopher's achievement when we say that he was a victim of conceptual confusion. And we do not necessarily waste our own time when we devote lengthy study to the unravelling of pseudo-problems.

(3) Comments on Salmon's 'Inductive Evidence'

HENRY E. KYBURG, Jr.

I would like to begin by saying that I think Salmon's reading of Hume's sceptical result is impeccable. It is indeed so clear and so faultless, that I would like to repeat it to you: 'Hume's argument shows not only that we cannot justify the claim that *every* inductive reference with true premises will have a true conclusion, but further that we cannot prove that *any* inductive inference with true premises will have a true conclusion.' This statement is clearly an important one to keep in mind when we talk about induction, inductive evidence, the justification of induction, inductive logic, and such things. Although I agree in the main with much of what Salmon says (indeed, with very nearly everything in the first section of his paper), there are places where I think he strays from the straight and narrow, and it will turn out that those places are precisely those places where he has inadvertently forgotten the conclusion of Hume's argument.

The problem of induction that Salmon is willing to take seriously—the problem which we may consider the new and valid problem of induction—is the problem of 'providing adequate grounds for the selection of inductive rules'. It is indeed the case, as Salmon himself has shown with elegance and finality, that some proposed inductive rules are better than others—that, for example, the counter-inductive rule is, in a sense, unsatisfactory. (It is unsatisfactory because it leads to conflicting predictions.) It is perfectly true that something concerning the selection from among possible rules needs demonstration and is amenable to demonstration. It is also true that Carnap has defined a whole continuum of inductive methods, and that the confirmation functions discussed there do not settle the problem of choosing an inductive rule.

On what basis, then, are we to choose among inductive rules? Salmon proposes[11] that there is a basis on which to choose, and a standard according to which to choose; and that to provide this standard (which of course will lead to the conventional rule which we all follow anyway) is a solution to 'Hume's problem of induction'. The basis on which we choose is the deductively established character of each of the possible inductive rules, and the standard is to be pragmatic. This kind of justification of induction, he calls (following Black) the 'practicalist's' justification.

A good part of Salmon's paper concerns a supposed analogy between

[11] [e.g. in the extract contained in pp. 85–97 of the present volume.—Ed.]

the justification of the ultimate *deductive* rules, and the justification of the ultimate *inductive* rules. It has been maintained, on the basis of this analogy, that ultimate inductive rules can only be justified on an intuitive basis, just as (it is claimed) ultimate deductive rules can only be justified on an intuitive basis. Salmon attacks that analogy; I shall attempt to defend it.

Feigl, long ago, introduced an appetizing distinction between validation and vindication. We can validate some deductive rules by reference to more 'ultimate' deductive rules; presumably we can validate (inductively) certain inductive rules by reference to more 'ultimate' inductive rules. But when it comes to the ultimate rules themselves, we can no longer seek *validation* (this would be self-contradictory, for validation *means* 'by reference to more ultimate rules'); we must seek vindication instead: that is, we must seek arguments to show that these ultimate rules will accomplish the purposes they are supposed to accomplish.

Salmon says (following Feigl) that the aim of deductive rules is to be able to draw true conclusions from true premises. This is one desideratum. Even better, of course, would be to have deductive rules that enable us to draw true conclusions from *any* premises. Furthermore, there *are* such deductive rules, e.g. 'From *P*, infer $2 = 2$.' But of course this desideratum, it is easy to show anyone except an absolute idealist or a dialectical materialist, is *inappropriate*, in the sense that we can't construct a system of deductive logic satisfying it which will also do the other things we want it to do. For example, we want it to organize our discourse in certain ways; we want it to be powerful enough to lead to the validation of our customary deductive rules of inference (the ones we learned at mother's knee).

One ultimate deductive rule that does seem to satisfy a large number of desiderata is *modus ponens*. (Of course it is only 'ultimate' in a particular system of logic—other systems might take other rules as 'ultimate'—but this leads to problems that I am willing to bypass.) The one desideratum that Salmon mentions for deductive rules is that they be truth-preserving. And he admits that we cannot *prove* that *modus ponens* is truth-preserving. Although we cannot prove that it is truth-preserving, we can reflect on it very carefully, and observe that it is difficult, impossible even, to 'conceive the possibility of any situation in which [its] use would lead from true premises to false conclusions'. These are Salmon's words.

But, he says, the situation with regard to inductive rules is quite different. I quote: 'After a small dose of Hume's *Enquiry* we can, without difficulty, imagine all sorts of states of affairs in which practically all—if not absolutely all—of our future inductive inferences with true premises turn out to have false conclusions.' We are, then, applying precisely the same standard to inductive rules that we applied to deductive rules: they are to be truth-preserving. But even the little dose of the *Enquiry* that appears early in Salmon's paper suffices to convince us that this standard is altogether *inappropriate* to inductive inference. It is inappropriate in precisely the way that the demand that deductive inference yield only true conclusions is inappropriate. Of course what we really want from deductive inference is the truth. Why hedge? Because, as we all know perfectly well, deductive rules with this highly desirable property, which are also deductively powerful and interesting, simply *are not available*. In precisely the same way, Hume's argument (the very one mentioned by Salmon) shows that inductive rules with the weaker but still desirable property (which does happen to be appropriate to deductive rules) that they lead from true premises only to true conclusions, or even inductive rules that we know have the property that they *sometimes* lead to true conclusions from true premises, *simply are not available*. They are no more available than acceptable deductive rules that are truth-insuring. And there's an end of the matter.

Since this is an inappropriate standard, and since Salmon, Hume, and I all agree that it is an inappropriate standard, it is clearly utterly irrelevant for Salmon to cloud the issue with the ghosts of Cartesian demons. *Of course* it is possible that inductive rules are not truth-preserving. The analogy that Salmon destroys here is not the relevant one. The relevant analogy, in bald terms, is this: An ultimate deductive rule (*modus ponens*, for example), which can no longer be validated, since it is ultimate, can be vindicated by (and this is Salmon's word) *reflection*: by reflecting on the rule very carefully, and failing, nevertheless, to 'conceive the possibility of any situation' in which it would fail to accomplish *what it may appropriately be expected to accomplish*. Similarly, an inductive rule which can no longer be validated, since it is ultimate (actually, here we should talk about the definition of probability that leads to the inductive rules) can be vindicated by reflecting on the rule very carefully, and failing, nevertheless, to conceive the possibility of any situation in which it would fail to accomplish what it may *appropriately* be expected to accomplish. Of course it can't appropriately be expected to be truth-preserving. We can appropriately expect it to lead to self-consistent predictions; we can appropriately expect it to be powerful enough to yield interesting results, and so on. And this, I think, is a requirement that is perfectly well satisfied, for example, by my own definition of probability, barring a few wrinkles. It is certainly a requirement that was (originally) intended to be satisfied by Carnap's c^*

(although things didn't work out that way). The appropriate thing to ask about an inductive rule (or a definition of probability) is not whether there is a universe where the inductive rule leads from true premisses to false conclusions (or where the definition of probability leads to inductive rules that are not truth-preserving), but whether we can conceive of a universe in which (for example) (1) all the A's that an individual has seen have been B's, (2) there is absolutely nothing else that that individual in that universe knows, and yet (3) it would be *irrational* for him to expect the next A to be a B. And this is indeed just the kind of argument that people who have proposed inductive notions of probability have used as litmus to test the soundness of their proposals. (The reference to the 'universe' in this example is gratuitous, of course; and that is precisely the point.)

Now what I have just gone through does no more than to rehabilitate the analogy that Salmon claims to have destroyed. I think that the only reason he makes the analogy seem to fail is that (*a*) he considers only one desideratum that a rule may satisfy, and (*b*) this desideratum is appropriate for deductive rules and inappropriate for inductive rules.

Salmon also says that the situation with respect to inductive rules is different from that with respect to deductive rules, because there are no live options for deductive rules. This isn't so. There is, e.g. the deductive rule I mentioned earlier; there is the deductive rule of affirming the consequent which Salmon mentions towards the end of his paper. There are no live options among deductive rules that do what we want them to do, and what we can legitimately expect them to do. True. And *I* don't think there are any live options among inductive rules (that is, among definitions of inductive probability) that do what we want them to do and can legitimately expect them to do.

Salmon asks if we can give reasons for preferring our conventional usage, intuitions, and behaviour to the alternatives. This applies with equal force to deductive rules and to inductive rules. To a very large extent, we *can* give adequate reasons, and, as Salmon says, this *is* a justification of induction. I agree with him wholeheartedly in his general conclusion—with the important exception that I think that in some sense our justification of inductive rules must rest on an ineradicable element of inductive intuition —just as I would say our justification of deductive rules must ultimately rest, in part, on an element of deductive intuition: we *see* that *modus ponens* is truth-preserving—this is simply the same as to reflect on it and fail to see how it can lead us astray. In the same way, we *see* that if all we know about in all the world is that all the A's we've seen have been B's, it is *rational* to *expect* that the next A will be a B.

There is one more loose end. Where does this leave the practicalist's justification of induction? I said that there were a number of desiderata that apply to inductive rules, just as there are a number of desiderata that apply to deductive rules. And I think that the practicalist's arguments serve very well to help select inductive rules (or theories of probability that lead to inductive rules) that meet these desiderata. Thus we may quite naturally want any rule of inductive estimation to have asymptotic properties; we may quite naturally desire that inductive rules lead to estimates that are consistent with each other (as the counter-inductive methods clearly do not).

It should be pointed out, of course, that these are *intuitive requirements*; they have *nothing at all* to do with our success in using these rules. Our use of the rules is necessarily only finite (in the long run we are all dead, as the first great inductive probabilist said), and in any finite run, we may, in point of fact, have better results with rules that are not asymptotic, and even with rules that actually lead to *inconsistent* estimates. What really counts, ultimately, even here on the practicalist's home ground, it strikes me, is inductive intuition. Our object should not be to try to replace that intuition with something else—in particular it should not be to try to replace it with just precisely *that* which Hume's argument tells us we can't replace it with—but it should be to attempt to reduce all the inductive rules that we use—those rules learned at our mother's knees—to the fewest and clearest and intuitively most acceptable principles we can possibly reduce them to.

(4) Rejoinder to Barker and Kyburg

WESLEY C. SALMON

PROFESSORS BARKER AND KYBURG agree, though on different grounds, that induction is justified because it is rational. Barker argues for an analytic relation, via probability, between induction and rationality, while Kyburg claims that the connection between induction and rationality is intuitively clear. In sharp contrast to my discussants, I maintain that the concept of rationality will not do the job by itself, but that it needs help from another quarter. A justification of induction must, I hold, hinge upon a relation between induction and frequency of truth-preservation or success. I do not deny, of course, that induction is rational; I claim it is rational *because of* its relation to truth-preservation. Barker and Kyburg, on the other hand, assert that the use of inductive methods is rational *regardless of* any relation to success. Both agree that, no matter how infrequently inductive methods might yield true conclusions from true premisses, and no matter how frequently some perverse anti-inductive method might be successful, induction would still be justified because it is rational. I reject this answer.

Much of the burden of the controversy rests upon the analysis of the concepts of rationality and probability. It is perfectly true, as Barker emphasizes, that terms like 'probable' and 'rational' sometimes function as terms of cognitive appraisal. They are used to commend beliefs, assertions, propositions, etc. We are taught various criteria for the application of these terms by our parents, our teachers, and our society. The same holds for 'good', 'beautiful', 'immoral', and other terms of ethical or aesthetic evaluation. To say that a painting is beautiful is (at least in part) to take a stand in favour of admiring it. To say that an act is immoral is (at least in part) to express disapproval of it. To say, in some contexts, that a conclusion is probable is (at least in part) to recommend its acceptance. Thus, our social group evolves a common morality, a common aesthetic, and a common methodology for appraisal of factual beliefs. When an object satisfies certain descriptive characteristics we commend it aesthetically; when an act satisfies certain descriptive characteristics we commend it morally; when a conclusion satisfies certain descriptive (logical) characteristics we commend it cognitively. Furthermore, the usual canons of induction certainly do play a basic part in the criteria of cognitive evaluation.

This situation obviously gives rise to fundamental problems. We all recognize the importance of the moral (or aesthetic) critic. According to the common morality, a certain practice is acceptable, but the moral critic asks whether it is really acceptable. Cannibalism, murder, rape, and slavery have each been accepted, and even commended, by some prevailing moral code. We are more civilized than we would otherwise have been because men challenged, criticized, fought, and rejected the common morality. I cannot accept the view that the common morality is above criticism because of our ordinary use of words. For precisely the same reasons, I cannot agree that induction needs no justification just because it happens to conform to the common methodology.

There is a familiar ambiguity in terms like 'good'. One meaning stems from the common morality and merely reflects the accepted standards. To say that something is good in this sense means merely that it is commended by society in general. A morally deeper meaning is that of being *worthy of commendation* regardless of what society as a whole may think. When an act is good in the former sense, the question remains whether it is good in the latter sense. Does the fact that most people in a particular group call something 'good' mean that it is good? Is an act (such as lynching or church bombing) which is commended in a given society actually deserving of commendation? Such questions had better not turn out to be meaningless!

Barker states explicitly that he does not embrace a view that rules out criticism of common moral practices. He suggests, however that such criticism must be piecemeal; it amounts to seeking some sort of coherence within the accepted morality. He expresses serious doubt about the possibility of calling the whole moral framework into question. This account seems to me inadequate. Consistency—even in a fairly extended sense—is not a sufficient basis for moral criticism; internal inconsistency alone cannot provide grounds for extensive moral reform. Despite many serious attempts to show otherwise, it seems entirely possible for an individual or a society to be highly immoral without violating any canons of logic. Furthermore, we can and do reject common practices, not on the basis of inconsistency, but on such grounds as simple abhorrence. Coherence theories of morality are, I suggest, just as inadequate as coherence theories of truth, and for just about the same reasons.

This obviously is not the place to discuss the grounds of moral judgement, so I shall say no more about the various meanings of moral terms. The fundamental ambiguity is clear enough. Barker has drawn an analogy between moral (or aesthetic) evaluation and cognitive evaluation. He regards this analogy as damaging to my view that induction stands in need of justification. I have tried to show that this analogy, like Strawson's legal analogy, tends to support the view that there is a real problem of justifying induction which is not amenable to dissolution by tracing the ordinary uses of words. We *can* ask whether moral practices commended by our society are worthy of commendation, and we *can* ask whether the inductive practices commended by our society are worthy of commendation.

The aesthetic, ethical, and legal analogies we have been discussing may have considerable persuasive value, but they can hardly have much probative force. The serious grounds for denying that there is a problem of justifying induction, while illustrated by these analogies, are quite distinct. Barker takes up two closely related ones. The first is that there are no more fundamental principles in terms of which the justification could be carried out, and the second is that we simply do not have the language in which to pose the problem coherently. Both of these arguments seem to me to suffer the fatal defect of failure to take account of Feigl's extremely fruitful distinction between validation and vindication.[12] Feigl has shown that there is a kind of justification—vindication—which does not rely upon the existence of more fundamental justifying principles. Barker, however, seems to be maintaining that validation is the only kind of justification possible in ethics, aesthetics, or logic. He seems to be denying the very possibility of vindication, but in so doing he, like every other proponent of this argument I know of, simply ignores Feigl's important distinction. The only reason Barker seems to give for denying the possibility of vindication is that our language—which is, of course, an expression of our common sense, our common morality, and our common methodology—contains the ultimate validating principles. These principles are incapable of being vindicated because, apparently, they are so deeply ingrained in our language that we cannot coherently ask questions about their vindication.

While I agree with Barker that many of the words we want to use to discuss the problem of induction are 'permeated by commitment to the practice of induction, a practice which shapes our entire form of life', it still seems to me that he underrates the power of our language. The language to which Barker refers is the language in which Hume wrote; it is the language in which Feigl stated the distinction between validation and vindication and showed how this distinction bears upon the problem of induction; it is the language in which we explore the ambiguities of a host of words such as 'good', 'beautiful', 'immoral', 'probable', and 'rational'; it is the language in which Carnap presented a continuum of inductive methods, and in which I have on numerous occasions discussed alternative inductive rules. These are not 'inarticulate cries'!

I am not saying that it is completely apparent what would constitute a vindication of induction. If we could prove that induction is frequently truth-preserving, that would provide an easy answer, but we all agree that no such proof is possible. Kyburg suggests, and Barker might agree, that we vindicate induction by showing that it leads to rational results even though it may not lead to true results. This answer is, unfortunately, difficult to make intelligible.

[12] Herbert Feigl, 'De Principiis Non Disputandum . . . ?' In *Philosophical Analysis*, ed. Max Black (Cornell University Press, Ithaca, 1950). In my discussions of the problem of induction I have made extensive use of Feigl's distinction; see, for example, 'Should We Attempt to Justify Induction?' *Philosophical Studies*, vol. 8 (1957), pp. 33–48, and 'Inductive Inference' in *Philosophy of Science: The Delaware Seminar*, vol. II, ed. Bernard H. Baumrin (John Wiley, New York, 1963) [pp. 85–97 of the present volume are an extract from the latter paper.—Ed.].

Consider some of the most usual ways in which the term 'rational' and its cognates are used, noting particularly the situations in which we withhold the term. We deny that people are rational (and derivatively, their practices and their thinking) if they are exceedingly drunk, under the influence of certain drugs, just coming out of certain anaesthetics, extremely young, psychotic, completely lacking in common sense and practicality, unaware of the most familiar matters of fact, or extremely deviant in belief or behaviour. To a significant extent, 'rational' connotes basic agreement with the user. Those who are politically far right are likely to regard those of the far left as irrational and vice versa, while the moderate is apt to doubt seriously the rationality of all extremists (except, perhaps, those who carry moderation to an extreme). We can tolerate some factual disagreements, but it is harder to tolerate methodological differences. There is hope of resolving factual disagreements if there is common methodological ground, but it is harder to resolve methodological differences. When methodological disagreements are really deep and irresolvable we are strongly tempted to challenge the rationality of the other: 'You just can't reason with him!' To allow that a person is rational suggests that he does not differ methodologically to such an extent that reaching an agreement is insuperably difficult. Rationality involves a kind of social conformity.

The foregoing remarks about 'rational' are more pragmatic than semantic. Literally, 'rational' means 'capable of reasoning correctly'. People are called 'rational' if we think they reason well; arguments are called 'rational' if we think they are logically correct; and logical principles are called 'rational' if we think they are canons of correct logical argument. We all agree that certain familiar inductive methods are logically correct, so we call them and the people who use them 'rational'. In this discussion, however, the very problem at issue is what constitutes a correct inductive method. The fundamental question arises for cognitive evaluation just as it did for moral evaluation: Are the things we actually commend really worthy of commendation? Are the inductive methods we regard as correct really correct?

I submit that we commend the principles of deductive logic because we believe they are invariably truth-preserving. I submit that we commend the accepted principles of inductive logic because we believe they are frequently truth-preserving. We call such methods 'rational' because we believe they are frequently truth-preserving. Hume shows us, of course, that we cannot prove that they are in fact frequently truth-preserving, so Barker and Kyburg conclude that frequency of truth-preservation cannot provide a basis for vindication. Instead, they claim, rationality is the basis for vindication. We can, I agree, show without difficulty that certain inductive methods are rational if this means only that they are methods which are thought to be frequently truth-preserving, but that is no vindication of an inductive method. Such socio-psychological facts have no bearing upon justification.

The question I am raising is how to construe 'rational' in order to make sense of the thesis that induction is justified because of its rationality. Let me suggest several possibilities. (1) 'Rational' might mean 'logically correct' where 'logically correct' means 'frequently truth-preserving'. With this meaning of 'rational', as Barker and Kyburg rightly insist, inductive methods cannot be proved to be rational. (2) 'Rational' might mean 'regarded by most people in our circle as frequently truth-preserving'. With this meaning of 'rational', to show that an inductive method is rational is simply to establish the sociological fact that certain people think it is frequently truth-preserving. Unless we can find some ground for their opinion, this fact is without logical interest. (3) The meaning of 'rational', it might be urged, is determined by the criteria for its application we have absorbed in learning to speak our language. This, I suspect, comes close to the sort of answer Barker would give. It does not differ fundamentally from (2), for the criteria we learn are just those which single out the methods which our parents, our teachers, and our society regard as frequently truth-preserving. Finally, (4) 'rational' might mean 'conforming to the principles commended by our group'. This may or may not coincide with sense (2), for we may commend inductive methods because we believe them to be frequently truth-preserving or we may commend them for some other reason. Mere commendation by society is of no use for vindication unless we are more interested in social approval than in truth. If, however, there is some desideratum other than frequency of truth-preservation which underlies our commendation of inductive methods, then we want to bring it out and examine it. I do not know what it is. Barker and Kyburg have not told us what it is. If rationality is that desideratum, then it is very important that we be told what rationality is. In what sense is the term 'rational' now being used? 'Conforming to accepted inductive methods' is no answer, for that would just bring us back to the view that accepted inductive methods have the desirable (?) characteristic of being accepted inductive methods.

Kyburg argues that we cannot dispense with inductive intuition. After carefully examining the logical properties of possible inductive methods, we may still have to rely on intuition much as we do in the deductive case. We *see* that certain inductive methods lead to *rational* expectations, and that is all there is to it. Reluctant as I am to admit inductive intuition, I must concede that it may be necessary in the last analysis to depend upon it. If inductive intuition does prove indispensable, then accept it we must, but we should make every effort to postpone its admission as far as possible and minimize its role. Furthermore, if inductive intuition is required, it will, I believe, have to be an intuition concerning a relation between induction and frequency of truth-preservation, not between induction and rationality as Kyburg would have it. I know what it means to intuit that a particular inductive method is frequently truth-preserving. Though such an intuition might be utterly unreliable, I could recognize it if I had it. If, however, the rationality of an inductive method had nothing whatever to do with frequency of truth-preservation, I really do not know what it would be like to intuit its rationality. Would it be simply a matter of intuiting that the use of the method would earn social approval, no matter how unsuccessful it might otherwise turn out? It is of first importance that those who claim that rationality is the aim of induction should tell us what rationality is.

It may seem that I have taken this discussion up a blind alley. While calling into question the possibility of vindicating induction on the basis of rationality alone, I have been insisting that the only adequate ground for vindication is frequency of truth-preservation. We have all agreed from the outset, however, that we cannot prove that any inductive method is frequently truth-preserving. Where does this leave the argument? Kyburg has said that frequency of truth-preservation is not an appropriate desideratum for inductive methods, for methods which are ampliative and frequently truth-preserving are simply not available. This is not quite accurate. Methods which are ampliative and which can be demonstrated to be frequently truth-preserving are not available, but methods which are ampliative and frequently truth-preserving have been available, seem to be available now, and may be available in future. It is just that we cannot prove that any given one will turn out to have this very desirable characteristic. Nevertheless, we shall do our level best to find one that has it. The fact that we cannot prove that a given method will be frequently truth-preserving means only that the relationship between induction and frequency of truth-preservation by means of which induction is to be vindicated is more complex and indirect than we might have hoped before reading Hume.

Kyburg concludes his remarks by suggesting that the kinds of requirements I have elsewhere [13] endorsed for vindicating induction have no connection with frequency of truth-preservation. He regards them as intuitive requirements of rationality. Again, I must disagree. Reichenbach's con-

[13] [e.g. on pp. 85–97 of the present volume.—Ed.]

vergence requirement does have something to do with over-all success. To adopt a rule that violates the requirement is to ensure endlessly recurrent error. Requirements of consistency also have to do with over-all success. To adopt an inconsistent inductive logic is to forego systematically any distinction between truth and error. To be sure, the recalcitrant problem of the short run remains unsolved, but that means only that the job of vindication is not yet done. This I gladly acknowledge, but I insist that the work is not superfluous.

IV

SOME QUESTIONS CONCERNING VALIDITY

J. O. URMSON

THE programme of this paper is as follows. First of all I shall outline a method of argument which is often used in the work of modern philosophers, and which I take to be a perfectly legitimate type of argument in its proper place and when used for its proper purpose. This method of argument I shall call the appeal to the standard example or to the paradigm case. By it the philosophical doubt whether something is really an X is exposed as being in some way improper or absurd by means of a demonstration that the thing in question is a standard case by reference to which the expression 'X' has to be understood, or a doubt whether anything is X is exposed by showing that certain things are standard cases of what the term in question is designed to describe. In the second place I shall show how this sort of argument has been applied by some philosophers to the problems of the validity of deductive, inductive, and ethical argument, here, as later, with special reference to the latter two. As a first rough approximation one can say that the argument from standard examples has here been used to show that at least some arguments in each field must be valid since they are standard examples of validity in their sphere, by reference to which validity in that sphere must be elucidated, so that to query their validity must be absurd and improper. Thirdly, and finally, I shall try to show that because of the evaluative element in the meaning of 'valid' the argument from standard cases cannot be applied to these fields without considerable modification, and that after such necessary modification the argument does not prove all that many who have used it have wished to prove, though not entirely without weight. In particular, when thus modified the argument leads to a better formulation of the problems which it fails to solve. This is no mean achievment in such difficult fields.

From *Revue Internationale de Philosophie*, No. 25, (1953), pp. 217–29. Reprinted by permission of the author and the editor of *Revue Internationale de Philosophie*.

Whatever the merits or demerits of the general arguments of the article, the author is now clear that 'valid' can more plausibly be classed with non-scalar adjectives like 'right' and 'correct' than with scalar adjectives like 'good'.

1. THE NATURE OF THE ARGUMENT FROM STANDARD EXAMPLES

Suppose that someone looking at what we would regard normally as a typically red object expressed a doubt whether it was really red. He might indeed express doubts whether it was really red because he thought that the light was unusual, or that his eyes were bad, or something of that sort. But suppose that he expresses doubt for none of these reasons but doubts whether the term 'red' can properly apply to this sort of thing. We would then be at a loss and probably ask him what on earth he meant by red if he was unwilling to call this red, or say that by 'red' we meant being of just some such colour as this—'If we do not call *this* red then what would we?' Thus, using a simple form of the argument from standard examples, we can make him see that there is something absurd in his question, since there is no better way of showing what the word 'red' means than by pointing to things of this colour.

Now a slightly more sophisticated example to show what is here meant by the argument from standard examples. In his popular book, *The Nature of the Physical World,* in an attempt to bring out in a vivid fashion the difference between the scientific and everyday description of such things as desks, Eddington said in effect that desks were not really solid. Miss Stebbing, in her book *Philosophy and the Physicists,* used the argument from standard examples to show that this way of putting things involved illegitimate mystification; this she did by simply pointing out that if one asked what we ordinarily mean by *solid* we immediately realize that we mean something like 'of the consistency of such things as desks'. Thus she showed conclusively that the novelty of scientific theory does not consist, as had been unfortunately suggested, in showing the inappropriateness of ordinary descriptive language.

Two comparatively trivial uses of the argument from standard examples have been given to illustrate its character. Obviously to give more subtle examples would require much space, and at present we are concerned only with what the argument is, not with showing that it is valuable or important. But as for the rest of this paper I shall be attacking what I consider to be illegitimate uses of the argument it would be as well to say now that, usually in conjunction with other techniques, this type of argument can be used to clear up a number of vexatious philosophical problems. In particular, it can be used time and time again to show that problems have traditionally been incorrectly formulated; and every philosopher knows how important correct formulation of problems is.

It is to be hoped that enough has been said to show the general character of the argument from standard cases. A full discussion is not possible in the space available.

2. THE ARGUMENT FROM STANDARD EXAMPLES AS APPLIED TO VALIDITY

I shall now set out the use of this argument to solve some major problems about validity; in the first instance this must be done as persuasively as is consistent with extreme brevity. As I think that these uses of the argument are, in part, illegitimate, our argumentation will at this stage embody error: but we cannot expose error until we have it before us, preferably in an attractive guise. We shall first apply the argument to deductive reasoning, since it is instructive to compare its use here with other uses; we shall then apply it to inductive and ethical reasoning, which are for us now the central issues. The reader is asked to bear in mind throughout this section that I am putting a case, not expressing my own opinions.

(a) Deductive reasoning

Logicians, in so far as they have been concerned to understand the nature of reasoning and not to produce abstract calculi or 'languages', have not been producing arbitrary fiats for us to obey when they have put forward principles of valid inference. Nor, again, do these principles present themselves as truths independent of actual reasoning. The logician is attempting to make explicit principles of validity already implicit in our judgements of the validity or invalidity of actual arguments. Thus it is not the case that the validity of the syllogistic arguments is determined by their conformity to the rules of the syllogism; it would be more correct to say that suggested rules of the syllogism are to be accepted only if they recognize as valid what we would in any case recognize as valid, and nothing else. Rules of inference and principles of validity have to be abstracted from standard examples of valid arguments; a suggested rule is refuted if it makes valid a standard example of an invalid argument, or vice versa. This being so, it is simply meaningless to ask whether the standard examples of valid deduction are really valid, or to ask whether any deductive arguments are valid. The meaning of 'valid' with regard to deductive argument is determined by these standard examples—they are the ultimate standard and court of appeal. To ask whether a tricky argument is or is not valid is in the end to ask whether it is like the standard examples of valid arguments or not, though our direct appeal may be to principles.

(b) Inductive reasoning

Perhaps no one has wished to query the validity of straightforward deduction, so that our last paragraph may have seemed to stress the obvious. But we may argue similarly with regard to inductive reasoning; and the general validity of inductive reasoning has indeed been questioned; this is the celebrated problem of induction. Now sometimes when the general validity of induction has been questioned the doubters have indeed had an independent criterion by which to judge it; they have relied on the principles of valid deduction. But this is clearly an error. For inductive arguments are supposed to be inductive, not deductive, whereas if they answered to the criteria of deductive reasoning they would be deductive. A perfectly good cat would get low marks at a dog show, and be none the worse for that. But if we abandon the irrelevant criteria of deductive validity, how are we able to condemn all inductive reasoning as invalid? Whence come our principles of judgement? Do we not come near to the evident absurdity of saying that all men are abnormal, all perception illusory? When we in fact regard an inductive argument as invalid it is because it differs importantly from those which we regard as valid; a contrast is intended.

Here, then, it appears, as in the case of deductive reasoning, we must start from the standard examples of valid and invalid argument and elicit from them our principles of inductive validity. It is not required that the scientific reasoning of a Newton or a Pasteur should conform to textbook canons but that textbook canons should be based on a study of them. Except by reference to such examples no meaning can be attached to the term 'valid' in the sphere of inductive argument. If the validity of such examples is denied, by what standards is it being judged? If the irrelevant standards of deduction have not been dragged in, then surely there are no standards available. These examples set the standard.

That is how the argument runs with regard to induction. The problem whether any inductive arguments are valid is held up as absurd, and with it the traditional problem of induction.[1]

(c) Ethical reasoning

It is clear that we can use an exactly similar technique to prove that it is absurd to doubt generally the validity of ethical reasoning. Some writers

---

[1] To check my exposition of this argument readers may be referred to a few expositions of it. It is given *in extenso* in 'Russell's Doubts about Induction', by Paul Edwards, *Mind*, (1949), (reprinted in *Logic and Language*, vol. I, ed. Flew) [pp. 26–47 of this volume—Ed.]. For shorter versions, see, e.g., the last chapter of *An Introduction to Logical Theory*, by P. F. Strawson, and A. J. Ayer's introduction to *British Empirical Philosophers*, pp. 26–7.

on ethics have suggested that it is impossible to distinguish valid and invalid arguments about moral matters—C. L. Stevenson maintained this quite recently in his *Ethics and Language*. But it appears that just as inductive argument has been condemned for failing to conform to the standards of deductive reasoning, so ethical reasoning is condemned for not conforming to the standards of either deductive or inductive reasoning. But why should it? Yet if we do not use such irrelevant standards of criticism we can surely not condemn ethical reasoning in general in this way. For our conception of what is valid and what is invalid in ethical reasoning must be derived from a study of ethical reasoning—we have here, as in other spheres, standard examples of valid and invalid argument. 'Valid' and 'invalid' must be used to mark a distinction within moral reasoning. It is no more possible for all ethical arguments to be invalid than for all men to be small men. We learn how to use the expression 'valid argument' with regard to ethics by hearing it applied to some arguments and not to others. Our task as philosophers is to make explicit the principles which we already implicitly have for distinguishing valid from invalid arguments. To query whether any ethical argument is valid is to ask a pseudo-question, not to raise a serious philosophical problem. As Mr. S. N. Hampshire said in *Mind*, (1949), p. 471, 'If the procedure of practical deliberation does not conform, either in its intermediate steps or in the form of its conclusions, with any forms of argument acknowledged as respectable in logical textbooks, this is a deficiency of the logical textbooks.'

3. CRITICAL EXAMINATION OF THE FOREGOING ARGUMENTS

So far we have been concerned to present a reasonably plausible version of the argument from standard examples as applied to the question of the general validity of certain types of argument. I shall now try to show:

    (*a*) that the arguments that we have just considered only appear to be proper examples of the argument from standard cases because they have been mis-stated;

    (*b*) that when recast in a more correct form they are indeed the prolegomena to some very important philosophical investigations, but by no means dispose of the major philosophical problems, as many who have used them have thought they would. It will however be shown that they do require a change in the traditional formulation of these problems.

(*a*) *The arguments we have been considering are mis-stated*

If we ask, absurdly, whether such things as desks are solid, then the reply can be given that the meaning of 'solid' is determined by its application to just such things. As an explanation of what we mean by 'solid' it would not be wrong to say 'of the consistency of such things as desks'. Now if the argument from examples is to be applied to validity its main contention will be, put in its most succinct form, that 'valid' means 'like these standard examples in certain essential respects' and that 'invalid' means 'like these other standard examples in certain essential respects'. Which arguments are suitable standard cases and what respects are relevant will of course depend on whether we are considering deductive, inductive, or ethical arguments. But this is a mistaken contention, not merely in detail but in principle, and for a very simple reason. The reason is that to call an argument valid is not merely to classify it logically, as when we say it is a syllogism or *modus ponens*; it is at least in part to evaluate or appraise it; it is to signify approval of it. Similarly to call an argument invalid is to condemn or reject it. Therefore while it is plausible to say that 'solid' means the same as 'of the consistency of certain standard objects such as desks', it cannot be said that 'valid' means the same as 'of the same logical character as certain standard arguments such as a syllogism in Barbara': in the former case we are legitimately equating the meaning of two classificatory expressions, in the second we are illegitimately equating the meaning of a classificatory expression, pure and simple, with an expression which is, at least in part, evaluative in its meaning.

I take it that, once stated, it is obvious that 'valid' is an evaluative expression. To speak of a good argument is in most contexts equivalent to speaking of a valid argument, for example; it would be ridiculous if, when asked to produce an argument to support a position which I had taken up, I were to inquire whether valid or invalid arguments would be preferred. It seems that any detailed argument on this point would be otiose. What we can more importantly do is to consider how the arguments under review can be restated when amended in the light of the point just made and then to ask of them how much they prove in the more correct form.

As a preliminary to the restatement of the argument we must first say something in general about the logic of evaluative terms. Shortness of space compels me to put this portion of my argument very dogmatically, for which fact an apology is undoubtedly due to the reader. For my arguments in support of my views I must refer the reader elsewhere.[2]

Some evaluative expressions claim only to indicate a personal preference, as, for example, when we say that we like something. One is not compelled to give reasons for liking something, and, if one does, one's reasons are at the worst odd, not improper. But some evaluative expressions clearly

[2] 'On Grading', *Mind*, (1950).

claim a more general validity. If instead of saying that we like something we say that it is good then reasons are demanded, are counted as good or bad reasons, and may be argumentatively countered by reasons against. In general it would seem that the straightforward use of such terms as 'good' in a given field presupposes a set of agreed standards of goodness in that field amongst those who use it; giving reasons for or against a thing being good is to show that it conforms to these standards. Thus in a given circle the standards for goodness in apples may be a certain taste, size, shape, keeping qualities, absence of worm-holes, etc.; then to give reasons for saying that an apple is good is to show that it has these characters. If I sell as good apples which fall far short of the accepted standards I am liable to get into trouble; if I do not know what standards are being used when they peak of good apples, then in a good sense I do not fully understand them. here is thus a close logical connection between an evaluative expression d the accepted standards for its appropriate use; but this cannot be ntity of meaning, for no evaluation can be identical in meaning with a d ription. Here the analytic–synthetic distinction breaks down.

is surely clear that 'valid' is one of those evaluative terms which, like 'go ', claim to show more than a personal preference. It is more specialized than good' in its application, as are 'brave' and 'intelligent'; it is used only evaluate arguments and then only from a certain point of view—an inval rgument might indeed be preferable for the persuasion of stupid people nd as a valid argument may have false premisses validity never can inv ve total satisfactoriness. But it seems that in its logical character validity embles goodness very closely, and when the context is clear we often use alid' and 'good' indifferently. If there is this resemblance, then we may ex ct there to be factual criteria or standards for its use, whether implicit or plicit, and these criteria will have a close logical connection not amoun g to identity of meaning with the evaluative term itself. Let us see if we car eformulate our arguments from standard examples in a way which does j ice to this logical situation.

If amongst certain group of people the evaluative distinction between valid and inva arguments is recognized, whether the arguments in question be deducti inductive, or ethical, then we shall expect to find criteria of validity which are generally accepted by the group. Otherwise they will not be able to use he distinction but only at the best to argue about how to use it. If we want know what these standards are, we can only find out what these standar s or criteria are if we examine what are agreed to be valid and invalid a uments and elicit the criteria from them. Even if a list of theoretically reed standards is already available we shall still have to check this list against actual practice if we want to know what the standards actually are; the argument from standard examples must teach us that this is the final court of appeal on the question what the standards are, if it teaches us nothing else. So, as a reformulation of the argument from standard examples, we can at least say this: if we can elicit from the usage of a group a set of criteria for the validity of a certain kind of argument, then it is pointless to ask whether *for that group* there is any distinction between valid and invalid arguments of the kind in question, or to say that there is no such distinction for them; for we already know what the distinction is. But, we can now add, we ourselves are a group which makes such distinctions, so that it is pointless to ask whether we have, or to deny that we have, criteria for the validity and invalidity of all these kinds of argument. Even if we have not yet been able to make these criteria explicit, none the less the fact that we do succeed in all these fields in using the words 'valid' and 'invalid' in an intelligible way, the fact that there are standard cases of validity which outside his study no one would deny, shows that the doubt when expressed in the study is absurd or at least incorrectly formulated.

(b) *What does this argument in fact show?*

Now that we have reformulated the arguments with which we are concerned, or rather indicated a general way of reformulating them without elaborating each in turn, what value can we attach to them? Will they convince the philosophical sceptic?

When we have elicited the standards for counting an apple good which are current in a group—taste, size, absence of worm-holes, etc., we can no longer ask whether it is possible for that group to distinguish good and bad apples. But we can perfectly properly ask why they use these standards and whether we ourselves have any good reason for using them—a question which in the case of apples is not very difficult to answer. We may note, too, that the question may be asked in two quite different spirits. We may ask in a spirit of genuine doubt whether we should accept these standards, and whether there are any good reasons for doing so, or we may be quite happy in the employment of these standards but ask why we employ them in a spirit of philosophical inquiry.

It is surely clear that in the same way when we have elicited our standards of validity we shall still be faced with the further question: granted that this is the way in which we distinguish between valid and invalid arguments in this field, what good reason have we for evaluating arguments in this way? Once again, the question can be asked in a spirit of genuine doubt or as a philosophical inquiry. It is an unfortunate fact that philosophers have continually cast their question in the form of scepticism, when it is quite clear that in fact they have no thought of abandoning the distinction. Now it is a fact of usage that when someone is sceptical of standards he often formulates his query, not in the form 'Are there good reasons for using these criteria of goodness?', but in the form 'Are these things *really* good?' And so we get the question 'Are these arguments really valid?' One cannot say that this is incorrect, as those who employ the argument from standard examples often say, but one can deplore it.

We have the first-order question whether, say, an apple is good, and the second-order question why we count such apples good. It appears that we have the same two questions with regard to the validity of arguments. We can ask of a particular argument whether it is good (valid), to which the answer will sometimes be that it is a paradigm of good arguments. But we can also ask why we count such arguments good, and there seems to be nothing improper in asking such a question, however much we may deplore the pseudo-sceptical form in which it is often phrased. Professor Ayer has said:[3] ' . . . in the case of any belief about a matter of fact what counts as good evidence is inductive evidence. So to raise the general question whether inductive evidence is good, is to ask whether what counts as good evidence really is good evidence; and I do not think that this question is significant.' This may be correct, so long as we are clear that being inductive is a criterion of, not what is meant by, good evidence. But the question still remains why we count inductive evidence as good evidence; probably those who ask the question which Ayer regards as meaningless have in fact been asking this significant question in a misleading way.

Our arguments show, then, that there is something very misleading about the formulation of some traditional problems, and many philosophers have been misled by such formulations. It is wrong to ask whether inductive or ethical arguments are ever valid. But it would appear to be possible to reformulate these questions to run: 'Why do we count as valid those arguments, inductive or ethical, which we do count as valid?' When so reformulated the questions are quite proper. It is therefore a mistake to think that the arguments we have considered dispose of these basic problems, for they remain.

It is worth noticing that the serious muddles which have arisen elsewhere have not arisen in the case of deductive argument. It is true that some authors have spoken as though 'valid' were here a logical term of the

---

[3] *British Empirical Philosophers*, pp. 26–7.

same type as 'disjunctive', but this has not often caused trouble. In the case of deductive argument the higher-order question has never, or hardly ever, been formulated in the misleading way: 'Are deductive arguments ever valid', but in the form 'Why are they counted valid?', and in a spirit of philosophical inquiry. We may not be entirely satisfied with any answer to this question which has been given, but most discussion of the topic has been sane, and some of it has surely advanced the frontiers of knowledge. It is the ridiculous way in which the higher-order question has been put that has prevented similar sanity with regard to ethics and induction.

The argument from standard examples does not then do what it was intended to do in the field of validity, at least by some who have used it. But it does compel us to reformulate the traditional problems in a healthier way. This is no matter of pedantry; in philosophy the correct formulation of problems is half the battle. To move from the question 'Are any inductive arguments valid?' to the question 'What good reasons can be given for rating arguments of a certain type higher then arguments of another type?' is to make a real advance, before any answer is found. Above all, we get away from bogus doubt into methodical philosophical research. Above all, these arguments compel us to take seriously the need for a careful analysis of the nature of the inductive, ethical, and other types of argument that we actually use. We cannot ask for the reasons for the use of the criteria of validity that we do use without an actual examination of these criteria. In the past there has been too much *a priori* argument about the 'possibility of induction' based on equally *a priori* notions of what inductive arguments were actually like. It is a merit of those philosophers whose arguments we have been considering that they have seen the need for a careful examination of the forms of our arguments, even if it has often been a defect that they have not seen that further inquiries remain.

My main contention has been that the attempt to discuss the question of validity by means of an argument from standard examples is misconceived, leading to the attempted dismissal of genuine philosophical questions. There is indeed no important philosophical question 'Why do we call things of the consistency of desks solid?' If we assimilate the logical character of validity to that of solidity we are tempted not to notice, or to dismiss as absurd, the question 'Why do we count arguments of this and that sort as valid?' The evaluative character of 'valid' is here overlooked. Thus exaggerated claims have been made for the force of these arguments. Such problems as the central 'problem of induction' have been thought to vanish into thin air. But I have also wished to claim that these arguments have not been simply misconceived. There are two problems: what are the criteria for validity of arguments in a given field, and why do we employ these criteria? As a result of these arguments we reach a better formulation of the second problem, and the need for a thorough examination of the first becomes apparent. If it is wrong to deny the existence of the second problem, it is at least as wrong to fail to notice the autonomy of the first.

V

THE PRAGMATIC JUSTIFICATION
OF INDUCTION

WESLEY C. SALMON

A UNIQUE approach to Hume's problem, which differs radically from the traditional attempts to refute Hume and from the modern attempts to show that Hume's problem is not a genuine problem, was proposed by Reichenbach.[1] Reichenbach's 'pragmatic' justification of induction suffers from well-known difficulties, yet it is, in my opinion, the only promising approach to the problem. In this section I shall present his solution and indicate certain ways of dealing with some of the difficulties.

Reichenbach regarded the problem of the justification of induction as a genuine philosophical problem—one which cannot be dissolved by clearing up a few elementary linguistic confusions. Furthermore, he regarded as sound the conclusion that it is impossible to prove, either deductively or inductively, that inductions with true premises will always, or even sometimes, have true conclusions. Thus he agreed that, in the frequency sense of 'probable', it is impossible to show that inductive conclusions are probable. Nevertheless, Reichenbach maintained, we can prove deductively that a certain inductive method is the method best suited to fulfil the knowledge-extending function. Formulating his viewpoint very roughly, he held that we can demonstrate that if there is any method of inference whatever which fulfils the knowledge-extending function, then his rule of induction will also do so. This is not to say that the method of induction will succeed in establishing true conclusions on the basis of true premises, nor is it to say that the method of induction is the only method which will. His thesis is that induction will succeed if any method will. This is more than we can say for any other method.

An extract from a paper 'Inductive Inference' in *Philosophy of Science: The Delaware Seminar*, vol. II, ed. B. Baumrin (Interscience Publishers, New York and London, 1963), pp. 353–70. Reprinted by permission of the editor and the University of Delaware.

[1] H. Reichenbach, *Experience and Prediction* (The University of Chicago Press, 1938), and *The Theory of Probability* (University of California Press, Berkeley and Los Angeles, 1949).

I shall begin by formulating Reichenbach's argument very loosely, in order to give an intuitive idea of his strategy. A tighter formulation will then be presented.

Hume had pointed out that inductive inference may fail completely to establish knowledge of the unobserved if nature is not uniform. We cannot validly show, either *a priori* or *a posteriori*, that nature is uniform, prior to a justification of induction. Therefore, we cannot justify induction. Reichenbach agrees that we cannot, prior to a justification of induction, establish the uniformity of nature. We can, however, examine the two possibilities: that nature is uniform and that nature is not uniform. In either case, we can see what happens when we employ the standard inductive method and when we use other methods. The following table emerges:

	Nature uniform	Nature not uniform
Induction employed	Success	Failure
Other method employed	Success or failure possible	Failure

It is fairly clear that inductive inferences will successfully establish knowledge of the unobserved if nature happens to be uniform, and that they will fail if nature should turn out to be chaotic and lawless. This is not to say that every inductive inference with true premises will have a true conclusion if nature is uniform, but only that persistent use of the inductive method of science will eventually establish such knowledge. If nature is uniform there is the possibility that other methods of gaining knowledge may work, but, even on the assumption of uniformity, we have no proof that any alternative method will succeed. The crucial entry is the last in the table. Reichenbach asserts that even the alternative methods will fail if nature is not uniform. His reason for this assertion is that the continued success of any alternative method would constitute a uniformity, contrary to the assumption of non-uniformity. Another way of putting the same point is this. If an alternative method were to succeed consistently, this would constitute a uniformity to which induction could be applied. Thus, if an alternative method were to succeed, induction would also succeed in yielding knowledge of the unobserved. We have, therefore, everything to gain and nothing to lose by using induction. If induction fails, no other method could possibly succeed.

The foregoing presentation is excessively loose, because it suffers from a failure to specify what is meant by 'inductive method', 'success', and 'uniformity'. It fails, in addition, to take account of the fact that there may be varying degrees and kinds of uniformity, and that nature could be uniform in one domain but not in another. Reichenbach has rendered the same argument much more precisely, but to present the more precise version a few preliminaries are required.

Since we are concerned with foundational problems, it will be necessary to consider very rudimentary forms of inference. These elementary forms can be concatenated to produce more complex forms. This procedure is familiar and well established in studies of the foundations of mathematics. Reichenbach selects the rule of induction by enumeration as his fundamental rule of induction. This rule governs inference from an observed sample of a class to a conclusion about the whole class; roughly, the rule permits the inference that the whole class matches the sample. Reichenbach couples this rule with the frequency interpretation of probability, according to which probability is defined as the limit of the relative frequency of an attribute in an infinite sequence. The rule of induction by enumeration permits the inference that the limit of the relative frequency in the infinite sequence equals (or approximates within a small interval) the relative frequency of that attribute in the observed initial section of the sequence. This interpretation of probability demonstrably satisfies the axioms of the mathematical calculus of probability, so the whole machinery of this calculus is automatically available for use. The mathematical calculus, by itself, cannot produce any empirical probability statements, but it can transform given empirical probability statements into other related probability statements. The rule of induction by enumeration governs the establishment of fundamental empirical probability statements. Reichenbach has developed a complex theory of scientific inference, but it all hinges basically upon his justification of the rule of induction by enumeration.

We can now present his justification more precisely, using the foregoing loose presentation as a model. The basic kind of uniformity with which Reichenbach is concerned is the statistical regularity that consists in the existence of a limit of the relative frequency of an attribute in a sequence. Universal laws are special cases of this sort of uniformity. Reichenbach's argument is now easily translated into precise terms; the preceding table can be rewritten as follows:

	Sequence has a limit	Sequence has no limit
Rule of induction by enumeration adopted	Value of limit established	Value of limit not established
Another rule adopted	Value of limit may or may not be established	Value of limit not established

The argument is similar to the preceding one. The entries in the table are verified by examining the definition of 'limit' and the rule of induction by enumeration.

The statement that the relative frequency of an attribute in an infinite sequence has a limit means that there exists some number, the limit, such that the observed relative frequency in any sufficiently long initial section of the sequence matches that number as closely as you like. Let us use the symbol '$F^n(A, B)$' to designate the relative frequency with which the attribute B occurs among the first n members of the ordered class A. To say that there exists a limit P of the relative frequency means, more precisely:

There exists a number P such that, for any $\varepsilon > 0$, there exists an integer N such that, for any $n > N$, $|\, F^n(A, B) - P\,| < \varepsilon$.

This is tantamount to the assertion that, if there is a limit of the relative frequency, the persistent use of the rule of induction by enumeration, applied to larger and larger initial sections of the sequence, will establish the limit within any desired interval of accuracy $\pm\varepsilon$.

It is an immediate consequence of the definition of a limit that, if a sequence has a limit, the rule of induction by enumeration will successfully ascertain the value of that limit, in the sense just specified. Other methods may successfully ascertain the value of the limit if one exists. For example, we might write fractions on slips of paper and put them in a hat. By drawing one of these slips from the hat, we might get the correct value of a given limit, but obviously there is no necessity of such success, nor is there any necessity that repeated drawings will yield numbers arbitrarily close to the correct value. On the other hand, if there is no limit, no method can ascertain its value. Reichenbach's justification is this. There is no way to prove, either *a priori* or *a posteriori*, prior to a justification of induction, that a given empirical sequence of events will have a limit for the relative frequency of a particular attribute. We cannot know beforehand whether nature is uniform in this respect. Nevertheless, to attempt to establish the value of a limit of this relative frequency, it is advantageous to use the rule of induction by enumeration, for if there is a limit the rule of induction by enumeration will establish its value and if there is no limit no method can establish its value. If any rule will work, induction by enumeration will work.

Many objections have been brought against Reichenbach's attempt to justify induction by enumeration, but the most serious objection is one he was clearly aware of. There is an infinite class of rules—called 'asymptotic rules'—which are equally justified by the same argument. Any rule for inferring the limit of the relative frequency can be represented as follows:

$$\text{From } F^n(A, B) = m/n, \text{ to infer } \lim_{n \to \infty} F^n(A, B) = m/n + c$$

where c is a 'corrective' term which may be specified as we choose. The rule of induction by enumeration is the one that results by making c identically zero. An asymptotic rule results from any specification of c according to which c converges to zero as n goes to infinity. Obviously, there are infinitely many asymptotic rules, and they all share with induction by enumeration the property of successfully ascertaining the limit of the relative frequency if there is a limit. The problem is to find grounds for preferring one of these rules to the others. Reichenbach's selection on grounds of descriptive simplicity will not do.

I shall illustrate the problems which arise in attempting a selection from among all (not only asymptotic) rules for inferring the limit of the relative frequency by reference to the standard model. Suppose we have an urn containing marbles, and we are interested in the frequencies with which various colours are drawn. As usual, we assume the marbles are indestructible and that each one is replaced after each draw to ensure an infinite sequence. Now let us examine several rules for inferring the limit of the relative frequency of a certain colour. They are given in the following table:[2]

$$\text{From } F^n(A, B) = m/n, \text{ to infer } \lim_{n \to \infty} F^n(A, B) =$$

(1)	m/n	Induction by enumeration
(2)	$1/k$	*A priori* rule
(3)	$(n - m)/n$	Counter-inductive rule
(4)	$(m/n + 1/k/2)$	Compromise rule
(5)	$(n - m)/n(k - 1)$	Normalized counter-inductive rule
(6)	$[1/(n + 1)](m + 1/k)$	Vanishing compromise rule

In this table, n is the size of the observed sample, m is the number of times the colour in question has occurred in the sample, and k is the number of mutually exclusive and exhaustive colour predicates we distinguish.

---

[2] Any rule in this table can be written so that the inferred value of the limit is represented in the form set out above, $m/n + c$, by the simple expedient of adding and subtracting m/n. For example, in the *a priori* rule it becomes $m/n + (1/k - m/n)$. This shows, incidentally, that the foregoing characterization of rules is broad enough to include even rules which fail to utilize the empirical evidence resulting from the observation of samples.

Aside from the first rule, and possibly the last, these rules are hardly the kind anyone would seriously propose; however, if we can see what is wrong with them it will help in finding principles for justification of an acceptable inductive rule. It seems to me, in fact, that this is an excellent way of posing Hume's problem. Given the infinity of possible rules, how are we to justify the selection of a unique rule as superior to all others? This formulation has a great advantage over the traditional question, 'Are we justified in using induction?' When we are faced with the infinite number of candidates, the problem loses much of its apparent triviality.

Rules 1–3 exemplify three basic possibilities. In rule 1, past experience is a positive guide to the future; if red marbles have been drawn frequently, we infer that they will continue to be drawn frequently in the future. In rule 2, past experience is no guide to the future; it is irrelevant. Suppose there are three possible colours: red, yellow, and blue. The *a priori* rule permits us to conclude that the limit of the relative frequency of red is $\frac{1}{3}$, regardless of the frequency with which red has been drawn. According to rule 3, past experience is a negative guide to the future. If red has occurred often in the observed sample, rule 3 sanctions the inference that it will occur seldom in the long run; indeed, it sanctions the inference that the limit of the frequency of red equals the observed frequency of non-red. Rules 4–6 make some improvements upon rules 2 and 3.

Several of the rules in our list are non-asymptotic; namely, rules 2–5. Consider rule 3. Suppose that the limit of the relative frequency of red is, in fact, $\frac{1}{3}$. As we apply the counter-inductive rule to larger and larger observed samples, our inferred values of the limit of the relative frequency will approach $\frac{2}{3}$. This rule has the general property that (leaving aside the exceptional case in which the value of the limit is $\frac{1}{2}$) if the relative frequency has a limit, persistent use of the counter-inductive rule will lead to inferences which converge to a necessarily incorrect value. Reichenbach's argument shows, I believe, the superiority of his rule over any non-asymptotic rule.

Rule 3 has another disadvantage which is even more serious. Suppose again that there are three possible colours: red, yellow, and blue. Suppose, further, that these three colours occur with equal frequencies in an observed sample. Applying the counter-inductive rule for each colour, we get the result that the limit of the relative frequency is $\frac{2}{3}$ for each. This means that the limit of the relative frequency of the disjunctive attribute of being either red or yellow or blue is $\frac{2}{3} + \frac{2}{3} + \frac{2}{3} = \frac{2}{1}$. This is a logical absurdity, for relative frequencies, and limits thereof, must lie between zero and one. Furthermore, the sum of the limits of the relative frequencies of a mutually exclusive and exhaustive set of attributes must equal one. Let us use the symbol 'IV lim $F^n(A, B)$' to denote the inferred value of the limit of the relative frequency of B on the basis of the sample consisting of the first n members of A. We can lay down the following *normalizing condition*:

Let $B_1, \ldots, B_k$ be any set of attributes mutually exclusive and exhaustive within A. The following relations must hold:

$$\text{IV lim } F^n(A, B_i) \geq 0$$

$$\sum_{i=1}^{k} \text{IV lim } F^n(A, B_i) = 1$$

Rules which satisfy the normalizing condition are called 'regular'.

Rule 3 is the only non-regular rule in our list. In particular, rule 5, the normalized counter-inductive rule, is regular. Nevertheless, it shares with rule 3 the feature of making past experience negative evidence for the future. Furthermore, rule 5 is, as previously noted, non-asymptotic. This becomes obvious when we note that rule 5 coincides with rule 3 for $k = 2$.

Rule 2 is a purely *a priori* rule; results of observation do not enter into the inferences governed by this rule. Rule 1 is a purely empirical rule; no *a priori* 'corrective' term is added to the observed frequency in inferring the value of the limit. Rule 4 is a simple compromise which averages the results of rules 1 and 2. Rule 4, although regular, is clearly non-asymptotic.

Rule 6, the vanishing compromise rule, is similar to rule 4 in combining an empirical factor with an *a priori* factor, but in rule 6 the *a priori* factor carries less weight as the amount of empirical evidence increases. In the limit, rule 6 coincides with rule 1; that is, for arbitrarily large samples the difference between the results of these two rules becomes arbitrarily small. For this reason, rule 6 is asymptotic; in addition, it is regular.

It is worth while to pause a moment to assay our progress. Starting from an infinite class of possible rules for inferring values of limits of relative frequencies, we found good reasons for rejecting rules which are either non-asymptotic or non-regular. The question is, how many regular asymptotic rules are there? The answer is that there are infinitely many. Furthermore, although for any given sequence the results of all these asymptotic rules converge to the same value, i.e. the limit of the relative frequency, the convergence is non-uniform. In fact, for any sample size and any possible observed frequency in a sample of that size, we may choose arbitrarily any number in the closed interval [0, 1] for our inferred value of the limit and find a regular asymptotic rule to justify that inference.[3] In other words, we have made no effective progress in reducing the possible arbitrariness of inductive inference.

The vanishing compromise rule has, however, a different kind of defect —one which it shares with rules 2, 4, and 5. Consider again the *a priori* rule. The fact that the number k is mentioned in this rule signals a fundamental difficulty. This number can be considered in either of two ways; it may be the number of colour predicates we are using or it may be the number of colour properties that actually exist. Construing it in either way, we get into serious trouble.

Suppose, first of all, that k is the number of colour predicates we are using. For example, we assumed above that 'red', 'yellow', and 'blue' constituted a mutually exclusive and exhaustive set of predicates for our population of marbles drawn from the urn. Under these conditions, the *a priori* rule led to the inference that the limit of the relative frequency of red is $\frac{1}{3}$. Suppose now that we strengthen our language in a way which does not affect the meaning of 'red' at all. We introduce the terms 'light blue' and 'dark blue' as terms which are mutually exclusive and together equivalent to 'blue'. As a result of this purely terminological change, which has no bearing on the meaning of 'red', the *a priori* rule now sanctions the inference that the limit of the relative frequency of red is $\frac{1}{4}$. The *a priori* rule thus leads to a contradiction: the limit of the relative frequency of red equals both $\frac{1}{3}$ and $\frac{1}{4}$. We must introduce a condition to exclude rules of this sort. I have proposed the *criterion of linguistic invariance*:[4]

Given two logically equivalent descriptions (in the same or different languages) of a body of evidence, no rule may permit mutually contradictory conclusions to be drawn on the basis of these statements of evidence.

Rules 2, 4, 5, and 6 violate this criterion because each of them mentions k.

Since rule 6 is regular and asymptotic, the only objection to it is the violation of the criterion of linguistic invariance. Let us examine this violation. First, let us use a language with only two colour predicates, 'red' and 'non-red'; in this case $k = 2$. Second, let us use a language with the predicates 'red', 'yellow', 'blue', 'orange', 'green', and 'purple'; in this case

---

[3] Proof of this asssertion is given in W. C. Salmon, 'The Predictive Inference', *Philosophy of Science*, vol. XXIV (April 1957), p. 180.

[4] For discussion of this criterion, see W. C. Salmon, 'Vindication of Induction', in H. Feigl and G. Maxwell, eds., *Current Issues in the Philosophy of Science* (Holt, Rinehart and Winston, New York, 1961), and idem, 'On Vindicating Induction', in Henry E. Kyburg, Jr., ed., *Induction: Some Current Issues* (Wesleyan University Press, Middletown, Conn., 1964).

$k = 6$. We stipulate that 'red' means the same in both languages. Let us make five draws from the urn and apply the vanishing compromise rule at each opportunity. Because of the *a priori* factor, we can make an inference with no empirical evidence. The results are as follows:

n	Colour	$F^n(A, B)$	IV lim $(k=2)$	IV lim $(k=6)$	Difference
0	—	—	$\frac{1}{2}$	$\frac{1}{6}$	$\frac{1}{3}$
1	red	$\frac{1}{1}$	$\frac{3}{4}$	$\frac{7}{12}$	$\frac{1}{6}$
2	non-red	$\frac{1}{2}$	$\frac{1}{2}$	$\frac{7}{18}$	$\frac{1}{9}$
3	red	$\frac{2}{3}$	$\frac{5}{8}$	$\frac{13}{24}$	$\frac{1}{12}$
4	red	$\frac{3}{4}$	$\frac{7}{10}$	$\frac{19}{30}$	$\frac{1}{15}$
5	non-red	$\frac{3}{5}$	$\frac{7}{12}$	$\frac{19}{36}$	$\frac{1}{18}$

The difference converges to zero as n goes to infinity, but it does not vanish for any value of n. For $n = 5$, we have the following two inferences with logically equivalent premises and logically contradictory conclusions:

1. Of five observed marbles, three are red and two are non-red.

The limit of the relative frequency of red marbles is $\frac{7}{12}$.

2. Of five observed marbles, three are red and two are either yellow, blue, orange, green, or purple.

The limit of the relative frequency of red marbles is $\frac{19}{36}$.

We might propose to get rid of such contradictions by insisting upon the adoption of a complete set of colour predicates. Such an approach is hardly feasible. It requires that we be able to determine *a priori* how many distinct colours there are, and that this be some finite number. If there is, in fact, a continuum of colours, this programme will be impossible, for there is no non-arbitrary way of splitting up the continuum *a priori*. This is precisely the kind of difficulty which arises if we construe k to be the number of colours that exist instead of merely the number of colour predicates we utilize. We can hardly suppose it to be a truth of pure reason that there are precisely 347 colours. If one wishes to tread the futile path of attempting to justify induction through synthetic *a priori* truths, he will do better to stick to the principle of uniformity of nature or the principle of limited independent variety.

The kind of contradiction which arose from the vanishing compromise rule is just the sort of contradiction which dealt the death blow to the classical interpretation of probability. The classical interpretation made use of the principle of indifference, a principle which states that two possible occurrences are equally probable if there is no reason to suppose one will happen rather than the other. This principle gives rise to the Bertrand paradox, which is exemplified by the following case. Suppose a car has traversed a distance of one mile, and we know that the time taken was between one and two minutes, but we know nothing further about it. Applying the principle of indifference, we conclude that there is a probability of $\frac{1}{2}$ that the time taken was in the range of 1 to $1\frac{1}{2}$ minutes, and a probability of $\frac{1}{2}$ that the time taken was in the range $1\frac{1}{2}$ to 2 minutes. A logically equivalent way of expressing our knowledge is to say that the car covered the distance at an average speed between 30 and 60 miles per hour. Applying the principle of indifference again, we conclude that there is a probability of $\frac{1}{2}$ that the average speed was between 30 and 45 miles per hour, and a probability of $\frac{1}{2}$ that the average speed was between 45 and 60 miles per hour. Unfortunately, we have just been guilty of self-contradiction. A time of $1\frac{1}{2}$ minutes for a distance of one mile is an average speed of 40, not 45, miles per hour. On the basis of the same information, formulated in different but equivalent terms, we get the result that there is a probability of $\frac{1}{2}$ that the average speed is between 30 and 40 miles per hour, and also that there is a probability of $\frac{1}{2}$ that the average speed is between 30 and 45 miles per hour. Since it is not impossible that the average speed is between 40 and 45 miles per hour, the foregoing results are mutually incompatible.

Let us again assay our progress. We have examined six rules of inference and have three grounds for rejecting possible candidates. The results are as follows:

Rule	Asymptotic	Regular	Linguistically invariant
(1) Induction by enumeration	Yes	Yes	Yes
(2) *A priori*	No	Yes	No
(3) Counter-inductive	No	No	Yes
(4) Compromise	No	Yes	No
(5) Normalized counter-ind.	No	Yes	No
(6) Vanishing compromise	Yes	Yes	No

Each of these rules, except the first, can be rejected for failure to be regular or for failure to be linguistically invariant. This result can be generalized. It is demonstrable that every rule for inferring limits of relative frequencies, with the exception of the rule of induction by enumeration, fails to meet one or the other of these conditions.[5]

[5] See the articles referred to in n. 4, above.

I shall not reproduce the proof here, but the idea behind the proof is, perhaps, philosophically illuminating. Suppose, still, that we are dealing with some set of mutually exclusive and exhaustive attributes. It is a trivial truth of arithmetic that the sum of the relative frequencies of these attributes in any sample is one. It is an equally trivial truth of mathematical analysis that, if these relative frequencies have limits, the sum of these limits must equal one. If we add something to the observed frequency of one attribute in order to get the inferred value of the limit, we must take that amount away from the observed frequencies of other attributes to get the inferred values of the limits of their relative frequencies. On what basis might we decide which observed frequencies ought to be increased and which ones ought to be decreased? If we do it in terms of the words which are used to refer to these attributes, then we pave the way to violation of the criterion of linguistic invariance and to logical contradiction. If we do it in terms of the attributes themselves, we require a kind of synthetic *a priori* knowledge we could not possibly have. It might be supposed that we could do it strictly in terms of the observed frequencies themselves; for instance, we might try adding to smaller frequencies and taking away from larger ones—a kind of Robin Hood principle of robbing the rich to give to the poor—but this is mathematically impossible. The only admissible 'corrective' function, c, which is a function of observed frequencies alone, is that which is identically zero, in short, the one which gives rise to the rule of induction by enumeration. Any deviation from the rule of induction by enumeration leads to some unconscionably arbitrary biasing of the evidence. We can, therefore, select one unique rule of inference from the infinity of possible candidates. In fact, this selection can be made without reference to whether the rule is asymptotic. It turns out that the remaining candidate is asymptotic. Since all others have been rejected, we may use the asymptotic character of induction by enumeration to justify its acceptance. Reichenbach's justification of induction is now cogent.

The justification is as follows. There is only one rule for inferring limits of relative frequencies which is free from contradiction. Every rule except this one permits the establishment of a logical contradiction on the basis of consistent evidence. Such rules are unsatisfactory. We are left with a simple choice. Either we accept the rule of induction by enumeration for purposes of inferring limits of relative frequencies, or we forgo entirely all attempts to infer limits of relative frequencies. We cannot prove beforehand that we will be successful in inferring limits of relative frequencies by using induction by enumeration, for the relative frequencies of the attributes we deal with may not have limits. But we can be assured that, if such limits do exist, persistent use of induction by enumeration will establish them to any desired degree of accuracy.

REMAINING PROBLEMS

I am not suggesting that the results presented in this paper succeed in fully legitimizing the cognitive claims of science. At best, I hope we have a beginning in that direction, and I think we do. There are two grounds for optimism. First, the properties of rules herein considered are of fundamental importance. If an anti-scientific method can be presented with some degree of clarity, we can examine it from the standpoint of regularity, linguistic invariance, and convergence (asymptotic properties), and perhaps show its inferiority to scientific methods. Even if we cannot completely justify the methods of science, it is useful to be able to discredit various forms of irrationalism. Second, the results so far achieved will, I hope provide a basis for a full-blown inductive logic whose rules are justified. In conclusion, I should like to indicate what seem to me to be the most important outstanding problems that need to be solved before this programme can be completed.

1. The Goodman paradox

Goodman[6] has shown how the rule of induction by enumeration can lead to paradoxical results if applied in connection with certain peculiar sorts of predicates. This paradox can be turned into an argument to the effect that even the rule of induction by enumeration fails to meet the criterion of linguistic invariance. This paradox necessitates the imposition of certain restrictions upon the kinds of predicates admitted into our scientific language. I have tried, elsewhere, to show how this paradox is to be blocked.[7] My justification for saying, as I did above, that the rule of induction by enumeration is linguistically invariant hinges upon the successful elimination of the Goodman paradox.

2. The short run

It has often been correctly noted that we deal in practice with finite sequences only. Various attempts have been made to assure the applicability of inductive knowledge to finite classes of unobserved events.[8] One

---

[6] N. Goodman, *Fact, Fiction, and Forecast* (Harvard University Press, Cambridge, Mass., 1955).

[7] Salmon, 'On Vindicating Induction'.

[8] Salmon, 'The Short Run', *Philosophy of Science*, vol. XXII (1955), p. 214.

approach is to finitize the frequency interpretation of probability, so that probability is identified with the actual relative frequency in a finite sequence. Another approach is to attempt to justify a short-run rule for inferring the relative frequency in a finite sample from the value of the limit of the relative frequency in an infinite sequence. Another approach is to attempt to justify a rule for inferring directly from one finite sample to another non-overlapping finite sample. None of these approaches to the problem of application of inductive knowledge to finite numbers of unobserved cases has been worked out with complete success, but I know of no reason to regard any of them as hopeless.

3. Complex inductive inferences

It is obvious that science utilizes much more complex forms of inductive inference than any we have discussed. In particular, an essential feature of scientific inference is the confirmation of scientific hypotheses by means of the so-called 'hypothetico-deductive method'. More complex inductive rules must be validated or vindicated.[9] They may be capable of validation on the basis of induction by enumeration. Following Reichenbach's approach, it may be possible to show that the more complex forms are concatenations of inductions by enumeration. On the other hand, it may be necessary to provide a separate vindication of additional and more complicated rules. Either way, the task has yet to be completed.

[9] Salmon here uses the distinction between 'validation' and 'vindication' introduced by Feigl. See (e.g.) Kyburg's exposition of it on p. 63 of the present volume—Ed.

VI

PROBLEMS FOR THE PRACTICALIST'S JUSTIFICATION OF INDUCTION

JOHN W. LENZ

IT is not the purpose of this paper to deny that there is a problem of justifying induction. In this respect I agree with Mr. Salmon[1] and disagree with Mr. Black.[2] My purpose is to show that, despite Mr. Salmon's skilful answers to Mr. Black's objections, practicalists face other and graver difficulties in their attempt to answer this problem. I have three basic objections to Reichenbach's claims that he had 'pragmatically justified' induction, objections which practicalists must answer before their programme of vindicating induction can be called successful.

1. My first objection is based upon a point which Reichenbach himself made but whose implications he failed to grasp. He showed that not only his rule of induction, the 'straight rule', but an infinity of inductive rules, the 'asymptotic rules', will eventually 'find' the limit of the relative frequency of two events, if there is such a limit.[3] He correctly saw that predictions made on the basis of any of these rules converge towards the actual limit eventually, that is, as the evidence gets larger and larger; but what he failed to appreciate is that, before this happens, the predictions we

From *Philosophical Studies*, vol. 9 (1958), pp. 4–7. Reprinted by permission of the author, the editor of *Philosophical Studies* and D. Reidel Publishing Company.

[1] Wesley Salmon, 'Should We Attempt to Justify Induction?' *Philosophical Studies*, 8 (April 1957), 33–48. [See pp. 84–97 of the present volume for a more recent statement of Salmon's pragmatist (or practicalist) justification.—Ed.]

[2] Max Black, *Problems of Analysis* (Cornell University Press, Ithaca, 1954), pp. 157–225. [See pp. 127–34 and pp. 138–39 of the present volume for some of Black's views —Ed.]

[3] Hans Reichenbach, *The Theory of Probability* (University of California Press, Berkeley, 1944). Reichenbach states his rule of induction as follows: 'If an initial section of n elements of a sequence x_1 is given, resulting in the frequency f^n, and if, furthermore, nothing is known about the probability of the second level for the occurrence of a certain limit p, we posit that the frequency $f^i (i \supset n)$ will approach a limit p within $f^n \pm \delta$ when the sequence is continued' (p. 446). Reichenbach goes on to say, 'The posit f^n is not the only form of anticipative posit. We could also use a posit of the form $f^n + c_n$ where c_n is an arbitrary function, which is chosen that it converges to 0 with n increasing to infinite values. All posits of this form will converge asymptotically towards the same value, though they will differ for small n' (p. 447).

make vary tremendously depending upon which rule is used. Since we have, on Reichenbach's own terms, no decisive reason for choosing among these rules, our predictions will accordingly be almost entirely arbitrary. We simply shall not know what predictions to make.[4]

One of the 'asymptotic' rules may lead to the best predictions, as a simple illustration will show. Suppose that the limit of the relative frequency of two events is 3/5. Suppose that the observed relative frequency of these events has been 40/60. There exists an inductive rule, 'justified' in the practicalist's sense, which would predict, on the basis of this observed sample, that the limit of the relative frequency is exactly 3/5. This rule, if used in this case, would, therefore, actually be superior to Reichenbach's straight rule, which would predict that the limit was 2/3. The trouble is, of course, that we do not know in advance what the actual limit is, and accordingly we do not know which rule to use, which prediction to make.

Practicalists might argue, as Reichenbach seemed to at times, that inductive rules other than the straight rule can be justified only at an advanced state of knowledge. They might argue that only if we have inductive evidence that other rules lead to better predictions do we have reason to use such rules.[5] However, such an argument would vastly over-simplify matters. The point is that we have no reason, even on the practicalist's own terms, to use the straight rule in assessing other rules. Thus a point similar to one made by Mr. Black has a great deal of cogency.[6] There is indeed an infinity of inductive rules, any one of which can be arbitrarily picked to assess the others.

However, we must note here, against Mr. Black, that his suggested procedure of inductively justifying induction now has a difficulty in addition to the kind of circularity which does infect it.[7] The new difficulty is that we do not know which inductive rule to pick for the task of justification. Any answer seems so wholly arbitrary that we could hardly get started with this task.

Practicalists, who are in the main advocates of the frequency theory of probability, can learn much from the supporters of the logical theory. Carnap has stressed the difficulties raised by the existence of an infinite number of inductive methods.[8] These inductive methods are given a different interpretation in the two theories (in the frequency theory they

---

[4] Reichenbach does mention simplicity as a ground for choosing the straight rule, but this is surely a very weak ground and is, in any case, separate from his 'pragmatic justification'. Cf. Reichenbach, op. cit., p. 447.

[5] Ibid., p. 447.   [6] Black, op. cit., pp. 195, 208.   [7] Ibid., pp. 191–208.

[8] Rudolf Carnap, *The Continuum of Inductive Methods* (Chicago, University of Chicago Press, 1950).

lead to predictions, in the logical theory to logically true probability statements) but it is instructive to note that, despite this difference, both theories are confronted with an analogous problem, that of having too many rules of induction from which to choose and no apparent grounds upon which to make a choice.[9]

2. My second objection is that practicalists, despite their 'pragmatic justification' of induction, give no assurance that any of the predictions that science actually makes are correct or even probably correct. Reichenbach did succeed in demonstrating that, if there is a limit to the relative frequency of events, the repeated use of the inductive method will find that limit—eventually, that is, if, as the evidence increases, we make an indefinite number of tries. The crucial point is, however, that we do not know how many tries will be needed, and thus we have no assurance that any of our actual tries is correct or even probably correct. Mr. Black would be right to suggest here that the practicalist has redefined the aims of science, for it simply is not the aim of science to predict successfully eventually. This eventuality might come too late for all the practitioners of science.

Mr. Black says that, because the practicalist offers no assurance that there is a limit to the relative frequency of two events, he offers us no assurance that our predictions of that limit are correct.[10] This point, which the practicalist readily admits, is not the one I am making here. Mr. Black also says that, if there is a limit, we will need an infinite number of tries at finding it.[11] My point is not this either, for Reichenbach has demonstrated that, if there is a limit, it can be found in a finite, though indefinite, number of tries.[12] My point is that, even if there is a limit, and even if it can be found in a finite number of tries, we do not know how many tries are needed. I do not deny that some of the predictions made on the basis of induction might be correct, but I do insist that, if they are correct, we shall never know it on the strength of what the practicalist had demonstrated. One need not be a devotee of ordinary language to insist that it is strange for the practicalist to say that the method of induction will, if possible, *find* limits. At least this is a sense of 'find' in which one never knows that one has found that for which he looks.

It is true that Reichenbach argued that we can evaluate the specific predictions made on different evidence. He argued, for example, that we can

[9] John Lenz, 'Carnap on Defining "Degree of Confirmation"', *Philosophy of Science* (July 1956), pp. 230–6. I have in this article criticized Carnap's answer to this problem, but it is to Carnap's great credit that he sees the problem very clearly.

[10] Black, op. cit., pp. 168–73.   [11] Ibid., pp. 170–1.

[12] Hans Reichenbach, op. cit., p. 446.

inductively ascertain that predictions made on the basis of small samples have a lower probability of being correct than those made on the basis of large samples.[13] However, if what I have said above is right, we have no reason to trust such an inductive evaluation itself.

The existence of an infinity of inductive rules only increases the difficulty of answering my second objection. If we have no reason to suppose that the predictions we make on the basis of *any* inductive rule are correct, we have still less reason to suppose that the predictions made on the basis of a *specific* rule are correct. And were we to attempt, as Reichenbach suggested, to assess inductively the predictions we make, we now have the seemingly insuperable problem of knowing which inductive rule to use for this assessment. Here too we will get different evaluations depending on which rule we use.

3. My third objection is that so far the practicalists, in their pragmatic justification of induction, have not dealt with short-run relative frequencies. This is a traditional problem confronting the frequency theory and has been much stressed by the supporters of the logical theory. Here is another place in which Professor Black would be right in maintaining that practicalists have narrowed the aims of science. Certainly science is not usually content to predict long-run relative frequencies of events. It usually strives to predict the relative frequency of events in the short run. The practicalist's pragmatic justification gives us no assurance that such predictions of short-run frequencies are correct or even probably correct. Even Reichenbach admitted that the frequency theory could not handle short-run relative frequencies directly. If it can handle them at all, it can do so, I believe, only by showing us how to infer them from long-run relative frequencies. Accordingly my previous objection, that we cannot know long-run relative frequencies, is relevant here. There is also an additional problem. Even if we know the long-run relative frequency of two events, we still cannot know the short-run relative frequency of these events. We could do so only if we knew that short-run relative frequencies approximate those of the long run, but of this we have no assurance.

Conclusion: I do not pretend to have shown that the practicalist's programme of justifying induction is defunct. What I have shown is that any claim that induction can be pragmatically justified is very premature.

[13] Ibid., pp. 461–9.

VII

THE PREDICTIONIST JUSTIFICATION OF INDUCTION

R. B. BRAITHWAITE

THIS justification of induction was first explicitly proposed by C. S. Peirce in 1877–8;[1] it has in the last quarter-century gained many adherents among logicians. In order to discuss it we must express it more precisely than so far has been done.

What is meant by speaking of a policy as being 'predictively reliable'? Peirce in 1878 gave a criterion in terms of the proportion among the inferences from true premises covered by the policy of those inferences which lead to true conclusions. Peirce finds the germ of this doctrine in Locke, who having spoken of a man who assents to a mathematical theorem on the authority of a mathematician without taking 'the pains to observe the demonstration', went on to say: 'In which case the foundation of his assent is the probability of the thing, the proof being such as, for the most part, carries truth with it.'[2] Peirce takes this use of Locke's 'probability' to be the criterion of inductive validity: 'in a logical mind an argument is always conceived as a member of a *genus* of arguments all constructed in the same way, and such that, when their premises are real facts, their conclusions are so also. If the argument is demonstrative, then this is always so; if it is only probable, then it is for the most part so. As Locke says, the probable argument is "*such as* for the most part carries truth with it".'[3] And in the following article in the series he says that, in the case of synthetic inferences (inductions), unlike that of analytic inferences (deductions), 'we only know the degree of trustworthiness of our proceeding. As

---

From *Scientific Explanation* by R. B. Braithwaite (Cambridge University Press, Cambridge, 1953), pp. 264–92. Reprinted by permission of the author and publishers.

[1] 'Illustrations of the Logic of Science', six articles which appeared first in *Popular Science Monthly*, reprinted in *Chance Love and Logic* (London, 1923) and in *Collected Papers of Charles Sanders Peirce*, vols. 2, 5, 6 (Cambridge, Mass., 1932–5). *The Philosophy of Peirce*, ed. J. Buchler (London, 1940), contains the first, second, and fourth articles entire, most of the third and part of the fifth. These works will be denoted by *CLL*, *CP*, and *PP* respectively.

[2] John Locke, *An Essay concerning Human Understanding*, Book IV, Chapter 15.

[3] *CLL*, p. 67; *CP*, § 2·649; *PP*, p. 158.

all knowledge comes from synthetic inference, we must equally infer that human certainty consists merely in our knowing that the processes by which our knowledge has been derived are such as must generally have led to true conclusions.'[4]

I am sure that this account of Peirce's of the trustworthiness of inductive inference as the criterion of its validity is along the right lines—in that it makes inductive validity depend on some objective fact about the principles in accordance with which the inference is made. But to make this dependence a dependence upon the proportion of inferences covered by the policy which lead to true conclusions is to put it in a form which is, in two ways, badly suited for our purpose.

In the first place, since the conclusion of an induction is a general hypothesis, there is no time at which it is conclusively proved. The hypothesis may, of course, be established by the induction, but its establishment at one time will not prevent its refutation at a later time if contrary evidence occurs. It is desirable that our criterion should be such that known evidence will have conclusively proved that the criterion held of some at least of the inductions that have been made in the past.[5] That the criterion will also hold of some inductions which will be made in the future will, of course, be a proposition that cannot be proved but will be one which is only capable of being established for inductive reasons. But knowledge that the criterion held in the past we wish to be independent of inductive considerations. This can be secured if we substitute for the 'true conclusions' in Peirce's criterion 'conclusions which up to now have been confirmed in experience but never refuted'.

Expressed more exactly, the criterion for the reliability of the inductive policy Π will run: At any time t, more than half of the hypotheses which have been established by the use of Π at a time earlier than t have the joint property (1) of not having been empirically refuted at any time between the time of establishment and t, (2) of having been empirically confirmed at least once at a time between the time of establishment and t.

But this criterion is not yet satisfactory. What we want is a criterion which we can be fairly confident has held of inductions made in the past by the use of some, at least, of the reputable scientific inductive policies.

---

[4] CLL, p. 105; CP, § 2·693; PP, p. 188.

[5] The past participles in my second quotation from Peirce may show that he had this consideration in mind. Why Peirce did not explicitly treat of this point may be because he intended his criterion to cover inferences with non-general conclusions, and thus, by taking the class of reference to be all possible inferences of the sort in question, to connect the Locke–Peirce 'probability' with a Limiting-Frequency view of probability of events. See CLL, p. 68; CP, §§ 2·650 f.; PP, p. 159.

But can we be certain, of any of these policies, that more than half of the hypotheses established by the use of this policy have been empirically confirmed and have not been empirically refuted since their establishment? It would be an extremely rash historian who would venture to maintain such a proposition. To make it at all plausible it would be necessary to diminish the class of reference from being that of all inferences made in the past which were covered by the policy in question to that of all such inferences made by a reputable scientist after the scientist had tried out a large number of alternative hypotheses which experience had then refuted. For it is one of the best-known facts in the history of science—a fact as notorious as the predictive success of science—that scientific discovery (i.e. the well-establishment of scientific hypotheses) is largely a matter of patience and perseverance in invention, and that there are very few fields in which the scientist expects the first hypothesis which he has thought of to cover the known facts to survive after confrontation with new facts. And even with this qualification we should not have sufficient historical evidence to justify an assertion that most of the hypotheses invented by scientists after many disappointments have been confirmed and not refuted. Moreover, a limitation of the class of reference to include only such hypotheses is far too arbitrary a limitation to be used as a satisfactory criterion for the reliability of an inductive policy.

The escape from this difficulty is to be found, I believe, by the abandonment in Peirce's criterion of the requirement that a *majority* of the hypotheses established by use of the inductive policy should be confirmed and unrefuted. Instead of this requirement all that will be demanded will be that *many* of such hypotheses should be confirmed and unrefuted; however, since this would be satisfied if a bunch of such hypotheses established in the past had this property while newly established hypotheses failed to have it, it is necessary to require that there should be many of these confirmed and unrefuted hypotheses established during each period of time since some fixed date. The criterion thus has to take the somewhat complicated form:

Of every time t later than a fixed time t_0, and of every interval of time of a fixed length of years d lying within the interval $[t_0, t]$, it is true that many of the hypotheses established by the use of policy Π during the interval of d years (unless there are no such hypotheses) have the joint property (1) of not having been empirically refuted at any time between the time of establishment and t, (2) of having been empirically confirmed at least once between the time of establishment and t.

In this criterion there are three arbitrary elements. The first is the fixed time t_0, which can be taken as the date of Babylonian astronomy or of Archimedes or of Galileo according to taste; it is inserted in order that historical evidence may be sufficient to establish the truth of this criterion as applied to the reputable inductive policies. The second is the fixed length d of the intervals, which might be one year or ten years. The third is the meaning of the vague word 'many'. The second and the third of these arbitraries are related in that, the shorter the interval, the smaller will have to be the least number covered by 'many' in order that the criterion, restricted to past times, shall be known to have held of scientifically reputable policies.

There is also an implicit arbitrary element in the class of persons using the policy for whom the truth of the criterion in the past has been established. This class may be taken to be all human beings or all those with a scientific education or some other limited class of persons; and the other arbitrary elements will have to be adjusted to be appropriate to this class.

To save words, let us call a policy satisfying this criterion (suitable values having been assigned to the arbitrary elements) an *effective* policy, and let us call one satisfying the same criterion with 'Of every time t not later than the present time and' substituted for 'Of every time t' an *effective-in-the-past* policy. It is a historic fact that the inductive policies of good scientific repute are effective-in-the-past policies; it is a general hypothesis that they are effective as well as being effective-in-the-past.

There are two ways in which a policy, Π, may fail to be effective in the future. One way is if enough of the hypotheses established during some period in the past by the use of Π are refuted to contradict the statement that many will not be refuted. The other way is for these old-established hypotheses to continue to be confirmed and unrefuted, but for enough of the new hypotheses established by the use of Π in the future to be refuted to contradict the statement that many of them will not be refuted. An inductive policy, that is, may fail in the future either by its past successes turning out to be failures after all or by its failing to have future successes.

This possibility of refutation in the future dispels the suspicion, which might otherwise be entertained, that the design of the effectiveness criterion in such a way that the inductive policies of good repute are known at present to be effective-in-the-past may have resulted in the effectiveness of a policy being a logical consequence of the policy's effectiveness-in-the-past, so that the reputable inductive policies would as certainly be as effective in the future as they have been in the past. But, although the word 'many' is vague, if no old-established hypotheses were unrefuted in the future, or if no newly established hypotheses were unrefuted after their

establishment, the inductive policy concerned would be discovered empirically by future facts not to be effective. So the effectiveness of an inductive
policy is an empirical proposition which does not logically follow from the
policy's effectiveness-in-the-past.

If an inductive policy, Π, is found not to be effective in the future, this
does not imply that at some time it will then be unreasonable to believe a
hypothesis the only reason for believing which is its establishment by the
use of Π. It will not be reasonable to believe the hypothesis in the sense of
'reasonable' for which the effectiveness of the policy is the criterion; but it
may well be reasonable in some other way. Or rather, the truth is that, if a
policy Π which is at present effective-in-the-past turns out in the future not to
be effective-in-the-past so that it is not effective, we just shall not know what
to say as to the reasonableness or unreasonableness of belief in the
hypotheses established by the use of this policy. If the failure in effectiveness
of Π were not due to the refutation of hypotheses established by its use in the
past, but were due to the refutation of new hypotheses established by its
use, there would be an inclination to say that it was still reasonable to
believe in the old hypotheses, but that it would be unreasonable to believe
new hypotheses established by its means. This state of affairs might be expressed by saying that the old successful inductive policy had done all
that it could do in wresting her secrets from Nature, but that it was now
played out and new policies must be discovered and used. The state of
affairs would appear not so much as a breakdown of a particular policy
as an exhaustion of its field of profitable application. On the other hand,
there would also be an inclination to say that the failure of the inductive policy to yield new unrefuted hypotheses showed that we had been
unjustified in using it in the past, and that its supposed past successes
had been just lucky coincidences. We have no satisfactory way of choosing
between these two opposing considerations. There would be similar opposed
tendencies as to what should be said if the failure in effectiveness of Π were
due to the refutation of hypotheses established by its use in the past while
it continued to yield confirmed hypotheses in the future.

If the inductive policy broke down in both these ways at once so that
neither the old nor the new hypotheses established by its means continued
to be unrefuted, there would be a strong inclination to say that it would
then be positively unreasonable to believe these hypotheses. But suppose
that all the inductive policies broke down simultaneously. It would then, of
course, not be reasonable in the sense which used the criterion of effectiveness, or in the modified senses described in the last paragraph, to believe an
inductive hypothesis; but it might well be called 'reasonable' in some new

sense of the word. The sense of 'reasonable' as applied to belief in inductive conclusions is different from the sense of 'reasonable' as applied to belief in logically necessary propositions; the former use, in connection with policies of inductive inference, was developed exactly because these policies were found to have been effective-in-the-past. A discovery that these policies were not effective would remove the occasion for applying the epithet 'reasonable' to beliefs in hypotheses established by their means; but another use might then be found for the epithet as applied to an inductive hypothesis, and another rationale for that use. It is futile to speculate as to what inductive beliefs we should call 'reasonable' and what 'unreasonable' if all our present inductive policies proved ineffective; our language is fixed on the assumption of their effectiveness, and if they are all ineffective we have no criterion for the application of the term.

The situation can be inadequately expressed by saying that the criterion we have been expounding for the validity of an inductive inference and for the reasonableness of belief in its conclusion—the criterion of the effectiveness of the inductive policy concerned—is a *sufficient*, but not a *necessary*, criterion. Why this is an inadequate way of expressing the situation is that this way of talking presupposes that there is a necessary criterion for the reasonableness of belief in an inductive hypothesis. And this would be equivalent to being a sufficient criterion for the unreasonableness of a hypothesis—which it would be rash to take as being given by the ineffectiveness of the inductive policy concerned.

The thesis maintained in this chapter is that the effectiveness of the inductive policy concerned is a sufficient condition for the adjective 'valid' to be applied to an inductive inference from known evidence and for the adjective 'reasonable' to be applied to belief in the conclusion of the inference. But, if this condition—the effectiveness of the inductive policy—fails, we do not necessarily use this failure as a sufficient condition for the adjective 'invalid' to be applied to the inference or the adjective 'unreasonable' to belief in the conclusion; we may, if this situation ever occurs, make use of some new criterion unthought-of at present. Books on logic have almost always considered only definitions of terms where the definition holds whatever the facts may be. Here we are concerned with a partial definition, in the form of a sufficient criterion, where the applicability of this partial definition depends upon the truth of an empirical matter of fact. If policy Π is effective, then the use of policy Π in inferring an inductive conclusion from empirical data makes the inference a 'valid' one and the belief in the conclusion a 'reasonable' belief. But if policy Π is not effective, then here nothing is said. A justification of induction requires a criterion for the validity of an inductive inference; it does not require one for the invalidity of such an inference.

The Locke–Peirce criterion for the trustworthiness of an inference in terms of a majority of inferences of a certain sort being confirmed has been abandoned in favour of a criterion which substitutes 'many instances' for the 'most instances' of the Locke–Peirce criterion. This new criterion constitutes a very much weaker condition than the Locke–Peirce one. And, even though we have strengthened it into the requirement that there should be many confirmed and unrefuted hypotheses established during every fixed interval of time since a fixed date in the past, the criterion may still be criticized for being too weak. The criticism may be put in the form that, although 'valid' and 'reasonable' can, if we like, be defined in this way, this definition will make the concepts so weak as to be pragmatically valueless. What a man wants, it will be said, is to use the adjective 'reasonable' in such a way that its application to belief is related to its application to action, so that it will be reasonable for him to do an action which it is reasonable for him to believe is a means to a goal at which he is aiming. But if all that can be said in favour of using an inductive policy is that it frequently predicts successfully, is this a justification for basing actions upon beliefs obtained by such a policy? Other policies for obtaining beliefs might be more predictively successful; in which case surely it would be better to use them rather than the inductive policies, or at any rate to prefer them to the inductive policies when there is a conflict of results.

The reply to this criticism is that why it is possible plausibly to propose such a weak condition as effectiveness (as specified in this chapter) for the validity of inductive inference is because no policy for establishing scientific hypotheses other than the scientifically reputable inductive policies is effective in even this very weak sense. It is not as if there were competitors to the inductive policies in the predictive-reliability race so that it would be unreasonable to prefer the inductive policies unless we could depend on their swiftness in the race. The non-inductive policies are not starters. There is no general policy other than an inductive policy which there is good reason to believe has been effective in the past, i.e. has, during every interval of time of a fixed length since some fixed date in the past, established many hypotheses which have been confirmed and not refuted—the fixed lengths of the intervals and the fixed past date being the same as those used in the specification of the effectiveness criterion according to which there is no doubt that the reputable scientific inductive policies have been effective in the past.

Some logicians of the Peircean school (e.g. William Kneale[6]) say that there is no other way, or at least no other systematic way, of attempting to make true predictions except by pursuing an inductive policy. This, I think, is too sweeping; we can *try* to make true predictions by a policy of consulting a soothsayer selected in some predetermined way or by a policy of deep breathing followed by free-association or by any other systematic non-inductive policy we fancy. But experience has taught us that we shall not succeed by any of these ways, that none of these non-inductive policies are effective-in-the-past, and so none of them are effective. The case for employing the recognized inductive policies is thus not the negative fact that there is no other systematic way of *trying*, but the negative fact that there is no other way of *succeeding* in making true predictions, combined with the positive fact that pursuing inductive policies frequently does succeed. The justification for the use of an inductive policy in terms of its effectiveness must be read in the context of other predictive policies being known to be ineffective.

It may be objected to this line of thought that it involves supposing that the inductive policies of good repute among scientists at present are the only policies that it ever will be reasonable to think effective. But this is not the case. That policy Π is effective is an inductive hypothesis to be established by induction according to a principle of simple enumeration on the basis of its effectiveness-in-the-past. A policy which has never been tried before may be tested for its ability to yield confirmed and unrefuted hypotheses; if many of the hypotheses which it yields are confirmed and not refuted, then it will satisfy the criterion for effectiveness-in-the-past and its introduction into our inductive repertoire for establishing hypotheses can be justified by the effectiveness of the policy being established in accordance with an effective inductive policy of simple enumeration. For example, suppose that in the first instance I do not accept hypotheses on the strength of their being asserted by Savant M, but, through curiosity perhaps, record the hypotheses he asserts throughout a period of time. If many of these hypotheses are confirmed and unrefuted during this period, the simple-enumerative inductive policy may make it reasonable for me to believe hypotheses asserted by M on the grounds that they have been asserted by M; and I shall thereby have obtained a new predictive procedure which will be good while it lasts. To say that in fact no predictive policy other than the recognized inductive policies is at present known

[6] *Probability and Induction*, pp. 234, 235, 259.

which is effective-in-the-past does not imply that no such policy will be discovered. Indeed, the eliminative inductive policies and the policy of establishing functional laws have been so discovered, the latter only some 350 years ago; the justification for their use is their effectiveness, which was in each case established by a simple-enumerative policy. Similarly, a simple-enumerative policy may establish the effectiveness of new predictive policies in the future; if it does so, these new policies will enter into competition with the present inductive policies of good repute, and we shall be compelled to choose as to which policy to use if they lead to conflicting results. But at present there is no competition.

THE ALLEGED CIRCULARITY IN THE PREDICTIONIST JUSTIFICATION OF INDUCTION

The thesis of this chapter may be expressed not quite precisely by saying that the justification for inductive inference consists in the fact that a policy of passing, in accordance with an inductive principle, from true beliefs to beliefs in general hypotheses frequently enables us to accept hypotheses which are confirmed and not refuted by experience. This thesis is thought by many philosophers to involve a viciously circular way of looking at the matter. Their argument runs as follows: On the predictionist thesis the reason for believing an inductive conclusion consists in two premises, one being the evidence for the conclusion appropriate to the inductive principle concerned, the other being the proposition that the policy of making inferences in accordance with the inductive principle concerned is an effective one. And reasonableness of belief in the conclusion is due to the reasonableness of the belief in each of these premises. But, so it is said, this second premise is itself a general hypothesis, reasonableness of belief in which can only be established by another inductive argument. This second induction will similarly require as premise the proposition that the policy of making inferences in accordance with the inductive principle used in it is an effective one; and this premiss will again be a general hypothesis which will require justifying by a third inductive argument. Thus, either there will be an infinite regress with an infinite series of inductive policies the establishment of the effectiveness of each policy in the series requiring the establishment of the effectiveness of the succeeding policy in the series, or we shall arrive, in ascending the series, at one inductive policy the establishing of whose effectiveness will require the establishment of its own effectiveness.

Since the reason that could be given for the effectiveness of any inductive policy except those of induction by simple enumeration would be that it had frequently been predictively reliable in the past, i.e. that it had proved to be effective-in-the-past, the establishment of the effectiveness of any other policy would require the establishment of the effectiveness of a simple-enumerative inductive policy. (For the purpose of this argument it is unnecessary to distinguish different simple-enumerative policies; so they will be referred to in the singular as the policy of induction by simple enumeration.) Thus to establish the effectiveness of the policy of induction by simple enumeration would require its own effectiveness to be taken as a premiss; and the circularity horn of the dilemma would be the one upon which we should be impaled. If we care to use the word 'presupposition' the argument against the predictionist justification may be expressed by saying that, according to it, the validity of every inductive inference *presupposes* the validity of induction by simple enumeration, and the vadility of induction by simple enumeration *presupposes* its own validity; and this, it is alleged, is a viciously circular justification for induction.

Before trying to answer this charge of vicious circularity, the predictionist may be permitted a *tu quoque* retort. The accusation of circularity does not lie solely against the predictionist justification of induction but lies equally against any account of the validity of induction which makes such validity depend upon a premiss which can only be established inductively. Keynes's attempt to justify induction by means of a theory of probability falls into this class. On Keynes's theory inductive confirmation serves only to increase the probability of a hypothesis by multiplying it by another probability, so that if the hypothesis has a 'prior probability' of zero its 'posterior probability' remains zero, however much evidence there may be for it. And the only way to secure that every hypothesis should have a prior probability greater than zero is to assign some probability greater than zero to a proposition which limits the number of possible hypotheses (e.g. Keynes's Principle of Limited Independent Variety).[7] But such a proposition is itself an empirical hypothesis, which calls for an inductive justification. So Keynes's justification for induction is viciously circular—unless one cuts the circle by the improper expedient of 'postulating' the empirical hypothesis required.

The fact, however, that many other attempted justifications of induction are open to the accusation of vicious circularity does not excuse the predictionist from trying to show that the charge does not lie against his account. This rebuttal must now be attempted.

The first move in the rebuttal is that the proposition 'presupposed' in the predictionist justification of an inductive inference does not function

[7] J. M. Keynes, *A Treatise on Probability*, chapter XXII.

in the inference as an additional premiss. The inductive inference to the proposition that induction by simple enumeration is an effective policy does not make use of this proposition as a premiss, and so is not circular in the *petitio principii* sense of professing to infer a conclusion from a set of premisses one of which is the conclusion itself.

This point is so important that it is desirable to make it as precisely as possible. What we are concerned with is the sort of circularity, if any, involved in the establishment of the validity of induction by simple enumeration by means of an induction by simple enumeration. A few symbols will abbreviate the discussion.

Let Π be the inductive policy of adding belief in a hypothesis h to belief in a set of propositions which collectively constitute π-evidence for h, i.e. adequate evidence for inferring h in accordance with the principle of inference π, π being the principle of induction by simple enumeration.[8]

Let e be the proposition that the policy Π is effective.

Now to say that the truth of e is the justification for employing the inductive policy Π is not to say that the principle π of induction by simple enumeration requires that e should be added as an additional premiss to the otherwise adequate evidence; were this to be the case, the inference of e by means of the principle π would require the inclusion of e itself among the premisses believed. The alleged inference would then not be an inference at all, let alone a valid inference, since it would be professing to establish belief in a proposition which was already one of the believed premisses. But since e does not function in the argument as a premiss which has to be believed along with the other premisses, the argument by means of the principle π from the π-evidence for e to e does not commit the fallacy of *petitio principii*, and it is a genuine inference in which belief is acquired in a new proposition which was not believed before.

The cirularity in the argument is of a more sophisticated character. It is the circularity involved in the use of a principle of inference being justified by the truth of a proposition which can only be established by the use of the same principle of inference. To express the matter in the symbols we have used:

The truth of e justifies the use of policy Π; i.e. for every h the truth of e justifies an addition of belief in h to reasonable belief in π-evidence for h.

From which there follows, by the substitution of e for h: The truth of e justifies an addition of belief in e to a reasonable belief in π-evidence for e.

---

[8] The Greek capital letter Π has been used earlier in this chapter to denote any inductive policy. It will henceforth be restricted by this definition to denote only the simple-enumerative inductive policy.

In other words, if e is true, an addition of belief in e to reasonable belief in πe-vidence for e is justified.

I do not wish to deny that there is a sort of circularity involved in this statement, but it is a peculiar sort of circularity whose viciousness is by no means obvious. The statement does not commit the fallacy of *petitio principii* as would have been the case had it said that, *if e were reasonably believed*, an addition of belief in e to the believer's body of reasonable belief would be justified. For in the statement the sufficient condition for the addition of belief in e is, not that a premiss is believed, but that an empirical proposition is true. The peculiar circularity consists in the *truth* of the conclusion of an inference being a sufficient condition for the validity of the inference. Let us call this type of circularity 'effective circularity', since in the cases in which we are interested it is the effectiveness of the inferential policy which is the sufficient condition. The question before us is whether or not the presence of effective circularity renders an inference invalid, or whether it prevents an inference from being a genuine inference at all?

At this point it is worth remarking that there are deductive inferences in which a sufficient condition for the effectiveness of the principle of inference is exactly that proposition which is the conclusion of the inference itself.[9] But here the proposition which is the condition for the effectiveness of a deductive principle of inference must be a logically necessary proposition; and though, in the case we are considering, this logically necessary proposition is supposed to be established by being deduced from other logically necessary propositions within a pure deductive system which uses as principle of inference a principle the condition for whose effectiveness is the logically necessary proposition itself, yet this proposition could always be established in ways which do not involve this effectiveness. For there is no necessary order in the deducing of logically necessary propositions from one another. However, in our inductive case, the proposition stating the effectiveness of the induction-by-simple-enumeration policy is a logically contingent proposition which can be established in no other way than by the use of an induction-by-simple-enumeration policy.

Now for a consideration of 'effective circularity'. Is there anything wrong in the effectiveness of a policy of inference being a justification for the

---

[9] An example of this would be the deduction within a deductive system of the proposition $(p(p \supset q)) \supset q$ from the two propositions

$$(p(p \supset q)) \equiv pq, \qquad ((p(p \supset q)) \equiv pq) \supset ((p(p \supset q)) \supset q)$$

by the use of an 'implicative' detachment principle the condition for whose effectiveness is the necessary truth of $(p(p \supset q)) \supset q$.

inference to this effectiveness as conclusion? Is there anything wrong in obtaining a belief in a proposition by inference according to a principle whose validity as a principle of inference is attested by the proposition which is itself the conclusion of the inference? In order to answer these questions it is necessary to consider what exactly we mean by 'inference' and by an inference being 'valid'.

THE CONDITIONS FOR VALID INFERENCE AND FOR THE REASONABLENESS OF AN INFERRED BELIEF

Inference is the passage of thought from belief, or rational belief, in a set of propositions, collectively called the *premiss* of the inference, to belief, or rational belief, in a proposition called the *conclusion* of the inference, the premiss and the conclusion being related in accordance with some principle of inference. The question of the validity of a process of inference is the same as the justification for adding a belief in the conclusion to the believer's body of reasonable beliefs (his 'rational corpus'), in the case in which the premiss of the inference forms part of this rational corpus, or for associating a belief in the conclusion with the belief in the premiss, in the case where this belief is not part of the believer's rational corpus, in such a way that belief in the conclusion will be inferentially supported by the belief in the premiss. And vice versa the question of the reasonableness of a belief, except in the case in which the reasonableness of the belief consists in the proposition believed being known directly to be true, is that of the validity of an inference by which the belief could be supported.[10]

Different sorts of criteria can be given for the validity of an inference, or for the reasonableness of an inferentially supportable belief. In order to avoid complications due to differences of nuance in the meaning of the words concerned, these different possible sets of criteria will be considered in the first instance in the form of an abstract classification.

The two relevant propositions are the premiss p of the inference and the proposition r asserting the effectiveness of the inferential policy which uses the principle of inference concerned in passing from the premiss p to the conclusion q. The possible criteria for the validity of an inference from p to q are obtained by considering the possible combinations of a belief in p, or a rational belief in p, with the truth of r, or with a belief in r, or with a rational belief in r. Possible combinations with the truth of p will not be considered, since the truth of the premiss is not relevant to the validity of an

---

[10] Not 'has been supported', for a belief may be reasonable if the believer would support it by an inference if the reasonableness of his belief were to be disputed, although in fact he had not arrived at it by inference.

inference from it, though it is relevant to the question as to whether or not an inference to a conclusion constitutes a *proof* of the conclusion.[11]

There are ten possibilities for sufficient criteria for the validity of an inference by a person B of the conclusion q from the premiss p in accordance with a principle of inference the effectiveness of whose use is asserted by the proposition r:[12]

   I B believes p and believes r;
  II B believes p and reasonably believes r;
 III B believes p, and r is true;
 IV B believes p and believes r, and r is true;
  V B believes p and reasonably believes r, and r is true;

  VI B reasonably believes p and believes r;
 VII B reasonably believes p and reasonably believes r;
VIII B reasonably believes p, and r is true;
 IX B reasonably believes p and believes r, and r is true;
  X B reasonably believes p and reasonably believes r, and r is true.

Criteria VI–X are possible criteria for the validity of an inference regarded as justifiably adding a belief in q to B's body of reasonable beliefs; criteria I–V are possible criteria for the validity of an inference regarded as justifiably carrying a belief in q along with B's belief in p. Which of the five criteria in each case is chosen as *the* criterion for the validity of the inference is to some extent a matter of taste. The usage of the expressions 'valid inference' and 'reasonable belief' is not sufficiently fixed by common usage for any of the possibilities to be excluded from the outset.

But some of these possibilities will make some inferences circular, and these possibilities will have to be excluded for the case of these inferences; otherwise these inferences will be invalid, not in failing to satisfy one of the criteria, but in involving a vicious circularity. The inferences that will be invalid through circularity will be those satisfying any of the conditions

    I–X if B's belief in p includes a belief in q.
    I, II, IV, V, VII, and X if B's belief in r includes a belief in q.

It is important to notice that B's belief in r may include a belief in q without making inferences satisfying conditions VI and IX circular, for these

---

[11] My treatment of the validity of inference, which owes much to W. E. Johnson's discussion in his *Logic, Part II* (Cambridge, 1922), chapter I, disagrees with him here.
 [12] Criteria sufficient, that is, except for the possibility of a vicious circularity to the discussion of which this classification is a preliminary.

inferences are allegedly adding q to B's body of reasonable beliefs, and the fact that q is already a proposition which B believes does not invalidate an inference which proposes to move q from B's body of *beliefs* to his body of *reasonable beliefs*.[13]

Let us now turn to the case of inductive inference. Here p, the evidence for the inductive hypothesis q, is assumed to be reasonably believed; so the criterion for the validity of the inference will be one of the possibilities VI–X. Suppose that the conclusion q of the inference is the proposition stating the effectiveness of a policy of induction by simple enumeration, and that it is according to induction by simple enumeration that the inference is being made. Then the inference will be invalid through circularity only if its condition for validity is taken to be either VII or X. For it is only in these two cases that B's reasonable belief in the conclusion of the inference will be part of his reasonable belief in the effectiveness of the inferential policy. So if any one of the other three possible criteria for the validity of an inference is taken, i.e. any one of VI, VIII, or IX, an inference to a conclusion stating the effectiveness of the inferential policy will be valid without any circularity.

Having reduced the number of possibilities to three, we can conveniently give them specific names. Let us call an inference (leading to reasonable belief in a conclusion) 'subjectively valid' if it satisfies condition VI (i.e. if VI is a sufficient condition for its validity), 'objectively valid' if it satisfies condition VIII and 'both subjectively and objectively valid' if it satisfies condition IX. To justify the use of the policy of induction by simple enumeration by its effectiveness, as we have done, is to use criterion VIII for the objective validity of the inference to the hypothesis of its effectiveness. The inference made by a person B is then objectively valid in that B reasonably believes the evidence for the hypothesis and that the hypothesis justifying the principle of inference is itself true; no question of his belief, reasonable or non-reasonable, in the hypothesis itself is part of the condition for the validity (the 'objective validity') of the induction.

It may, however, be felt that such objective validity is not enough, and that an inference cannot be a properly valid inference unless the inferrer is in some way cognizant of the principle according to which he is making the inference and of the propriety of the principle for this purpose. Whether or not objective validity is thought to be enough depends upon whether the validity of the inference is being considered, as it were, from the outside

---

[13] Some accounts of inference would limit it to being a passage of thought leading to belief in a proposition not previously believed; but this would seem to involve an undesirably narrow definition of inference.

or from the inside. When considered from the outside the person making the inference is being regarded as a reasoning machine. The machine would first have fed into it a set of propositions which together make up π-evidence for e, and would thus take up a 'position' which would correspond to having a reasonable belief in this π-evidence for e. The machine would then be put in operation according to its principle of working, and would acquire a new position which would correspond to a reasonable belief in the proposition e. Obviously there is nothing objectionable in the machine arriving at a new position which corresponds to having a reasonable belief in a proposition asserting some general property of the method of working of the machine. From the external point of view the machine is making 'valid inferences' if it is working according to its working 'principle of inference' starting with a 'reasonable' position, and it can quite well arrive by such working at a position which corresponds to having 'validly inferred' a proposition which asserts some general property of its working 'principle of inference'.

Similarly, from an external point of view, a man may be considered to be making valid inferences from reasonably believed premises if his policy of inference is in fact an effective one, quite independently of whether or not he believes or knows that it is effective; and in this case there is no vicious circularity in his arriving by a valid process of inference at the conclusion that the policy of using the principle of inference according to which he is making this inference is an effective one.

An inference will be valid in the sense of being *objectively valid* (in the sense explained) if the inference proceeds from reasonably believed premises to a conclusion according to a policy of inference which is in fact effective, whether or not the inferrer knows or believes that it is effective or indeed whether he considers the question of its effectiveness at all. The inferrer, that is, is acting like a machine which works according to certain principles without being cognizant of these principles. He is not assumed to be wholly a machine, since he is supposed to start with a reasonable belief in the premises and to end with a reasonable belief in the conclusion, but the process by which he passes from his original reasonable belief to his final reasonable belief is supposed to be one which does not require his cognitive participation. This process may be regarded as analogous to the free-association used in adding up a column of figures, where the adder has consciously thought of the number written at the head of the page and again consciously thinks of the number to be written at the bottom of the page but does not consciously think of the arithmetical relationships which justify his calculating from the one to the other. The result of a calculation obtained in this automatic way may well be a statement which asserts the effectiveness of the method of calculation.

But if the machine becomes self-conscious and critical of its mode of working, it will not be satisfied with a criterion for the validity of inference which depends upon the effectiveness in fact of the method by which it is working, but will demand a condition, either as an alternative or as an addition, which states its belief in this effectiveness. From the inside, that is, criteria VI or IX will seem more appropriate criteria for the validity of an inference than the criterion VIII giving 'objective validity'. Since criterion IX combines the conditions of criteria VI and VIII, it is criterion VI that needs to be considered. It substitutes the requirement that the thinker should believe that the policy of induction by simple enumeration is effective for the fact that it is effective; in the terms we have used it ascribes 'subjective validity' rather than 'objective validity' to the inference leading to the conclusion that the policy is effective. Though belief in the effectiveness of this policy is one of the conditions for the subjective validity of an inference yielding a reasonable belief in such effectiveness, this fact does not (as we have seen) make the inference *ipso facto* circular, for the thinker is passing from a mere belief in this effectiveness to a reasonable belief in it. He is, as it were, moving it within his body of beliefs into the privileged position of being one of his body of reasonable beliefs.

So a critic who finds the objective validity criterion inadequate, in that it gives no place for the thinker's consciousness of the principle according to which he is making the inference, can be offered instead, without fear of vicious circularity, either the subjective validity criterion or the subjective-and-objective validity criterion for the validity of his inference. In none of these three cases is there any vicious circularity.

At this point, however, the question may well be raised as to whether either of the criteria VI or VIII are at all appropriate criteria for the validity, in any proper sense, of the inductive inference. The objector may perfectly well say that for an inference to yield a new reasonable belief the inferrer must not merely *believe* that the policy represented by the principle of inference is effective, but must *reasonably believe* this proposition. And he can point out that we have required reasonable belief, and not only belief, in the premiss in order that an inference may yield reasonable belief in the conclusion.

On the face of it this objection seems a very cogent one. To obtain a reasonable belief by inference, it says, we must have reasonable belief all along the line, reasonable belief in the effectiveness of the policy of inference no less than reasonable belief in the premiss. But the rejoinder can be made that such a requirement would invalidate the majority of inferences, deductive as well as inductive, that are actually made in the course of reasoning. For the requirement would admit only deductions in which the proposition authenticating the principle of inference used was either seen directly to be true or was seen directly to be a logical consequence (in a chain of proof sufficiently short to be taken in at one glance) of a proposition seen directly to be true. Any other way of attaining belief in the effectiveness of the policy of deduction, e.g. by citing authority, or by remembering that one had satisfied oneself of its truth in the past, would involve inductive steps, and would thus not permit the belief to be 'reasonable', since the inference by which it had been obtained, or upon which it could be based, would not satisfy this stringent condition for validity. So to insist that an inference is only valid, and a belief in the conclusion of the inference only reasonable, if the inferrer's belief in the effectiveness of a policy of inference is already a reasonable one would exclude a great number of the inferences, and a great many of the beliefs, which would normally be considered to be valid or to be reasonable.

The objector may, of course, say at this point that he is not concerned with the application of the terms 'valid' and 'reasonable' in our ordinary slovenly everyday language; what he is concerned with is a purified use of these terms after the user of them has been purged by a course of treatment with methodological doubt. In a purified sense the objector may decline to admit valid inferences in which the effectiveness of the policy of inference is not reasonably believed—even if this were to exclude most so-called 'valid' inferences. But then it is difficult to see what the argument is about. It started presumably because the objector wished to dispute the justification of induction by simple enumeration in terms of the effectiveness of this policy, the ground of his objection being that such an attempted justification was circular. We then replied that this justification would not be open to this criticism if the criterion of valid inference did not require reasonable belief in the effectiveness of the policy of inference, but only required alternatively either the fact of this effectiveness or belief in this effectiveness. And we maintained that a reasonable belief in this effectiveness was not an essential part of the criterion for validity of the sorts of passages of thought which are normally thought of as valid inferences. If the objector has decided beforehand to decline to admit as a valid inference any inference in which the effectiveness of the policy is not reasonably believed, his valid inductive inferences will be bound to suffer from circularity (unless, indeed, he takes the desperate course of regarding the effectiveness of the policy as a logically necessary truth). But the vicious circularity will be of the objector's own making.

It is illuminating to compare the senses in which we have called inferences 'objectively valid', 'subjectively valid' and 'both objectively and subjectively valid' with various senses in which an action may be said to be 'right'.

Whether the rightness of an action is held to consist in its fittingness to a certain situation or in its having a certain characteristic or producing effects having that characteristic or in some blend of these two, it will in all cases be possible to distinguish two senses of rightness—one an objective sense, when the action in fact is fitting to the situation or in fact has the characteristic or produces effects having the characteristic, whether or not an action is right in this sense being entirely independent of whether or not the agent believes it to be right; the other a subjective sense in which what determines the rightness of the action is whether or not the agent believes the action to be fitting to the situation or to have the characteristic or to produce effects having the characteristic, i.e. whether or not the agent believes the action to be right in the first, objective sense of the word. And a third sense of rightness can then be given in which an action is right if it is both objectively right and subjectively right.[14]

The objective sense of rightness of an action may be compared with the objective sense of validity of an inference, that in which the policy of inference is in fact effective; the subjective sense of rightness of an action may be compared with the subjective sense of validity of an inference, that in which the policy of inference is believed to be effective. The third, composite sense of rightness may then be compared with the sense of validity of an inference which is both objective and subjective. And there would similarly be comparable senses of reasonable belief in a proposition which had either been derived by inference or would be defended against criticism by citing an inference by which it might have been derived. An objectively reasonable belief, associated with an objectively valid inference, would be compared with an objectively right action; a subjectively reasonable belief, associated with a subjectively valid inference, would be compared with a subjectively right action; and there would be a similar com-

---

[14] Further distinctions can be made for the cases in which an action is subjectively right without being objectively right according as the agent's erroneous belief as to the objective rightness of his action is due to his being in error on a matter of fact (as to the nature of the situation or as to what effects the action will in fact have) or in his moral evaluation. Such further distinctions are not relevant for the purpose of our comparison.

parison in the case of a belief which was both objectively and subjectively reasonable.

The enlightenment produced by making these comparisons seems to me to be as follows. Whatever be the sense of rightness appropriate to describing other moral situations, it is almost undisputed that the sense of rightness which is appropriate to the imputation of moral praise or blame is the subjective sense of rightness. A man, that is, is not considered blameworthy for doing an action which is objectively wrong provided that, at the time of doing it, he believed it to be objectively right, nor is he considered praiseworthy for doing an action which is objectively right if he believed it to be objectively wrong.

Now to say of a man that he is reasonable in holding a belief q, or that his belief in q is reasonable, is in many contexts to make a judgement which is either a moral judgement or closely resembles one. It is a moral judgement if reasonably holding beliefs is regarded as one of the modes of moral goodness of a man; it is closely related to a moral judgement if reasonably holding beliefs is regarded, not as itself a manifestation of moral goodness, but as a positive symptom for moral goodness in a man. In either case to say of a man that he is unreasonable in holding a belief q is to make, or to imply, a hypothetical moral criticism of him. For it is to imply that the man would be morally better were he not unreasonably to hold the belief q. It does not imply that he ought not unreasonably to hold the belief, for it may not be in his power either to hold it reasonably or to abandon the belief. But, whether these possibilities are in his power or not, the fact that he unreasonably holds the belief makes him worse than would be the case were he not unreasonably to hold it.

In any context in which reasonableness is ascribed with this moral implication, to the extent that the reasonableness of a man's belief is derived by a valid process of inference, this reasonableness must depend not upon the actual effectiveness of the policy of inference but upon the man's belief in this effectiveness. For otherwise a man would be regarded as blameworthy for holding a belief in a scientific hypothesis which he had inferred from reasonably believed evidence by following an inductive policy which, although the man believed it to be effective, was not in fact an effective one. And he would be regarded as praiseworthy for holding an inductive belief which he had inferred by a policy which was in fact effective, even though he did not believe that it was effective. Such judgements would be contrary to our moral sense as displayed in our use of moral language, which makes 'unfortunate' and 'fortunate' more appropriate epithets than 'blameworthy' and 'praiseworthy' to ascribe to these two cases. So, in the contexts in which reasonableness is associated with praiseworthiness and unreasonableness with blameworthiness (and these are the most frequent contexts), what we have called the subjective sense of reasonableness will have to be taken—just as it is the subjective sense of rightness that has to be associated with praiseworthiness.

This comparison with subjective rightness further supports the view that the sufficient condition for the subjective reasonableness of an inductively supported belief, so far as the effectiveness of the inductive policy is concerned, is simply the belief that this policy is effective, without the qualification that this belief should be a reasonable one. For we think that a man is acting rightly if he does what he believes to be the objectively right action, irrespective of whether or not this belief of his is a reasonable one. If we think that his belief is an unreasonable one, and that he might, for example, by a previous more diligent study of the facts of the situation, have prevented himself from having this unreasonable belief, and instead have acquired a different and reasonable belief, we may blame him for his past sin of omission in not having taken the steps he might have taken to acquire a more reasonable belief. But we do not blame him for acting on his present belief, whether this be reasonable or unreasonable. Similarly, we should consider a man reasonable in following an inductive policy which he believed to be effective, independently of the question as to whether or not his belief was a reasonable one. Thus, in the sense of reasonableness which is comparable with subjective rightness, it is belief in the effectiveness of the inductive policy, whether or not this belief is well grounded, that is a condition for the validity (in the subjective sense) of the inductive inference and for the reasonableness (in the subjective sense) of belief in the inductive conclusion.

But may not this comparison with subjective rightness be pushed further so that the reasonableness of belief in the premiss is as irrelevant to the reasonableness of belief in the inductive conclusion as is the reasonableness of belief in the effectiveness of the inductive policy? If so, the criterion for the reasonableness of an inductive belief would be criterion I, namely, that the thinker believes both the premiss of the inductive inference and that the inductive policy is effective. In defence of selecting this criterion it might be argued that a man might defend himself against criticism for holding an inductive belief q by saying that he believed the evidence from which he derived his belief in q by following an inductive policy in whose effectiveness he believed, without thinking it necessary to maintain that his belief in the evidence was a reasonable one. But I do not think that this would be a good defence. If the reasonableness of a belief is to be defended by the belief's having been inferred or being able to be inferred from other beliefs, these other beliefs must themselves be reasonably held. The process of obtaining new reasonable beliefs by inference is one of adding new beliefs to the thinker's body of reasonable beliefs (his rational corpus) on the basis of some of the beliefs already in this corpus. If the beliefs to which the new belief is added by the inference fall within the body of the thinker's beliefs but not within his rational corpus, the inference may well be valid in the sense of justifiably supporting his belief in q, but the inference does not justify him in including q in his rational corpus.

The situation in the criterion for reasonable belief in an inductive conclusion is thus different in respect of the roles played by belief in the inductive premiss and by belief in the effectiveness of an inductive policy pursued. The former belief has to be a reasonable one, in order that the inference should build upon a stable foundation. But what is required of the latter proposition—that the inductive policy pursued is effective—is, for the subjective sense of reasonable, that this proposition should be believed, for the objective sense of reasonable, that this proposition should be true. In neither the subjective sense nor the objective sense nor the combined sense is a reasonable belief in the policy's effectiveness a requirement for a belief which has been obtained by the use of the inductive policy from a reasonably believed premiss to be a reasonable belief.

The result of this discussion is, I hope, to uphold the thesis that there are three proper criteria yielding three proper senses for the 'validity' of an inductive inference made by a man B, and also three corresponding senses for the 'reasonableness' of B's belief in a conclusion arrived at by, or that would be based upon, an inductive inference. All three criteria agree in requiring that the premiss of the inference—the inductive evidence—should be reasonably believed by B; they agree in requiring something which is concerned with the effectiveness of the inductive policy pursued. They differ as to what is this something required. The objective criterion requires that the proposition asserting the effectiveness of the inductive policy should be true, the subjective criterion requires that this proposition should be believed by B. The both-objective-and-subjective criterion requires both that the inductive policy should in fact be effective and that its effectiveness should be believed by B. Let us now re-examine the accusation of vicious circularity in the light of this triple distinction.

CIRCULARITY RE-EXAMINED

The conditions for it to be subjectively valid for a man to infer e, the proposition that the policy Π of induction by the principle π of simple enumeration is effective, from π-evidence for e, and correlatively that this belief obtained or supportable by this inference is a subjectively reasonable belief are, first, that he should reasonably believe the evidence for e, and secondly, that he should believe e. Since neither of these conditions include the requirement that his belief in e should be a reasonable one, there is no explicit circularity in his reasoning. Nor is there any implicit circularity, since he can quite well reasonably believe both that he is reasonable in believing the π-evidence for e and that he is believing e without reasonably believing, or indeed believing, that he is reasonable in thus believing e. The critic will thus be compelled to withdraw his charge of circularity. But, of course, he will fall back upon saying that this criterion for the validity of an inductive inference and for the reasonableness of an inductive belief is too weak a one.

In which case the critic can be offered the stronger criterion for the man's inference to be both subjectively and objectively valid and for his inductive belief to be both subjectively and objectively reasonable. This criterion adds a third condition to the two conditions for subjective validity, namely, that e should in fact be true. Since this third condition no more than the other two includes the requirement that the man should reasonably believe e, there is again no explicit circularity. But the critic will then insist that here there is an implicit circularity in that to have a reasonable belief in this third condition for the validity of the inference requires an inference of exactly the same sort to establish it.

There is one consideration which is worth mentioning at this point, since it may perhaps serve to mitigate this implicit circularity. Let us consider the new inference whose premiss is the conjunction of the three conditions for the both subjective and objective validity of the inductive inference whose conclusion is e, i.e. whose premiss is the conjunctive proposition

> (B reasonably believes the π-evidence for e) and (B believes e) and (e is true),

and whose conclusion is the proposition that it is both subjectively and objectively reasonable for B to believe e. Since with this sense of 'reasonable' it is a logically necessary proposition that the premiss in this new inference is a sufficient condition for the conclusion, this new inference is a deduction. Now think of this new inference, not as adding a belief in the conclusion to B's body of reasonable beliefs but as carrying with it B's belief in the conclusion by deducing the conclusion from a premiss which B believes. Criteria I–V (p. 115) then become the relevant criteria for validity; and, if B believes the conjunctive premiss, belief in which is equivalent to a conjunction of three beliefs held by B—a belief that he reasonably believes the π-evidence for e, a belief that he believes e, and a belief in e—this triple belief justifiably carries with it a belief that it is both subjectively and objectively reasonable for B to believe e, provided that, if criteria I, II, IV, or V are used, B believes that the conjunctive premiss is logically a sufficient condition for the conclusion, and, if criteria II or V are used, that this belief of B's is a reasonable one. So B's second-order belief that he is both subjectively and objectively reasonable in believing e is a belief justifiably carried along with a first-order belief in e, together with a second-order belief that he has this belief, a second-order belief in the reasonableness of a belief in the π-evidence for e and—in the case of some of the criteria—a belief or a reasonable belief in a logically necessary proposition. If we take the second-order belief that he has a belief in e as going along automatically with a belief in e, and if we take for granted the second-order belief in the reasonableness of a belief in the π-evidence for e and the belief or reasonable belief in the logically necessary proposition, what we have said can be reduced to the statement that, if a man believes e, this belief justifies his holding along with it the second-order belief that he is both subjectively and objectively reasonable in believing e. Thus a belief in e is self-rationalizing—not, of course, in the sense that believing e makes this belief itself reasonable, but in the sense that believing e carries along with it a belief that this belief in e is reasonable.

The critic may object that all this farrago is like taking in one another's washing, and goes no way to producing any argument which is not circular for a belief in e to be reasonable in a sense of 'reasonable' which is not merely subjective. I can say no more than that the account of objective validity of an inference which has been given is in terms of the right working of an inference-machine, and that the implicit circularity only arises from the inference-machine becoming self-conscious about the way in which it operates. The predictionist can offer to the circularity-mongering critic two alternatives—a weak subjective sense of reasonableness with no suspicion of circularity, or a stronger sense of reasonableness, objective as well as subjective, with no explicit circularity but with an implicit circularity which depends essentially upon the inferrer being regarded as an inference-machine and the validity of his inference depending upon his operating, *qua* inference-machine, according to an efficient mode of operation (with the rider that, if the inferrer believes that he, *qua* inference-machine, is operating efficiently, that belief is self-rationalizing in the way explained in the last paragraph). If neither of these alternatives, nor the third alternative of the purely objective sense of reasonableness, satisfies the critic, and if he is not prepared to be satisfied by one sense of reasonableness in some contexts and another in other contexts but still demands a method of establishing the effectiveness of an inductive policy which is not to be obtained by following an inductive policy, he must be told outright that what he is demanding is that the effectiveness of an inductive policy should not be an empirical proposition. But if so, induction would be deduction, there would be no inductive problem to puzzle our heads over, and this chapter tediously worrying at the problem would have been altogether unnecessary.

VIII

SELF-SUPPORTING INDUCTIVE ARGUMENTS

(1) MAX BLACK

THE use of inductive rules has often led to true conclusions about matters of fact. Common sense regards this as a good reason for trusting inductive rules in the future, if due precautions are taken against error. Yet an argument from success in the past to probable success in the future itself uses an inductive rule, and therefore seems circular. Nothing would be accomplished by any argument that needed to assume the reliability of an inductive rule in order to establish that rule's reliability.

Suppose that inferences governed by some inductive rule have usually resulted in true conclusions; and let an inference from this fact to the probable reliability of the rule in the future be called a *second-order* inference. So long as the rule by which the second-order inference is governed differs from the rule whose reliability is to be affirmed, there will be no appearance of circularity. But if the second-order inference is governed by the very same rule of inference whose reliability is affirmed in the conclusion, the vicious circularity seems blatant.

Must we, then, reject forthwith every second-order inductive argument purporting to support the very rule of inference by which the argument itself is governed? Contrary to general opinion, a plausible case can be made for saying, No.[1] Properly constructed and interpreted, such 'self-supporting' inferences, as I shall continue to call them, can satisfy all

(1) is from *Journal of Philosophy*, vol. 55 (1958), pp. 718–25, (2) is from *Analysis*, vol. 22 (1962) pp. 138–41, where it was originally published under the title of 'The Circularity of a self-supporting Inductive Argument'. (3) is from *Analysis*, vol. 23 (1963), pp. 43–4, where it was originally published under the title of 'Self-support and Circularity. A Reply to Mr Achinstein'. (4) is from *Analysis*, vol. 23 (1963), pp. 123–7, where it was originally published under the title 'Circularity and Induction'. The papers are republished by permission of the authors, the editor of the *Journal of Philosophy* and Basil Blackwell.

[1] See Max Black, *Problems of Analysis* (Ithaca, N.Y., 1954), chapter 11, and R. B. Braithwaite, *Scientific Explanation* (Cambridge, 1953), chapter 8 [pp. 102–126 of the present volume.—Ed.].

the conditions for legitimate inductive inference: when an inductive rule has been reliable (has generated true conclusions from true premisses more often than not) in the past, a second-order inductive inference governed by the same rule can show that the rule deserves to be trusted in its next application.

The reasons I have given for this contention have recently been sharply criticized by Professor Wesley C. Salmon.[2] In trying to answer his precisely worded objections, I hope to make clearer the view I have been defending and to dispel some lingering misapprehensions.

My original example of a legitimate self-supporting inductive argument was the following:[3]

(a) In most instances of the use of R in arguments with true premisses examined in a wide variety of conditions, R has been successful.

Hence (*probably*):

In the next instance to be encountered of the use of R in an argument with a true premiss, R will be successful.

The rule of inductive inference mentioned in the premiss and the conclusion of the above argument is:

R: To argue from *Most instances of A's examined in a wide variety of conditions have been B* to (probably) *The next A to be encountered will be B.*

Thus the second-order argument (a) uses the rule R in showing that the same rule will be 'successful' (will generate a true conclusion from a true premiss[4]) in the next encountered instance of its use.

The rule R stated above is not intended to be a 'supreme rule' of induction, from which all other inductive rules can be derived; nor is it claimed that R, as it stands, is a wholly acceptable rule for inductive inference. The unsolved problem of a satisfactory formulation of canons of inductive in-

---

[2] See Wesley C. Salmon, 'Should We Attempt to Justify Induction?' *Philosophical Studies*, vol. 8, no. 3 (April 1957), pp. 45–7.

[3] See *Problems*, p. 197, where the argument is called '(a_2)' and the rule by which it is governed 'R_2'. At that place, I also presented another self-supporting argument with a more sweeping conclusion of the *general* reliability of the corresponding rule. But since I was unable to accept the premiss of that argument, or the reliability of the rule it employed, I shall follow Salmon in discussing only the argument presented above.

[4] Here and throughout this discussion, I assume for simplicity that all the premisses of any argument or inference considered have been conjoined into a single statement.

ference will arise only incidentally in the present discussion. The rule R and the associated argument (a) are to serve merely to illustrate the logical problems that arise in connection with self-supporting arguments: the considerations to be adduced in defence of (a) could be adapted to fit many other self-supporting arguments.

The proposed exculpation of the self-supporting argument (a) from the charge of vicious circularity is linked to a feature of the corresponding rule R that must be carefully noted. Inductive arguments governed by R vary in 'strength'[5] according to the number and variety of the favourable instances reported in the premiss. So, although R permits us to assert a certain conclusion categorically, it is to be understood throughout that the strength of the assertion fluctuates with the character of the evidence. If only a small number of instances have been examined and the relative frequency of favourable instances (A's that are B) is little better than a half, the strength of the argument may be close to zero; while a vast predominance of favourable instances in a very large sample of observations justifies a conclusion affirmed with nearly maximal strength. The presence of the word 'probably' in the original formulation of R indicates the variability of strength of the corresponding argument; in more refined substitutes for R, provision might be made for some precise measure of the associated degree of strength.

Variability in strength is an important respect in which inductive arguments differ sharply from deductive ones. If a deductive argument is not valid, it must be *in*valid, no intermediate cases being conceivable; but a legitimate inductive argument, whose conclusion may properly be affirmed on the evidence supplied, may still be very weak. Appraisal of an inductive argument admits of degrees.

Similar remarks apply to inductive rules, as contrasted with deductive ones. A deductive rule is either valid or invalid—*tertium non datur*; but at any time in the history of the employment of an inductive rule, it has what may be called a *degree of reliability* depending upon its ratio of successes in previous applications. A legitimate or correct inductive rule may still be a weak one: appraisal of an inductive rule admits of degrees.

Now in claiming that the second-order argument (a) *supports* the rule R, I am claiming that the argument raises the degree of reliability of the rule, and hence the strength of the arguments in which it will be used; I have no

---

[5] In *Problems*, p. 193, I spoke, with the same intention, of the 'degree of support' given to the conclusion by the premiss. If the latter has the form *m/n A's examined in a wide variety of conditions have been B*, it is natural to suppose that the strength of the argument increases as m increases, and also as m/n increases. A plausible formula for the 'strength' of the argument might be $(1 - e^{-m})(2m/n - 1)$.

intention of claiming that the self-supporting argument can definitively establish or demonstrate that the rule is correct. Indeed, I do not know what an outright demonstration of the correctness or legitimacy of an inductive rule would be like. My attempted rebuttal of Salmon's objections will turn upon the possibility of raising the degree of reliability of an inductive rule, as already explained.

The contribution made by the second-order argument (a) to strengthening the rule R by which it is governed can be made plain by a hypothetical illustration. Suppose evidence is available that $\frac{4}{5}$ of the A's so far examined have been B, and it is proposed, by an application of the rule R, to draw the inference that the next A to be encountered will be B. For the sake of simplicity the proposed argument may be taken to have a strength of $\frac{4}{5}$.[6] Before accepting the conclusion about the next A, we may wish to consider the available evidence about past successes of the rule R. Suppose, for the sake of argument, that we know R to have been successful in $\frac{9}{10}$ of the cases in which it has been previously used. If so, the second-order argument affirms with strength $\frac{9}{10}$ that R will be successful in the next instance of its use. But the 'next instance' is before us, as the argument whose premiss is that $\frac{4}{5}$ of the A's have been B. For R to be 'successful' in this instance is for the conclusion of the first-order argument to be true; the strength of the second-order argument is therefore immediately transferred to the first-order argument. Before invoking the second-order argument, we were entitled to affirm the conclusion of the first-order argument with a strength of no better than $\frac{4}{5}$, but we are now able to raise the strength to $\frac{9}{10}$. Conversely, if the second-order argument had shown R to have been unsuccessful in less than $\frac{4}{5}$ of its previous uses, our confidence in the proposed conclusion of the first-order argument would have been diminished.

There is no mystery about the transfer of strength from the second-order argument to the first-order argument: the evidence cited in the former amplifies the evidence immediately relevant to the latter. Evidence concerning the proportion of A's found to have been B permits the direct inference, with strength $\frac{4}{5}$, that the next A to be encountered will be B. It is, however, permissible to view the situation in another aspect as concerned with the extrapolation of an already observed statistical association between true premisses of a certain sort and a corresponding conclusion. The evidence takes the form: In 9 cases out of 10, the truth of a statement of the form *m/n X's have been found to be Y's* has been found associated in a

---

[6] This means taking m/n as the measure of strength, rather than some more complicated formula like the one suggested in footnote 5 above. The argument does not depend upon the exact form of the measure of strength.

wide variety of cases with the truth of the statement *The next X to be encountered was Y*.[7] This is better evidence than that cited in the premiss of the original first-order argument: it is therefore to be expected that the strength of the conclusion shall be raised.

It should be noticed that the evidence cited in the second-order argument is not merely greater in amount than the evidence cited in the first-order argument. If R has been successfully used for drawing conclusions about fish, neutrons, planets, etc. (the 'wide variety of conditions' mentioned in the premiss of the second-order argument), it would be illegitimate to coalesce such heterogeneous kinds of objects into a single class for the sake of a more extensive *first-order* argument. Proceeding to 'second-order' considerations allows us to combine the results of previous inductive inquiries in a way which would not otherwise be possible.

Nothing in this conception of inductive method requires us to remain satisfied with the second-order argument. If circumstances warrant, and suitable evidence can be found, we might be ledt o formulate third- or even higher-order arguments. These might conceivably result in lowering the measures of strength we at present attach to certain arguments in which R is used. But if this were to happen, we would not have been shown to have been mistaken in previously attaching these measures of strength. Nor is it required that a first-order argument be checked against a corresponding second-order argument before the former can properly be used. If we have no reason to think that R is unsuccessful most of the time, or is objectionable on some logical grounds, that is enough to make our employment of it so far reasonable. The function of higher-order arguments in the tangled web of inductive method is to permit us to progress from relatively imprecise and uncritical methods to methods whose degrees of reliability and limits of applicability have themselves been checked by inductive investigations. It is in this way that inductive method becomes self-regulating and, if all goes well, self-supporting.

Salmon's objections to the foregoing conception are summarized by him as follows:

The so-called self-supporting arguments are . . . circular in the following precise sense: the conclusiveness of the argument cannot be established without assuming the truth of the conclusion. It happens, in this case, that the assumption of the truth of the conclusion is required to establish the correctness of the rules of inference used rather than the truth of the premisses, but that makes the argument no less viciously circular. The circularity lies in regarding the facts stated in the

---

[7] We might wish to restrict the second-order argument to cases in which the ratio m/n was close to $\frac{4}{5}$. Other refinements readily suggest themselves.

premisses as *evidence* for the conclusion, rather than as evidence against the conclusion or as no evidence either positive or negative. To regard the facts in the premisses as evidence for the conclusion is to assume that the rule of inference used in the argument is a correct one. And this is precisely what is to be proved. If the conclusion is denied, then the facts stated in the premisses are no longer evidence for the conclusion.[8]

Comments: (1) Salmon's reference to 'conclusiveness' smacks too much of the appraisal of deductive argument. An inductive argument is not required to be 'conclusive' if that means that its conclusion is entailed or logically implied by its premisses; it is, of course, required to be correct or legitimate, but that means only that the rule of inductive inference shall be reliable—shall usually lead from true premisses to true conclusions. The correctness of an inductive argument could only depend upon the truth of its conclusion if the latter asserted the reliability of the rule by which the argument was governed. But this was not the case in our argument (a). The conclusion there was that R would be successful in the next instance of its use: this might very well prove to be false without impugning the reliability of R. Salmon was plainly mistaken if he thought that the falsity of (a)'s conclusion entails the incorrectness of the rule by which (a) is governed.[9]

(2) Can the *correctness* of argument (a) be 'established without assuming the truth of the conclusion' of (a)? Well, if 'established' means the same as 'proved by a deductive argument', the answer must be that the correctness of (a) cannot be established at all. But again, a correct inductive argument in support of the rule governing (a) can certainly be constructed without assuming (a)'s conclusion. We do not have to assume that R will be successful in the next instance in order to argue correctly that the available evidence supports the reliability of R.

(3) Salmon says: 'To regard the facts in the premisses as evidence for the conclusion is to assume that the rule of inference used in the argument is a correct one.' In using the rule of inference we certainly *treat* it as correct: we would not use it if we had good reasons for suspecting it to be unreliable. If this is what Salmon means, what he says is right, but not damaging to the correctness of (a). But he would be plainly wrong if he maintained that an assertion of the correctness of (a) was an additional premiss required by (a), or that an argument to the effect that (a) was correct must precede the

[8] Salmon, loc. cit., p. 47.
[9] I conjecture that Salmon was led into making this mistake by forgetting the conclusion of the argument that he correctly reproduces at the foot of page 45 of his article. It is a sheer blunder to say 'A given inductive rule can be established by a self-supporting argument, according to Black' (p. 45)—if 'established' means the same as 'proved reliable'. The self-supporting argument can *strengthen* the rule, and in this way '*support*' it.

legitimate use of (a). For if this last demand were pressed, it would render deductive inference no less than inductive inference logically impossible. If we were never entitled to *use* a correct rule of inference before we had formally argued in support of that rule, the process of inference could never get started.

I shall end by considering an ingenious counter-example provided by Salmon. He asks us to consider the following argument:

(a'): In most instances of the use of R' in arguments with true premisses in a wide variety of conditions, R' has been *un*successful.

Hence (probably):

In the next instance to be encountered of the use of R' in an argument with a true premiss, R' will be successful.

The relevant rule is the 'counter-inductive' one:

R': To argue from *Most instances of A's examined in a wide variety of conditions have not been B* to (probably) *The next A to be encountered will be B.*

Salmon says that while (a') must be regarded as a self-supporting argument by my criteria, the rule here supported, R', is in conflict with R. From the same premisses the two rules 'will almost always produce contrary conclusions'.[10] This must be granted. But Salmon apparently overlooks an important respect in which the 'counter-inductive' rule R' must be regarded as illegitimate.

In calling an inductive rule 'correct', so that it meets the canons of legitimacy of *inductive* rules of inference, we claim at least that the rule is reliable, in the sense of usually leading from true premisses to true conclusions. That is part of what we *mean* by a 'correct inductive rule'. It can easily be shown that R' must fail to meet this condition.

Suppose we were using R' to predict the terms of a series of 1's and 0's, of which the first three terms were known to be 1's. Then our first two predictions might be as follows (shown by underlining):

$$1\ 1\ 1\ \underline{0}\ \underline{0}$$

At this point, suppose R' has been used successfully in each of the two predictions, so that the series is in fact now observed to be 1 1 1 0 0. Since 1's still predominate, direct application of the rule calls for 0 to be predicted next. On the other hand, the second-order argument shows that R' has been successful each time and therefore demands that it not be trusted next time, i.e. calls for the prediction of 1. So the very definition of R' renders it impossible for the rule to be successful without being *incoherent*.[11] The suggested second-order argument in support of R' could be formulated only if R' were known to be unreliable, and would therefore be worthless. So we have an *a priori* reason for preferring R to its competitor R'. But it is easy to produce any number of alternative rules of inductive inference, none of which suffers from the fatal defect of R'. The choice between such rules, I suggest, has to be made in the light of experience of their use. I have tried to show in outline how such experience can properly be invoked without logical circularity.

(2) PETER ACHINSTEIN

1. MANY philosophers regard as circular, and hence illegitimate, any justification of a principle of induction which makes reference to the success of that principle in the past. Taking issue with this position, Max Black has defended the thesis that the appeal to the past performance of an inductive rule in order to provide support for its future success need involve no circularity whatever, and may indeed constitute a legitimate argument in favour of the rule.[12] As an example, he considers the following inductive rule of inference:

R: To argue from *Most instances of A's examined under a wide variety of conditions have been B* to (probably) *The next A to be encountered will be B.*

In defence of R, Black proposes the following 'self-supporting' argument which he claims to be free from circularity:

(a): In most instances of the use of R in arguments with true premisses examined in a wide variety of conditions, R has been successful.

Hence (probably):

In the next instance to be encountered of the use of R in an argument with a true premiss, R will be successful.

---

[11] A parallel situation would arise in the use of R in predicting the members of the 1-0 series only if R were to be predominantly *un*successful. But then we would have the best of reasons for assigning R zero strength, and the second-order argument would be pointless.

[12] Max Black, *Problems of Analysis* (London, 1954), chapter 11.

Argument (a) uses R as its rule of inference and purports to support the use of R in the next instance of its application by citing the fact that R has been successful in the past. As Black points out, the premiss of (a) is neither identical with the conclusion nor the conclusion in different words, nor is the conclusion a premiss of any argument used to support the premiss of argument (a). Hence, he emphasizes, one cannot attribute circularity to (a) on grounds such as these.

Despite Black's attempts to defend (a),[13] it has been maintained by Wesley Salmon that the argument is circular.[14] Salmon attributes its circularity to the fact that in proposing (a) one must '. . . assume that the rule of inference [R] used in the argument is a correct one. And this is precisely what is to be proved'. Undaunted by such criticism, Black offers a detailed reply to the charge of circularity.[15] Because I do not find Salmon's formulation sufficient to expose the circularity, nor Black's attempt to defend argument (a) successful, I wish to open the issue once more by considering the cogency of a 'self-supporting' argument such as (a).

2. When any argument is proposed for the purpose of showing that a certain proposition is probable, the correctness or validity of the argument, and hence of the rule of inference which governs the argument, is obviously assumed. Now to claim that a non-deductive rule of inference is correct or valid is to imply, at least for one thing, that the rule will generally be successful, and in particular, that it will probably be successful in the next instance of its use, i.e. that in the next argument with a true premiss the rule will afford an inference to a conclusion that is probably true. This is part of the concept of a correct or valid non-deductive rule of inference. Black, indeed, would seem committed to the latter point when he writes: 'In order for an inductive argument to be correct the rule to which it conforms must be *reliable*. A rule is reliable if it yields true conclusions in *most* cases in which it governs arguments having true premisses.'[16] (If a rule leads to success in most cases—and Black here is speaking of future as well as past successes—then I take it to be an analytic consequence that it is probable that it will be successful in its next application.)

It should be noted that although the claim that a non-deductive rule of inference is correct or valid does not entail that it will definitely be successful in its next application, it does entail that it will probably be so. This

[13] See ibid., pp. 198–206.
[14] Wesley C. Salmon, 'Should We Attempt to Justify Induction?', *Philosophical Studies*, 8 (1957), 33–48.
[15] Black, 'Self-Supporting Inductive Arguments', *Journal of Philosophy*, 55 (1958), 718–25 [pp. 127–34 of the present volume.—Ed.].
[16] *Problems of Analysis*, p. 194.

means that if the next application of the rule turns out to be unsuccessful, the rule is not thereby shown to be incorrect. (Although, of course, too many such failures certainly would affect its claim to correctness.)

What follows from these considerations is this. The assumption that argument (a) is correct logically involves the assumption that the rule of inference R which sanctions (a) will probably be successful in its next application. This means that the assumption that (a) is correct involves the assumption that (a)'s conclusion (which is that R will be successful in its next application) is probable. Now, as we observed earlier, in using an argument to show that a proposition is probable the correctness of the argument must be assumed. It follows, therefore, that in using (a) to show that the proposition 'R will be successful in its next application' is probable, it must already be assumed probable that R will be successful in its next application. And it is precisely this fact which renders (a) circular.

3. By way of defending and further expounding the present charge, it will be helpful to consider how Black defends argument (a) against the type of criticism offered by Salmon.

In his first two rebuttals Black complains—with some justification—that when Salmon writes 'The conclusiveness of argument (a) cannot be established without assuming the truth of its conclusion', he seems to be treating (a) as if it were a deductive argument, and furthermore he is mistaken in maintaining that (a)'s conclusion must be assumed to be true when the argument is proposed. Thus, Black emphasizes, the validity of (a) does not depend upon the truth of its conclusion, since the conclusion of (a) could turn out false and not impugn the validity of the rule of inference involved.

However, while Salmon was incorrect in suggesting that the validity of (a) depends upon the truth of (a)'s conclusion, it is nevertheless the case, as we observed earlier, that the assumption that (a) is valid (an assumption which is made in proposing (a)) does involve the claim that (a)'s conclusion is *probable*. It is this assumption which suffices to render (a) circular, since (a) purports to show that its conclusion is probable. And the claim that (a)'s conclusion is probable would not be shown to be unfounded if (a)'s conclusion turned out false.

It is Black's third reply to the charge of circularity which seems centrally important in his defence of argument (a): Here Black agrees that in using rule R we assume that it is correct ('treat it as correct'); but, he argues, this does not suffice to expose circularity in (a). For to assume that R is correct is not to assume its correctness as a premiss of the argument itself, nor as a premiss of any argument used to establish the premiss of (a). That is, Black seems to be maintaining, the only assumptions which could justify a charge of circularity in (a) would have to be assumptions expressed actually as premisses of (a) or as premisses of other arguments whose conclusions are used to support the premisses of (a). It is this claim that merits closer examination.

When one proposes an argument in support of a certain proposition one makes at least two kinds of assumptions: those expressed as premisses of the argument (or as premisses of other arguments used to establish these premisses), and those involving the claim of the correctness or validity of the rule of inference which sanctions the argument. As Black rightly remarks, assumptions of the latter sort cannot be expressed as premisses of the argument itself, on pain of infinite regress. Nevertheless, an assumption of the correctness of the rule of inference governing an argument is made by one who claims that the argument supports or establishes a certain conclusion. Suppose, now, that a proposition *p*, as well as being required to be assumed by one who proposes a certain argument, constitutes also the conclusion of that argument. Then the proponent of the argument must assume *p* (assume that *p* is probable) in order to establish *p* (or show that *p* is probable). And this is what is essentially involved in circular reasoning, whether or not *p* is actually a premiss of the argument.

The fact that an argument whose conclusion neither appears as, nor is presupposed by, a premiss can nevertheless be circular will become even more patent if we consider the following (non-valid) *deductive* rule D and the corresponding 'self-supporting' argument (b) in its favour:

D: To argue from *No F is G* and *Some G is H* to *All F is H.*

The 'self-supporting' argument (b) can now be formulated as follows:

(b): No argument using D as its rule of inference is an argument which contains a premiss beginning with the term 'All'. Some arguments containing premisses beginning with the term 'All' are valid.

Therefore:

All arguments using D as their rule of inference are valid.

Argument (b), each of whose premisses is true, uses D as its rule of inference and purports in its conclusion to demonstrate the validity of D. Furthermore, the conclusion of (b) is not the same as its premisses, nor is it presupposed by them. According to Black's reasoning, then, (b) could legitimately be employed to demonstrate the validity of the unacceptable rule

D. However, the circularity, and hence illegitimacy, of (b) lies in the fact that the validity of D must be assumed when one uses (b) in trying to demonstrate the validity of D.

Black, then, would seem to be mistaken in his claim that circularity can only be imputed to arguments whose conclusions are included in their premises, or whose conclusions must be the premises of other arguments which are used to establish the premises of the arguments in question. Any defence of argument (a) which rests on such a claim must be considered unsatisfactory.

Accordingly, in his replies to the charge of circularity, Black does not appear to succeed in demonstrating the logical cogency of a 'self-supporting' argument such as (a).

(3) MAX BLACK

1. LET R be the following rule of inductive inference:

R: To argue from *Most instances of A's examined under a wide variety of conditions have been B* to (probably) *The next A to be encountered will be B.*

In the past[17] I have argued that the following inductive argument in support of R is not reprehensibly circular:

(a): In most instances of the use of R in arguments with true premises examined in a wide variety of conditions, R has been successful.

Hence (probably):

In the next instance to be encountered of the use of R in an argument with a true premiss, R will be successful.

Here, 'successful' means leading from true premises to a true conclusion.

2. Nearly everybody who looks at (a) feels that it somehow begs the question. The rule in (a) is R itself: surely, one wants to say, there is something wrong in using R itself in trying to provide a good reason for using R again. Yet nobody has so far succeeded in showing what, if anything, is wrong with (a).

[17] See chapter 12 of *Models and Metaphors* (Ithaca, N.Y., 1962) [originally published in *Journal of Philosophy* and republished on pp. 127–34 of the present volume.—Ed.] and chapter 11 of *Problems of Analysis* (London, 1954).

3. In a recent paper,[18] Mr. Peter Achinstein has proposed a new reason for rejecting (a). The gist of his objection is as follows: Anybody who offers argument (a) in good faith must make a certain assumption[19] which entails that R will probably be successful in its next application. 'It follows, therefore,' according to Achinstein, 'that in using (a) to show that the proposition "R will be successful in its next application" is probable it must already be assumed probable that R will be successful in its next application. And it is precisely this fact which renders (a) circular' (p. 136 above).

4. Let S be the proposition 'R will be successful in its next application' and let T be the proposition 'S is probable'; S and T are clearly different propositions and T does not entail S. Achinstein says that if I present (a) I must assume the truth of T. His remark is irrelevant, whether true or not. Suppose he is right in claiming I must assume T to be true; what then? The conclusion of (a) is S, not T, and T does not entail S. Even an argument that had T as an explicit premiss and S as its conclusion would not be circular. Achinstein may have been misled by the presence of the word 'probably' in the statement of (a). But I hoped I had made it quite plain that the parenthetical occurrence of 'probably' in the statement of (a) was to indicate that inductive arguments, unlike deductive ones, admit of various degrees of 'strength'. Whatever the strength of (a), its conclusion, S, not T, is asserted categorically. It would be pointless to take the conclusion of (a) to be T rather than S, because in that case, so far as I can see, the new argument would be a valid *deductive* one.[20] Perhaps, after all, Achinstein is committing the old mistake of treating an inductive argument as if it aspired to be deductive. At any rate, his objection fails because it is not applicable to the argument he took himself to be discussing, but at best to some other argument.

[18] 'The Circularity of a Self-supporting Argument', *Analysis*, 22.6 (June 1962), pp. 138–141, [pp. 134–8 of the present volume.—Ed.].

[19] The supposed 'assumption' is that R is reliable, i.e. that it usually leads from true premisses to true conclusion. It is at best misleading to call this an assumption. In using my pencil I do not need to assume that it usually works; nor do I assume R's reliability when I use the rule—I just use it. Had I good reasons to suspect the rule of being unreliable, I should not use it, but it is, after all, reliable in the intended sense and I have good reasons, not themselves part of argument (a), for thinking so.

[20] I am not sure about this, if only because it is not clear to me what Achinstein means by talking about S being probable. I would have thought that T would have to be exponible into a proposition relating S to the premiss of (a), for S is surely not probable *per se*, but is so in view of the facts used in (a). If this reading is correct, assuming T's truth amounts to 'assuming' that (a) is a sound argument. If this were a misdemeanour, it would be committed in the course of every argument.

(4) PETER ACHINSTEIN

1. RECENTLY[21] I suggested why an argument proposed by Max Black, which attempts to support an inductive rule by citing its past success, suffers from circularity. The inductive rule under discussion is this:

R: To argue from *Most instances of A's examined under a wide variety of conditions have been B* to (probably) *The next A to be encountered will be B.*

The argument in favour of the rule is as follows:

(a): In most instances of the use of R in arguments with true premises examined in a wide variety of conditions, R has been successful.

Hence (probably):

In the next instance to be encountered of use of R in an argument with a true premiss, R will be successful.

I argued that in proposing (a) for the purpose of showing that (a)'s conclusion is probable it must already be assumed that (a)'s conclusion is probable; hence the circularity. Professor Black objects[22] on the ground that (a)'s conclusion is not '*Probably* in the next instance . . . R will be successful' (T), but simply 'In the next instance . . . R will be successful' (S); and, he claims, the most I have shown is that T must be assumed, not S. Hence, the spectre of circularity vanishes, he maintains, for 'even an argument that had T as an explicit premiss and S as its conclusion would not be circular'.[23] This claim appears to reflect his general assumption that an argument with a premiss of the form 'it is probable that p' cannot be considered circular if its conclusion is simply 'p'.

Black's reply raises important issues which merit closer examination.

2. In the case of some inductive arguments, the premises involved, although they do not deductively entail the conclusion, nevertheless provide overwhelming support for it. E.g., Black cites the following as an illustration of one type of inductive reasoning: 'All kinds of acids under all sorts

[21] 'The Circularity of a Self-Supporting Inductive Argument', *Analysis*, 22.6 (June 1962) [pp. 134–8 of the present volume.—Ed.].

[22] 'Self-Support and Circularity: A Reply to Mr. Achinstein', *Analysis*, 23.2 (December 1962), 43–4 [pp. 138–9 of the present volume.—Ed.].

[23] Ibid., p. 44 [p. 139.—Ed.].

of conditions have invariably turned blue litmus red; hence, acids turn blue litmus red.'[24] An argument of this type is such that if we know its premiss(es) to be true, and we are using a correct mode of inference, we are justified in claiming that (we know) the conclusion is true also. When we employ such an argument we may be said to have shown that its conclusion is true.

Other inductive arguments are such that while the premisses involved do not provide overwhelming support for the conclusion, nevertheless they do provide some support for it. Consider, e.g., the following argument: In a random selection of housewives interviewed, four out of five were found to play bridge; hence (probably) the next housewife to be interviewed will be found to play bridge.[25] An argument of this type is such that if we know its premiss(es) to be true, and we are using a correct mode of inference, we may claim, not that we know the conclusion to be true, but rather that (we know) the conclusion is probable. When we employ such an argument we may be said to have shown that its conclusion is probable.

These observations reflect the fact that to classify something as an (inductive) argument is not merely to say that it is a set of sentences with a certain form. One must consider as well the use to which the sentences are, or can be, put. If I utter a sentence of the form 'p, hence (definitely) q', I am arguing only if I am using these words to show that 'q' is (definitely) true. Similarly, if I utter a sentence of the form 'p, hence (probably) q', I may be considered to be arguing only if I am using these words to show that 'q' is probable (probably true). (In the latter case, I cannot claim, without reservation, that the argument shows that 'q' is true; nor can I claim only that the premiss *supports* the conclusion—of course it does do this, but, if the premiss is true, I can go on to claim that the conclusion is shown to be probable.) To determine whether my argument is circular, then, one must examine not merely the sentences I employ but also what it is that I am using these sentences to show. And, in employing the argument, if I must assume what the argument purports to show, then I am arguing circularly.

Now, two types of circularity may be distinguished within both *deductive* and *non-deductive* arguments. In the deductive case, the first type can be illustrated, e.g., by reference to the following mode of argument:

(I):   p
     hence
        p

---

[24] *Problems of Analysis* (London, 1954), p. 192.   [25] Cf. ibid., p. 192.

An argument of form (I) would be considered reprehensibly circular if it were the case that we claim we know its premiss 'p' to be true where our justification for this claim is that the argument itself shows that 'p' is true.

In the non-deductive case, the first type of circularity can be illustrated by reference to the following mode of argument:

(II): It is probable that p
     Hence (*probably*)
  p

Such an argument would be reprehensibly circular if it were the case that we claim we know the premiss, 'it is probable that p', to be true where our justification for this claim is that the argument itself shows that it is probable that p, and hence that the premiss is true. In this case, of course, as the argument is formulated above, the conclusion 'p' is not the same as the premiss 'it is probable that p'. Nevertheless, such an argument must be considered circular *when used to show that* '*p*' *is probable*. Indeed, if it were legitimate to employ an argument of form (II), we could obviously show that any proposition whatever is probable. Accordingly, I conclude that Black is mistaken in his claim that circularity cannot be imputed to an argument whose premiss is 'it is probable that p' and whose conclusion is 'p'. Such a claim involves a failure to recognize an important type of non-deductive circularity.

The second type of circularity involves employing an argument where the truth, or probability, of the conclusion must be assumed by one who proposes the argument, although this assumption is not one of the premisses, nor is it used to support a premiss. As an example of *deductive* circularity of this second type, consider the following argument each of whose premisses is true:

(b): No argument using **D** as its rule of inference is an argument which contains a premiss beginning with the term 'All'. Some arguments containing premisses beginning with the term 'All' are valid.

Therefore:

All arguments using **D** as their rule of inference are valid.

The (non-valid) deductive rule of inference in question is this:

D: To argue from *No F is G* and *Some G is H* to *All F is H*.

The circularity of (b) lies not in the fact that we assume the conclusion of (b) *as a premiss*, but rather in that in employing the argument to demonstrate the conclusion of (b) it must be assumed that the rule of inference governing the argument is valid. And it is this assumption that one who employs the argument is attempting to establish; hence, the circularity.

Now, my claim is that Black's argument (a) is an example of an *inductive* argument plagued by circularity of this second type. One who employs (a) is presumably attempting to show that its conclusion is probable. (Since the premiss of (a) does not provide overwhelming support for the conclusion, we cannot maintain, without reservation, that the argument shows that the conclusion is (definitely) *true*.) But in utilizing the argument to show that its conclusion is probable one must assume that its rule of inference is correct. And this, I attempted to show in my original paper, involves the assumption that its conclusion is probable; hence, the circularity.

3. Professor Black objects to my statement that in using an argument we must *assume* that the rule governing the argument is correct (and therefore reliable). He maintains that 'it is at best misleading to call this an assumption. In using my pencil I do not need to assume that it usually works; nor do I assume R's reliability when I use the rule—I just use it.'[26] Now surely Black does not want to say that we may use any arbitrary rule we wish. Rather it would seem necessary that the rule of inference employed in an argument is correct if the argument is to be considered correct. Hence, a claim that the argument is correct involves a claim, or assumption, that the rule of inference involved is correct. And a claim that an argument is correct is at least implicitly made by one who maintains that the argument establishes, or supports, its conclusion. Of course, when I employ a certain argument I needn't *formulate* my claim that the rule of inference involved is correct; nor if I were to formulate this claim would I express it as a premiss of the argument itself, on pain of infinite regress; nor need I defend this claim in order to make it. If this is Black's point I quite agree. But it does not follow from this that in using an argument to show that a certain proposition is true, or probable, we make no assumption concerning the correctness of the rule of inference involved. Indeed, Black seems to agree that we do make such an assumption, when he writes: 'In using the rule of inference [R] we certainly *treat* it as correct: we could not use it if we had good reasons for suspecting it to be unreliable.'[27]

Black also confesses that he finds my use of the term 'probable' unclear, since, he maintains, the sentence '(a)'s conclusion is probable' 'would have

[26] 'Reply', p. 44, footnote 1 [p. 139, footnote 19.—Ed.].
[27] *Models and Metaphors* (Ithaca, N.Y., 1962), p. 216, italics his [p. 132.—Ed.].

to be exponible into a proposition relating S [(a)'s conclusion] to the premiss of (a), for S is surely not probable *per se*, but is so in view of the facts used in (a)'.[28] This, of course, is to reopen the issue of the relativity of probability statements, an issue which cannot profitably be discussed in this short space. I shall restrict myself to making the following claims, which indicate briefly the general viewpoint I would defend: (1) I cannot accept the thesis that a statement of the form 'p is probable' literally *means* 'evidence e supports p', or 'p is probable relative to e', though, to be sure, evidence is used to support the claim that 'p' is probable. (2) Black's reasoning in the passage quoted does not establish his thesis about probability statements: of course a proposition is probable *in view of* the relevant facts (the same might be said of 'true'); but this is at least equally well explained by admitting that relevant facts are needed to support a probability statement, and does not necessitate the claim that a statement of the form 'p is probable' contains an ellipsis.

[28] 'Reply', p. 44, footnote 2 [p. 139, footnote 20.—Ed.].

IX

ONE FORM OF SCEPTICISM ABOUT INDUCTION

KEITH CAMPBELL

SOME principles of thought are so fundamental that they cannot coherently be called in question; any successful denial of such a principle's validity must itself depend on what it would impugn. The 'laws of thought', notably those of contradiction and excluded third (fourth, fifth, . . .), are commonly held to be of this kind. The characteristic is shared also by some inductive principles, in particular by A: *At least one inductively established result is justifiable*.

Let 'regular concomitance' be taken as synonymous with 'repetitive concomitance in accordance with some law'. Let a *sub-predictive generalization* be any assertion of the form 'There is a regular concomitance of characteristics α and β throughout a substantial segment of space-time, past and present'. These assertions are labelled *sub-predictive* because, although any such assertion does entail that given favourable conditions for confirmation, for every occurrence of α up till now, an occurrence of β would be found to have been its concomitant, yet it makes no claim about future occurrences of α. Each is a *generalization* because it makes an assertion about the whole class *occurrences of α hitherto* in a situation where it is not known that more than a proper part of that class has been examined.

In all that follows, it is to be understood that no analytic relations hold between α and β. So a sub-predictive generalization can only be established by taking the cases of α observed up till now as establishing a law of concomitance, and using this law as the basis for a general claim concerning αs. That is, its mode of establishment is inductive, but as a sub-predictive generalization does not claim that the concomitance in question will continue, the inductive process is a weak one. It is, consequently, the less likely to be dispensable. Whether the generalization is regarded as inferred from, or confirmed by, the relevant observational truths is here irrelevant.

For brevity, sub-predictive generalizations connecting two characteristics

From *Analysis*, vol. 23 (1963), pp. 80–3. Reprinted by permission of the author and Basil Blackwell.

will be referred to by descriptions of the form 'the sub-predictive generalization that αs β', or 'the inductive result that αs β'.

Consider now the sceptical assertion Ā: *No inductive generalization, of any
kind, is justifiable.* Any use of a language to communicate evinces faith in
the inductive results that language utterers are language understanders, that
sound patterns are propagated in air without radical distortion, that human
beings can distinguish areas of light and dark on a page under normal conditions, and so on. And any successful use of language for communication
entails the truth of some of these propositions. So the communication of Ā
involves the falsehood of Ā. That is, denial of A, in any inter-personal use
of language, depends on the truth of A.

But, language once learned, is it perhaps possible to embrace silence and
Ā together, keeping thought pure of induction because private? A negative
answer to this question may be established by either of two theses, a strong
and a weak. The results obtainable from the theses diverge at a later stage
in the argument.

The strong thesis: *The employment, even in thought alone, of every general
term involves at least one sub-predictive generalization.*

A necessary condition for the use of a general term is that, among
entities and possible entities, a class may be distinguished whose members
are all significantly related in some way to one another, and in this way to
no non-member. And a necessary condition for distinguishing such a class,
and for correlating a term of language with that by which the class is distinguished, is a certain minimum permanence of the members, and a
certain minimum stability of class-membership.

This permanence and this stability are established, if at all, by inductive
means at least as powerful as sub-predictive generalization. To illustrate,
consider the general term 'stoat'. In the assertion 'That's a stoat', made as
a rodent runs away ahead of us, use of 'stoat' involves the sub-predictive
generalization that what has the directly observable characteristics of a
stoat has the biography, hitherto, of a stoat. Use of 'A stoat swam across
the Thames' depends, among others, on the sub-predictive generalizations
that macroscopic volumes of relative impenetrability last an appreciable
time and change relatively slowly throughout that time, and, more specific
to the case of 'stoat', that 'being self-moving during its healthy waking life
hitherto' is a concomitant of whatever cluster of characteristics suffice for
the identification of this entity as a stoat.

To each possible use of a general term corresponds some such set of sub-
predictive generalizations: in general, to a different use corresponds a
different set.

These generalizations establishing the necessary stability and permanence of the class distinguished by a general term must hold over a substantial range of every dimension of their space-time segments. This is easily shown: the permanence requires extension in time directly; and extension in time, coupled with the possibility of rapid movement, and the wide limits within which spatial position is irrelevant to class membership, require extension in space.

Succinctly, applicability of a general term depends on the existence of a suitable stable class of relatively permanent entities. That there is such a class can be established only by sub-predictive generalization, or some stronger inductive method. So if any general term can be used, some inductive generalization is justifiable. The inductive generalization need only be sub-predictive, for a general term does not lose its utility as the world's end approaches.

From the strong thesis, the weak one: *Any use of the general term 'generalization established inductively' depends on at least one generalization established inductively*, follows as a special case. It can also be established independently, by production of a suitable example. One such is 'The silent thinker's memory is reliable in analytic matters'. For as 'inductively established generalization' is a general term it must be possible to distinguish real from merely apparent inductive results. And to do this the thinker will need to recall all the steps by which the analysis of the generalization is made, and then judge these steps by remembered criteria.

From either thesis it follows that Ā, the proposition that no generalization established inductively is justifiable, depends on just such a generalization. If true, it involves its own negation. So A, the proposition that at least one inductive generalization is justifiable, is indeed a principle of the type mentioned, viz. one whose truth is necessary to the possibility of its own denial.

Faced with this situation, a sceptic might make the even wider claim that the use of general terms is never proper. This claim is, however, afflicted with a like incoherence to that of Ā, for 'general term' is a general term.

Or he might react by attempting to eschew all inductive results. If all assertions concerning induction involve inductions, can one express suspicion of them Cratylus-wise, not by denying anything, but by refraining from their use?

The weak thesis, if true, does leave some room for manoeuvre to one who would avoid commitment to inductive procedures. He may merely refrain *ad hoc* from using the term 'inductively established generalization' and any other term for which it can likewise be shown that its use depends on such generalization; more generally, he may avoid all use of terms of the type of any term shown to carry the inductive involvement. He may, indeed, abandon use of all general terms, on the ground that if one can be shown to be tainted, none is safe; but he can never be forced by the weak thesis alone to this total renunciation.

The strong thesis, if true, leaves no such choice open. It requires that if commitment to inductive procedures is to be avoided, all use of general terms must be abandoned. Nor can any singular term be retained. To apply a singular term we must distinguish, by its properties, an individual to be its reference. And for the term applied to count as a genuine singular term, this individual must possess the stability and permanence which fit it for the application of general terms and hence, through re-identification, for repeated application of the singular term. Hence the use of a singular term involves the applicability to an individual of descriptions employing general terms. On the strong thesis, inductive generalizations can only be avoided by the abandonment of language in its entirety.

It is well known that one cannot act, or speak, without relying on inductively established results. The strong thesis shows that one cannot think without them either, and weak one, when extended to further particular cases, that such thinking would be gravely confined.

It is a consequence of either thesis that the general, unrestricted denial of the propriety of induction cannot coherently be made.

Scepticism concerning particular inductive procedures is proper and doubtless often warranted. The genuine problem of induction is that of finding criteria whereby acceptable procedures may be distinguished from unacceptable. There are instances of both types.

X

CAN THERE BE NECESSARY CONNECTIONS BETWEEN SUCCESSIVE EVENTS?

NICHOLAS MAXWELL

I

THE aim of this paper is to refute Hume's contention that there cannot be logically necessary connections between successive events. I intend to establish, in other words, not 'Logically necessary connections do exist between successive events', but instead the rather more modest proposition: 'It may be, it is possible, as far as we can ever know for certain, that logically necessary connections do exist between successive events.'

Towards the end of the paper I shall say something about the *implications* of rejecting Hume's contention.

It should perhaps be noted at the outset that Hume does not, in a sense, deny the *idea* of necessary connections between events: but he does deny the possibility of the objective existence of logically necessary connections between events. According to Hume the *idea* results from habit or custom after the observed frequent conjunction of two events. Thus he declares: 'Upon the whole, necessity is something that exists in the mind, not in objects . . . Either we have no idea of necessity, or necessity is nothing but that determination of the thought to pass from causes to effects, and from effects to causes, according to their experienced union.'[1] In other words we may, if we wish, hold that Hume does not reject, but merely gives an analysis of, the notion of 'necessary connection', but in this case we must admit that his analysis excludes the possibility of the existence of any kind of logically necessary connections between events. Looked at in this way, the main task of this paper is to analyse, or interpret, 'There exists a logically necessary connection between two successive events E_1 and E_2', in such a way that this statement cannot be refuted on *a priori* grounds.

From *British Journal for The Philosophy of Science*, vol. 19, (1968), pp. 1–25. Reprinted by permission of the author and Cambridge University Press.

[1] D. Hume, *A Treatise of Human Nature*, vol. I (London, 1911), 163–4.

It must be admitted of course that it is *propositions*, and not *events*, that can be logically related or connected, and hence that there is something ill-formed about the assertion 'There exists a *logically* necessary connection between E_1 and E_2'. In view of this I suggest that this statement is to be analysed as, or is to be interpreted to mean:

(1) At the time of occurrence of E_1 there exists that which can only be completely described by propositions, P_1, which logically imply propositions, P_2, that state that E_2 occurs subsequently.

The essential requirement here is that, at the time of occurence of E_1, there exists something, X say, which is such that *any* propositions which completely describe X, logically imply propositions which state that E_2 occurs subsequently. No one denies that propositions, P_3 say, which *incorporate* a description of what exists at the time of occurrence of E_1 can logically imply propositions which state that E_2 occurs subsequently. But if P_3 only *incorporate* a description of what exists at the time of occurrence of E_1, it is possible that, by whittling away at P_3, one can arrive at propositions, P_4 say, which (*a*) give just as complete a description as P_3 of what exists at the time of occurrence of E_1, (*b*) do *not* logically imply propositions which state that E_2 occurs subsequently. Thus the fact that propositions which *incorporate* a description of what exists at the time of occurrence of E_1 can logically imply propositions which state that E_2 occurs subsequently, does not suffice at all to establish the existence of a logically necessary connection between E_1 and E_2 in the sense of (1) above.

As far as I can see, (1) above successfully captures all that anyone could hope or want to mean by 'There exists a logically necessary connection between E_1 and E_2'. Granted the truth of (1), that which exists at the time of occurrence of E_1 determines the subsequent occurrence of E_2 with logical necessity, in the sense at the time of occurrence of E_1 there is that which exists—X say—which is such that *any* propositions which completely describe X logically imply propositions which state that E_2 occurs subsequently. The 'logical connection' is of course between the propositions P_1 and P_2, not between the events E_1 and E_2: nevertheless this 'logical connection' arises not merely as a result of the way in which we choose to think of, or describe, E_1 and E_2; it arises as a result of *that which exists* at the time of occurrence of E_1. In asserting (1) one makes an *existential* claim, namely that at the time of occurrence of E_1 there *exists* that which can be completely described only by propositions which logically imply propositions which state that E_2 occurs subsequently.

I assume here that Hume, in denying the possibility of the existence of logically necessary connections between events, would wish to deny the possibility of (1) being true, for any two successive events E_1 and E_2. In what follows I shall occasionally employ 'There exists a necessary connection between E_1 and E_2' as a shorthand expression for (1).

I turn now to a consideration of arguments, including Hume's, which may be deployed against the thesis that it is possible, conceivable, as far as we can ever know for certain, that (1) is true, for some pairs of successive events E_1 and E_2.

These arguments fall into three categories. In the first place it may be argued that (1) is *meaningless*. Secondly, it may be argued that (1) is analytically false, that it is not a conceptual possibility that (1) could be true. But finally it might be argued that (1) is analytically *true*. The point is that in asserting (1) of two events, E_1 and E_2, one is making an *existential* claim. If the thesis that it is possible that (1) is true is to amount to anything, then (1) must be interpreted in such a way that it is not true in any universe whatsoever, i.e. not analytically true.

One main argument employed by Hume can be dismissed without much discussion. Hume argues, essentially, that it cannot be meaningful to assert that there exists a necessary connection between two events E_1 and E_2 because there is no *impression* which could give rise to the *idea* of such a necessary connection. A basic tenet of Hume's *Treatise* is '*all our ideas are copied from our impressions*'.

In somewhat more modern terminology this argument might be presented as follows:

(*a*) Only those words (sentences) which can be given a phenomenalistic analysis, i.e. which can be analysed in terms of words (sentences) that refer to sense data, are meaningful.

(*b*) 'Necessary connection' as employed in the sentence 'There exists a necessary connection between E_1 and E_2' cannot be given such an analysis. Hence 'There exists a necessary connection between E_1 and E_2' cannot be meaningful.

I assume without discussion that no one today would wish to defend any such phenomenalistic criterion of meaning as (*a*) above.

Much of Hume's discussion concerning causation may be construed as a defence of the *epistemological* thesis that it is impossible *to know with complete certainty* that any particular observed event, which we describe perhaps as E_1, will be followed by an event that we describe as E_2. This *epistemological* thesis I accept without reservation: we must just admit that it is always possible, as far as we can ever know for certain, that things may suddenly cease to happen as we expect or predict. However this *epistemological* thesis does not imply that the *ontological* thesis 'There exist necessary connections between successive events' (where this is understood as in (1)) is false. These two theses are in fact perfectly compatible. For suppose the ontological thesis is true. Suppose that at the time of occurrence of a particular observed event E_1 there exists that which can only be completely described by propositions P_1 which logically imply a proposition P_2 that states that E_2 occurs subsequently. It is perfectly compatible with this to assert that at the time of occurrence of E_1 it is impossible to know for certain that E_2 will occur subsequently, for of course it may well be impossible to know for certain that P_1 is true.

I would wish in fact to argue that there is no empirical statement that can be known to be true with complete certainty. I support, in other words, Einstein's dictum: 'In so far as propositions refer to reality they are not certain: in so far as they are certain they do not refer to reality.'[2]

Briefly, then, the position defended here is this: (*a*) we cannot be certain that E_2, say, will follow a particular event we observe and describe perhaps as E_1; but equally (*b*) we cannot be certain that E_2 does not necessarily follow E_1 (in the sense of (1)).

Another argument, due to Hume, which may be deployed against the thesis that (1) is possibly true, runs, briefly, somewhat as follows. Given any two successive events, E_1 and E_2, it is always possible that E_1 should not be followed by E_2, possible in the sense that (*a*) we can imagine that E_1 is not followed by E_2, or (*b*) no contradiction is involved in asserting that E_1 is not followed by E_2. (In what follows the first criterion is ignored, since we are here concerned with *logical* necessity.) Since it is logically possible that E_1 is not followed by E_2, it cannot be logically necessary that E_1 is followed by E_2.

But *is* it always logically possible, given any two successive events E_1 and E_2, that E_1 should not be followed by E_2? *Is* the statement 'E_1 is not followed by E_2' invariably non-contradictory? Suppose E_1, that which exists at the instant in question, is such that any complete description, or specification, of E_1 logically implies propositions which state that E_2 occurs subsequently. Suppose that the meaning of 'E_1' is such that the statement 'E_1 occurs' logically implies some such statement as 'E_2 occurs subsequently'. In this case 'E_1 is not followed by E_2' *is* a logical contradiction. Of course no doubt if one gives only a certain kind of true descrip-

---

[2] Einstein's remark referred specifically to *mathematical* propositions: see A. Einstein, *Geometrie und Erfahrung*, Springer (Berlin, 1921), pp. 3–4.

tion of the two events—a description in terms of what the two events look like, for example—so that E_1 is described as 'E'_1', E_2 as 'E'_2', let us say, then it may well be that 'E'_1 is not followed by E'_2' is invariably non-contradictory. But *this* result does not establish the inconceivability of (1).

Clearly in order to show that (1) cannot possibly be true it is necessary to show that that which exists at any instant *cannot conceivably be such that* only propositions which logically imply some proposition which states that such and such occurs subsequently, can completely state what it is that exists at the instant in question.

This thesis may be defended as follows. Given any two successive events, E_1 and E_2, if a proposition, P_1, which is intended to be a description of E_1, logically implies that E_2 follows E_1, then 'P_1' must include some such statement as 'This event is followed by E_2' or 'E_1 is followed by E_2'. But 'E_1 is followed by E_2' cannot be interpreted as referring exclusively to what exists at the time of occurrence of E_1. 'E_2 follows E_1' refers to a *relational* property of E_1; it can no more be said to refer exclusively to what exists at the time of occurrence of E_1 than say 'A is to the left of B' can be said to refer exclusively to what exists at the place where A is. Hence (1) cannot possibly be true of any events.

My reply to this argument is as follows. There are at least two distinct ways in which 'event', 'object' and 'change' may be conceived, two conceptual schemes, which I shall call C_1 and C_2. The above 'relational' argument against the possibility of (1) being true is valid granted C_1, invalid granted C_2.

I shall give here only a brief, informal description of C_1 and C_2.

C_1 and C_2 may be contrasted as follows. C_1 is committed in the first instance to an ontology of 'events' or 'time-slices', statements about objects that persist and change being analysable in terms of, or reducible to, statements about successive 'events' or 'time-slices'. C_2, on the other hand, is committed in the first instance to an ontology of persisting, changing objects, statements about instantaneous events being reducible to statements about persisting, changing objects.

According to C_1 the universe is a sort of four-dimensional array of point-events. The ultimate entities of C_1 are point-events, and the ultimate properties are properties that can be ascribed to point-events. Just as there are *spatial* relations between point-events, such 'x is above y', so there are *temporal* relations between point-events, such as 'x is earlier than y'. (Of course both 'above' and 'earlier than' presuppose conventionally assigned 'directions', which may however be suggested by certain pervasive features of the array of point-events.) Just as spatial relations are the essence of Space, so temporal relations are the essence of Time.

Notions of 'object', 'persistence' and 'change' can be defined in terms of the above as follows. A homogeneous spatio-temporal array of point-events can be termed an 'object': objects are thus four-dimensional entities. If the object has a temporal length of t units, then the object 'persists' for those t units. If the point-events at one 'temporal end' of the object differ in a systematic way from the point-events at the other 'temporal end', then the object 'changes' in the interval t. At different moments or instants throughout t, there exist different temporal parts of the object just as different spatial parts exist at different places.

Granted this conceptual scheme one can, I think, legitimately argue that just as the spatial relation 'B is to the left of A' can scarcely be said to exist exclusively at the place where A exists, so the temporal relation 'E_2 is later than E_1' can scarcely be said to exist exclusively at the time of occurrence of E_1.

According to C_2 notions of 'persistence' and 'change' are of the essence of time, and are not derivable notions. Each presupposes the other. If something persists then something must change, for if there was no change, nothing would happen, there would be no 'passage of time', and hence no persistence. Again, if a thing changes then that thing must persist throughout the change. And even if it is simply the case that there are changes, without there being any one thing which suffers these changes, nevertheless a place must be identified throughout the changes, and this requires the persistence of *something*.

The ultimate entities of C_2 are objects which, by definition, persist and change. Ultimate properties of C_2, which are ascribable to objects, *presuppose the notions of persistence and change*. A description of an instantaneous event states what is true of *objects* at that instant; such a description thus presupposes the notions of persistence and change. In other words, whereas, in C_1, statements about persisting, changing objects presuppose statements about successive instantaneous events that do not involve the notions of 'persistence' and 'change', in C_2, *statements about instantaneous events presuppose statements about persisting changing objects*.

According to C_2, objects have spatial parts, but no temporal parts. Objects are three-dimensional, not four-dimensional, entities. Certainly objects persist and change; but to say this is not to say that objects are composed of their successive instantaneous states. It is not an object, but rather the *life-history* of an object, that is composed of the successive states of that object. And an object is not to be identified with its life-history.

It is, I think, clear that the ordinary commonsense way of conceiving the world presupposes C_2 rather than C_1. Physical things—tables, stones, birds, etc.—are clearly 'objects' in the sense of C_2 rather than C_1. 'Object' in the sense of C_1 we should ordinarily translate as 'life-history of an object'. Instead of thinking of an object as a spatio-temporal array of events (which presupposes C_1), we ordinarily think of an event as the instantaneous state of a number of persisting, changing objects (which presupposes C_2).

We tend however to think of 'Time' in spatial terms. This is perfectly compatible with C_2 if it involves no more than simply thinking of persistence/change, i.e. time, in *metrical* terms. But if it involves thinking of objects that persist and change as being *extended* in time, as being four-dimensional entities made up of temporal parts, then clearly thinking of time in spatial terms is completely inconsistent with C_2. The fact that we do tend to 'spatialize' time in this second sense explains much of our ordinary puzzlement about the nature of Time. Any picture of Time which has the Present moving up an extended time-line constitutes a hopeless, contradictory fusion of C_1 and C_2.

If one accepts C_2, the above 'relational' argument against the possible existence of necesssry connections between successive events, or states of affairs, is no longer valid, since the analogy between temporal and spatial relations collapses. I assume here that the world can legitimately be conceived in terms of C_2, and that physical theories can be formulated in terms of C_2.[3]

It may be objected: But if there is to be any change in the world, objects must have different properties, or be in different states, at different times. Now suppose an object, X, is in the state S_1 at time t, S_2 at time $t + dt$. Then any description of what exists at time t, which logically implies 'X is S_2 at time $t + dt$', must incorporate some such statement as 'X is ϕ at time t', where the *meaning* of 'ϕ' is such that an object is ϕ at time t only if it is S_1 at time t and S_2 at time $t + dt$. But here ϕ-ness is not the sort of property that can conceivably exist at an instant, that an object can conceivably have at an instant. That which exists at time t, and is described by 'X is ϕ at time t', is also described by 'X is S_1 at time t'. And this latter description does not logically imply 'X is S_2 at time $t + dt$'. Hence it is not the case that which exists at time t is such that any description of

---

[3] For a defence of what is, in effect, the thesis that the special theory of relativity is compatible with C_2, see W. Sellars, 'Time and the World Order', in H. Feigl and G. Maxwell, eds., *Scientific Explanation, Space and Time, Minnesota Studies in the Philosophy of Science*, vol. 3 (University of Minnesota Press, Minneapolis, 1962).

this logically implies 'X is S_2 at time $t + dt$'. In other words, *even if C_2 is presupposed*, (1) above cannot conceivably be true.

My answer to this argument is as follows. The above argument assumes that any statements of the form 'X is ϕ at time t', where these entail some statement about how X is, or is not, *changing* at time t, can invariably be reduced to a set of statements of the form 'X is S_0 at time t', 'X is S_1 at time t_1', 'X is S_2 at time t_2' ... where $t < t_1 < t_2 < ...$, and where not one of these statements, taken on its own, entails any statement about how X is, or is not, changing at the instant in question. The above argument assumes, in other words (to state the thing a little more generally), that any statement about an object that involves the notions of 'change' or 'persistence', can be reduced to, or translated into, a set of statements that attribute similar and dissimilar properties to the object at different times, where none of these statements, taken individually, involves the notions of 'change' or 'persistence'. *But it is precisely this assumption which must be rejected if C_2 is accepted or presupposed.* Within C_2, there are predicates applicable to objects which presuppose the notions of 'persistence' and 'change', and which cannot be reduced to predicates which do not presuppose these notions. The thesis that there are such predicates is absolutely essential to C_2. For the basic entity of C_2 is the 'object', which, by definition, 'persists' and 'changes'; and to say this is to say that to any object of C_2 a predicate can be applied which presupposes the notions of 'persistence' and 'change', and which cannot be reduced to predicates which do not presuppose these two notions.

At this point one might almost be tempted to conclude: If C_2 is incompatible with the above assumption, with the assumption, that is, that any predicates involving the notions of persistence and change can be reduced to predicates that do not involve these notions, then *so much the worse for C_2*. However, in the next section I shall defend a thesis, which I shall call 'dispositional realism', which entails that the above assumption is *false*.

One last remark about the distinction between C_1 and C_2. It has sometimes been suggested that the question of whether one accepts a basic ontology of 'events', or of 'changing persisting things' (i.e. whether one accepts C_1 or C_2), depends on, or is related to, the question of whether one's basic language is *tenseless* or *tensed*.[4] The two questions are however *entirely* distinct. How one answers the question: Are propositions basically *tensed* or *tenseless*? depends simply on what one chooses to mean by the term 'proposition'. If one chooses to employ the term 'proposition' in

[4] This suggestion has been defended at length by W. Sellars, see ibid.

such a way that a proposition can, with the passage of time, *change its truth-value*, then *tense* will indeed be basic and uneliminatable. According to this use of 'proposition', 'Harold Wilson is talking', for example, expresses, at different times, the *same* proposition: thus one and the same proposition can be true at one time, false at some other time. Attempts to eliminate the tense of 'Harold Wilson is talking' must fail, for such attempts will produce sentences of the form 'Harold Wilson is (tenseless) talking at time *t*'; and this sentence expresses *different propositions at different times*, granted the above interpretation of the term 'proposition'.[5]

One may, however, of course employ the term 'proposition' in such a way that propositions do not change their truth-value with the passage of time. In this case the sentence 'Harold Wilson is (tenseless) talking at time *t*' expresses *the same* proposition at all times, whereas 'Harold Wilson is (tensed) talking' expresses *different* propositions at different times. In this case tense can be eliminated simply by reformulating any tensed sentence so that the time to which the sentence refers does not depend on the time at which the sentence is uttered.

All this has nothing whatsoever to do with whether one accepts C_1 or C_2. For one accepts C_1 if and only if one accepts that all predicates which presuppose the notions of persistence and change can be reduced to predicates which do not presuppose these notions. And one accepts C_2 if and only if one rejects the above thesis.

The *temptation* to associate C_2 and C_1 with the above two theses about tensed propositions might arise in the following kind of way. On the one hand it is tempting to think that if the world consists, in the first instance, of persisting, changing objects, then, in the first instance, one's propositions must also persist and change, i.e. must change their time-reference and truth-value with the passage of time. But a consequence of employing the term 'proposition' in this kind of way is that tense cannot be eliminated from propositions. Thus C_2 becomes associated (for wholly fallacious reasons) with the thesis that tense cannot be eliminated. On the other hand it is also tempting to think that if one employs the term 'proposition' in such a way that propositions do not change their time-reference and truth-value with the passage of time (so that tense *can* be eliminated), then one is committed in the first instance to an ontology of 'events', or 'time-slices'. In this way the thesis that tenses can be eliminated becomes associated with C_1.

[5] For recent developments in 'tense logic' (which is based on the idea that a proposition can have different truth-values at different times), see A. Prior, *Past Present and Future* (Oxford University Press, 1967).

II

So far I have been arguing against objections to the thesis that it is conceivable that (1) is true, for some two events E_1 and E_2. In a sense, therefore, I have not yet said anything directly in support of the conceivability of (1). There remains the problem: Is it conceivable that that which exists at some instant is such that it can only be completely described by propositions which logically imply that some event occurs subsequently? In order to answer this question it will be convenient to examine whether or not the kind of descriptions we ordinarily give of things, and the descriptions of physics, could ever logically imply descriptions of subsequent states of affairs. Ultimately I hope to establish the conceivability of (1) by establishing that:

(*a*) It is conceivable that a *certain type* of realistic, comprehensive, deterministic physical theory is true.

(*b*) If a theory of this type is true, then (1) is true for successive states of affairs E_1 and E_2.

Although the ordinary descriptions we give of things do not logically imply descriptions of subsequent states of affairs, nevertheless such descriptions do carry implications about how the things described *change*. In describing something as 'solid', 'inflammable', 'soluble', 'magnetic', 'elastic', 'hot', 'heavy', 'soft', 'sticky', or 'brittle', for example, we not only attribute a property to that thing, but we also imply that the thing will, in certain circumstances, 'behave' or 'change' in certain definite ways. This applies also to such descriptions as 'stone', 'copper', 'water', 'salt', 'glass', 'petrol', 'oxygen', etc., in that such substances have certain properties, of the above type, *by definition*.

The point to note is this: It is not just a contingent matter of fact that, for example, solid objects are objects which do not pass effortlessly through each other. It is implicit in the *meaning* of the term 'solid' that one solid object does not pass effortlessly through another solid object. Similarly it is implicit in the *meaning* of the term 'inflammable' that an object which is inflammable, and which is exposed to a naked flame, itself bursts into flames. In other words, the meaning of the term 'inflammable' is such that 'X is inflammable at time t' and 'X is exposed to a naked flame at time t', taken together, logically imply 'X bursts into flame at time t'. Similar considerations arise in connection with the meaning of the other terms mentioned above, 'soluble', 'magnetic', 'elastic', etc.

There is, however, a very simple reason why statements of the above type, which attribute the above type of properties to objects at some instant, cannot logically imply statements which attribute properties to the objects at some subsequent instant. The reason is this: It is always a logical possibility that any object which possesses any property of the above type might suddenly and inexplicably cease to possess this property. A liquid that is inflammable at one instant might suddenly cease to be inflammable at a subsequent instant: a solid object might suddenly melt, evaporate, explode or vanish.

Of course in giving the above kind of descriptions of things we ordinarily presuppose that objects will not inexplicably vanish, petrol inexplicably cease to be inflammable, etc.; we presuppose that, in general, the above kind of properties will change only in the customary known ways. In fact a sort of general inter-related stability in the way in which properties persist and change is essential if the kind of descriptions we ordinarily give of things is to have any application at all. Inflammability, solidity, elasticity, etc., constitute properties that objects either do or do not possess only in the context of the hypothesis that these properties in general change and persist only in certain constant, inter-related ways. It is only because it is presupposed that in general an object only becomes or ceases to be inflammable under certain specific circumstances (e.g. when soaked in petrol or water) that an assertion such as 'X is inflammable at time t', where X is not exposed to a naked flame at time t, qualifies as a description of what exists at that instant. If nothing can be presupposed about the way in which the inflammability of an object does and does not change, then it would make, in a sense, no difference whatsoever whether one ascribed inflammability or non-inflammability to an object at a moment when it was not exposed to a naked flame, for whatever happened subsequently when the object was exposed to a naked flame, one could always argue that the object had become, remained, or ceased to be inflammable (as the case might be) in the intervening time.

The fact remains, however, that there is no precise, exceptionless, comprehensive hypothesis about the way in which such properties as inflammability, solidity, elasticity, etc., do and do not change incorporated explicitly in the meaning of the words 'inflammable', 'solid', 'elastic', etc. It is essentially for this reason that the ordinary descriptions we give of things cannot logically imply descriptions of subsequent states of affairs.

Nevertheless, the following at least can be maintained: The ordinary descriptions we give of things, the ordinary, commonsense way in which we conceive the world, presuppose that:

(2) There are irreducible properties, possessed by objects at an instant, which are such that any statement which attributes such a property to an object at a time *t* will, when combined with some further statement which merely states something about the state of affairs at time *t*, logically imply a statement about how the object is *changing* at time *t*.

I should perhaps add that this does not mean that *any* attribution of a 'disposition' to something constitutes ascribing a *property* to that thing. In saying of someone that he is a cigarette-smoker, for example, one says just that the person smokes cigarettes from time to time. It is not logically possible for a person to be a cigarette-smoker and never smoke a cigarette. 'X is inflammable', on the other hand, does not mean 'X bursts into flames from time to time'. An object may be inflammable even though it never bursts into flames.

I must now consider two possible objections to the claim that the ordinary descriptions we give of things presuppose thesis (2), or 'dispositional realism' as this thesis might be called.

In the first place it may be objected: An object or substance which is inflammable may not burst into flames when exposed to a naked flame for any number of different reasons: There may not be enough oxygen present; the object may be slightly damp; the flame may not be hot enough, etc. Hence the meaning of 'inflammable' cannot be such that 'X is inflammable at time *t*' and 'X is exposed to a naked flame at time *t*' *logically* imply 'X bursts into flames at time *t*'. Similar considerations arise in connection with all the other 'dispositional properties'—solidity, elasticity, etc.

But this argument simply exploits a certain *vagueness* in the meaning of 'inflammable'. In saying that an object is inflammable one might mean anything from 'If this object is heated to 6,000° C. in an atmosphere of pure oxygen, after an hour or so the object will show slight signs of oxidation', to 'The object ignites spontaneously at room temperature when exposed to the air'. In other words, the above objection no longer applies once a *precise* meaning has been assigned to 'inflammable'.

In the second place it may be objected: To ascribe inflammability or solidity, etc., to an object at some instant is not to ascribe a property to the object at that instant. Objects burst into flames or fail to ignite: but at those moments when they are not exposed to naked flames, objects do not possess some mysterious additional property of inflammability or non-inflammability. To assert 'X was inflammable at time *t*', assuming X was not exposed to a naked flame at time *t*, is to assert no more than 'If X had been exposed to a naked flame at time *t*, X would have burst into flames'. In this manner any reference to a property such as inflammability, solidity, elasticity, etc., can be eliminated. Thus despite appearances to the contrary, the statement 'X is inflammable' does not *really* attribute any property to X.

I shall now attempt to refute this thesis.

The first point to note is that the thesis leaves utterly obscure what *is* to count as an ascription of a property to an object at an instant. For presumably any statement that 'supports a counter-factual conditional', i.e. implies a statement of the form 'If such and such were the case, then such and such would happen', cannot, if the above thesis is accepted, be construed as a straightforward description of what exists. But any ordinary description of things, events, states of affairs, in the world, *will* support 'counter-factual conditionals'. Bereft of such statements as 'X is solid', 'X is heavy', 'X is hot', 'X is fluid', 'X is soft', etc., and 'X consists of water', 'X consists of copper', etc., one is left entirely in the dark as to what precisely *can* be attributed to objects at any given instant.

Here then is a major objection to the thesis that reference to dispositional properties can be eliminated. Interpreting 'X is inflammable at time *t*' to mean 'If X were exposed to a naked flame at time *t*, X would burst into flames at time *t*' does not help to eliminate reference to dispositional properties, because 'is exposed to a naked flame' and 'bursts into flames' are just as dispositional as 'is inflammable'. For example, the sudden appearance of a wavering light about an object does not mean that that object has burst into flames if the object is in no way changed or consumed with the passage of time.[6]

One obvious reply to this objection is that only those statements which ascribe properties to *sense-data* can qualify as irreducible descriptions of what exists at an instant. But this thesis is equivalent to phenomenalism, and there are well-known objections to phenomenalism, which I shall not discuss here.[7]

Granted that phenomenalism is untenable, the thesis that the ordinary descriptions we give of things do not presuppose (2) must, it seems, be rejected.

[6] That ordinary descriptive predicates are *dispositional* predicates, and presuppose the truth of laws or theories, has been repeatedly emphasized by Popper: see, for example, K. Popper, *The Logic of Scientific Discovery* (Hutchinson, London, 1959), pp. 422–6.

[7] For criticisms of phenomenalism, see, for example, J. J. C. Smart, *Philosophy and Scientific Realism* (Routledge and Kegan Paul, London, 1963), chapter 2; and W. Sellars, *Science, Perception and Reality* (Routledge and Kegan Paul, 1963), chapter 3.

But in any case, what possible reason can there be for holding that statements that incorporate dispositional terms should be reducible to statements that incorporate only non-dispositional terms? Why should it be thought desirable to be able to analyse any dispositional terms such as 'inflammable' in terms of purely non-dispositional terms?

One answer to this question might of course be the following: The basic descriptive terms should be such that it is always possible to verify or falsify conclusively whether a particular description is true of a particular object. But any description that incorporates a dispositional term cannot always be conclusively verified or falsified. 'X is inflammable', or 'X is solid', for example, cannot be conclusively verified or falsified at those times when X is not being tested for inflammability.

The simple answer to this is, of course, that *no* descriptions, however 'epistemologically basic', can be conclusively verified or falsified. Even on those occasions when X *is* being tested for inflammability or solidity, one still cannot conclusively verify or falsify 'X is inflammable' or 'X is solid', for this would require the conclusive verification of certain other descriptive statements which would in turn incorporate dispositional terms. It is only when certain low-level assumptions have been made about how relevant dispositional properties are correlated and conserved—assumptions presupposed by such 'basic' statements as 'X is a material object', 'X is water', 'X is copper', etc.—that any singular description such as 'X is inflammable at time *t*' can be verified or falsified. Assumptions about how dispositional properties are correlated and conserved can of course be tested individually: they cannot however be tested *en masse*, for then the whole machinery of testing would break down. No observation at one instant would have any relevance to any observation at any other instant, and the fully fledged Humean nightmare would be upon one.

Of course if one wishes to defend phenomenalism, if, in other words, one accepts a sort of updated version of Hume's thesis 'All our ideas are copied from our impressions', then the meaning of terms such as 'inflammable' will seem wholly obscure unless they can be defined phenomenalistically, and hence non-dispositionally. But once phenomenalism, and the above criterion of meaning, have been rejected, there seems to be no very good reason why it should be thought to be *desirable* to define dispositional predicates in terms of non-dispositional predicates.

There is perhaps one other reason why it might be felt that dispositional predicates require analysis in terms of non-dispositional predicates if they are to have any clear meaning. Dispositional predicates clearly presuppose the notions of persistence and change. From statements that attribute dispositional properties to objects at some time *t* one can deduce statements about how some object is *changing* at that instant. Further, it is only in the context of assumptions about how dispositional properties are correlated and conserved—i.e. in the context of assumptions about how dispositional properties persist and change—that it becomes meaningful to attribute dispositional properties to objects at all. It may be assumed however that any statement which ostensibly attributes a property to an object at some instant, but which presupposes the notions of persistence and change, ought to be analysable in terms of statements which attribute similar and dissimilar properties to the object at successive instants, where none of these statements, taken individually, involves the notions of persistence and change. But, as I remarked in the previous section, *it is precisely this assumption which must be rejected if C_2 is accepted.* In other words, if C_2 is accepted, one has no cause whatsoever to be disturbed by the fact that the ultimate properties of things are *dispositional* properties.

Despite the undesirability and impossibility of reducing dispositional terms to non-dispositional terms, various philosophers have persisted in the attempt. And as a result, what requires analysis is not so much the meaning of 'inflammable' etc. but rather the meaning of terms coined by philosophers in their attempts to analyse 'inflammable' etc.

In the first place, the whole 'problem' of 'subjunctive conditionals' or 'contrary-to-fact conditionals' or 'counter-factual conditionals' seems to have arisen simply as a result of a refusal to countenance the idea that, for example, 'X is inflammable at time *t*' might ascribe a property to X at time *t*, where the meaning of 'inflammable' is such that the above statement, together with 'X is exposed to a naked flame at time *t*', logically implies 'X bursts into flames at time *t*'. For if one insists that 'X was inflammable at time *t*' must be interpreted as 'If X had been exposed to a naked flame at time *t*, X would have burst into flames at time *t*', one then creates the problem of how this *latter* statement is to be analysed.

Some philosophers have argued that this so-called 'problem of counter-factual conditionals' is to be solved along the following lines: a counter-factual conditional makes an implicit appeal to a universal conditional, where this is to be understood as asserting 'nomic' as opposed to 'accidental' universality. According to this kind of view a statement asserts 'nomic' universality if it is a universal statement that meets certain 'logical and epistemic requirements'.[8]

But according to the position developed here, this sort of approach puts

[8] For this kind of quasi-Humean approach, see E. Nagel, *The Structure of Science* (Routledge and Kegan Paul, London, 1961), pp. 56–73.

the cart before the horse. For, according to the view defended here, the meaning of a counterfactual conditional such as 'If this object had been exposed to a flame at time t, it would have burst into flames', at least under one legitimate interpretation, *poses no problem whatsoever*; the statement means simply 'This object was inflammable at time t (and was not exposed to a naked flame at time t)'. Hence, if the terms 'nomic universality' and 'counterfactual conditional' are linked analytically, if in other words 'A statement that asserts nomic universality supports counterfactual conditionals' is *analytic*, then 'nomic universality' should be analysed in terms of 'counterfactual conditional' and not the other way round. This can be done very simply as follows.

Consider for example the following statement:

(3) All the screws in Smith's car are rusty.

If this statement is interpreted as asserting 'accidental' universality only, it can be written as:

(4) (x) $((x$ is a screw & x is in Smith's car$)$ $\supset$ x is rusty$)$.

If (3) is interpreted as asserting 'nomic' universality, then it can be written as:

(5) $(x)(x$ is a screw $\supset$ x is R$)$

where 'R' is a predicate such that 'x is R at time t' and 'x is in Smith's car at time t' together logically imply 'x is rusty at time t'. (Here R-ability is a property analogous to inflammability or rustability: 'R-able' and 'rustable' differ of course because, roughly speaking, it is exposure to Smith's car, not to air and water, that rusts an R-able object.)

It is I hope clear that (5) asserts 'nomic' universality because it supports counterfactual 'If this screw were in Smith's car at time t it would be rusty at time t', where this means simply 'This screw is R'. (4) on the other hand asserts only 'accidental' universality because it does not support this counterfactual conditional. Any assertion of (3) would of course be interpreted as asserting only 'accidental' universality, simply because no one wishes to attribute the property R to screws.

This interpretation of the term 'nomic' universality is not put forward as the only conceivable interpretation: it is put forward simply as a legitimate interpretation, granted that there is the above analytic tie-up between 'counterfactual conditional' and 'nomic universality'. In particular it must be stressed that the phrase 'asserts nomic universality', as employed here, is not intended to be equivalent to 'is a law-like statement', or 'asserts a physical law'. Clearly a statement that asserts nomic universality must satisfy further conditions before it can be called a physical law: one might, for example, stipulate that a physical law can contain no reference, explicit or implicit, to a particular object or a particular spatio-temporal region.

It may, however, be held that any reasonable interpretation of 'nomic' universality must be such that asserting nomic universality constitutes, if not a sufficient, then at least a *necessary* condition for a statement to be a physical law. And, it may be held, there are many universal statements which we wish to regard as statements of physical laws, which do not assert 'nomic' universality in the above sense.

Consider, for example, Newton's law of gravitation. If this asserts 'nomic' universality then it supports the following kind of counterfactual conditional:

(6) If this object had been over there during the interval $\varDelta t$, then it would have moved in accordance with Newton's law.

But this statement, according to the above interpretation, is equivalent to attributing a dispositional property—gravitational charge—to the body during the interval $\varDelta t$ in question. Hence Newton's law of gravitation can only be interpreted as asserting 'nomic' universality if it is interpreted as attributing the dispositional property of gravitational charge (proportional to mass) to all bodies. But this interpretation amounts to the kind of 'essentialist' interpretation defended for example by Cotes, but rejected by Newton himself. And although Newton rejected this interpretation, he clearly did not regard the law of gravitation as asserting 'accidental' universality only. How then can one interpret a law as asserting 'nomic' universality, in the above sense, if the law is not given an 'essentialist' interpretation, i.e. if it is not interpreted as ascribing a dispositional property to objects?

The answer to this question is, I suggest, as follows: a law which is not, for one reason or another, given the above type of 'essentialist'[9] interpretation may nevertheless justifiably be interpreted as asserting 'nomic'

---

[9] By 'essentialist' interpretation of a law I mean only that the law is interpreted as attributing a dispositional property—such as gravitational charge—to objects of a certain kind.

universality, in the above sense, as long as it is held to be conceivable that there is an essentialist law which entails or replaces the first law. Newton, for example, did not reject essentialism as such; he merely rejected as unacceptable the dispositional property of gravitational charge. Any theory which entailed or replaced the law of gravity, and which attributed dispositional properties to corpuscles which did not involve the notion of 'action at a distance', and which supported the counterfactual (6), would have been, it may be presumed, entirely acceptable to Newton.

To this it may be objected: But to insist that physical laws should assert 'nomic' universality in this sense is to commit physics to 'essentialism' in an important sense, even if not all acceptable physical laws are required to be essentialistic. But there are overwhelming objections to committing physics to 'essentialism' in this way. Hence physical laws cannot be required to assert 'nomic' universality in the above sense.

In reply to this objection I shall make just two comments.

(a) If there are overwhelming objections to committing physics to 'essentialism', then what the above discussion has shown is that in a perfectly straightforward, entirely legitimate, sense of 'nomic universality', physical laws do not assert nomic universality.[10]

(b) However, in the next section I shall in effect argue that there are no general objections to committing physics to an essentialistic programme.

III

In the last section I argued that statements that attribute dispositional properties to objects at some time t can logically imply statements about how some object is *changing* at time t. Further, I argued that it is only in the context of assumptions about how such dispositional properties are correlated and conserved—i.e. in the context of assumptions about how such dispositional properties persist and change—that it becomes meaningful to attribute dispositional properties to objects at all. It was maintained however that ordinary descriptions of objects at some instant cannot logically imply descriptions of subsequent states of affairs because there are no *precise, comprehensive, exceptionless* assumptions about how dispositional properties persist and change incorporated explicitly in the meaning of the terms which refer to these properties. Thus statements which ascribe

---

[10] It might be noted that if there is a perfectly straightforward (but non-Humean) sense in which only 'essentialist' laws can assert 'nomic' universality, there is also a perfectly straightforward (but non-Humean) sense in which only 'essentialist' laws can qualify as *explanatory* laws.

inflammability, solidity, etc., to objects cannot logically imply statements about subsequent states of affairs because it is always *logically possible* that the objects might suddenly and inexplicably cease to be inflammable, solid, etc.

This suggests that in order to arrive at propositions which both qualify as descriptions of what exists at one instant and logically imply descriptions of what exist at subsequent instants, it will be sufficient to formulate a precise, comprehensive hypothesis about how things do and do not change, a comprehensive deterministic physical theory, in other words, which is explicitly incorporated in, or presupposed by, the meaning of the terms of the hypothesis in question.

More precisely, I suggest that in order to establish the conceivability of (1), it will be sufficient to establish that it is conceivable that that which exists at some instant is such that only propositions which incorporate terms whose meanings presuppose the truth of some comprehensive deterministic physical theory, can completely describe that which exists at the instant in question.

No one denies of course that it is conceivable that propositions, **P** say, which specify (*a*) relevant deterministic physical laws, (*b*) so-called initial conditions, at some instant, can logically imply propositions, P_2, which describe some subsequent state of affairs. But to acknowledge the conceivability of *this* is not to acknowledge the conceivability of (1), for of course the propositions P merely *incorporate* a description of what exists at the instant in question. The propositions P specify, not just the initial conditions, but also physical laws. In order to establish that (1) is conceivable, it is necessary to establish that it is conceivable that propositions, P_1, which specify or describe no more than the initial conditions can logically imply propositions, P_2, which describe some subsequent state of affairs. Or, more precisely, in order to establish that (1) is conceivable, it is necessary to establish that it is conceivable that that which exists at some instant—the initial conditions—is such that only propositions which incorporate terms whose meanings presuppose the truth of a comprehensive, deterministic physical theory can completely describe that which exists at the instant in question.

In order to clarify precisely what it is that I am proposing here, let us suppose that the world consists entirely of spherical, perfectly elastic particles, which interact by means of three kinds of forces, gravitational, 'electrical', and elastical. Suppose that the following somewhat crude Newtonian, atomistic, comprehensive physical theory, T, is true. The postulates of T are as follows:

(i) If a material has elasticity E (with Young's modulus = Y, Poisson's ratio = σ, Y and σ being specific constants), then:

(a) $F = \dfrac{Y \cdot \varDelta L \cdot A}{L}$, where L is the unstressed length of a rectangular rod of the material, $\varDelta L$ is the increase in length corresponding to a force F, A = unstressed area of cross-section of the rod, and Y = Young's modulus

(b) $\dfrac{\varDelta w}{w} = -\dfrac{\sigma \cdot \varDelta L}{L}$, where w and L are the unstressed width and length of a rectangular rod of the material, $\varDelta w$ is the decrease in width corresponding to an increase in length $\varDelta L$, and σ = Poisson's ratio.

(ii) For any two particles with charges $\pm q_1$, $\pm q_2$

$$F = \frac{(\pm q_1) \cdot (\pm q_2)}{d^2}$$

(iii) For any two particles with masses m_1 and m_2

$$F = \frac{G \cdot m_1 \cdot m_2}{d^2}$$

(iv) $\overline{F} = m \cdot \bar{a}$

(v) If two forces $\overline{F}_1$ and $\overline{F}_2$ act on a body, then the resultant force $\overline{F} = \overline{F}_1 + \overline{F}_2$.

(vi) Any particle of mass m, charge $\pm q$, unstressed radius r, elasticity E, interacts with any other particle with mass m, charge $\pm q$, unstressed radius r, elasticity E in such a way that m, $\pm q$, r, E remain constant.

(vii) The world consists entirely of particles mass m, charge $\pm q$, unstressed radius r, elasticity E.

Granted that T is true, then propositions, formulated in terms of T, which specify initial conditions, which describe what exists at any instant, will be of the following type: 'At x,y,z,t, there is a particle, mass m, charge $+q$, elasticity E, velocity v, which is a sphere of radius r when unstressed, but whose present shape and size is such and such'. Now suppose that that which exists at some instant is such that it can only be completely described if the descriptive terms employed, e.g. 'E', 'm', 'q', *presuppose the truth of the postulates* (i)–(vi) of T. Suppose, in other words, that that which exists at some instant is such that it can only be completely described in terms of T if the meaning of the terms 'E', 'm', 'q' are interpreted in such a way that the postulates (i)–(vi) of T are *analytic* statements. In this case a complete description of what exists at some instant, formulated in the terms of T, will presuppose the truth of postulates (i)–(vi) of T, and will thus logically imply descriptions of subsequent states of affairs. In other words, that which exists at some instant will be such that any set of propositions which gives a complete description of this will logically imply propositions which describe subsequent states of affairs.

It should be noted that the fact that the postulates (i)–(vi) of T are analytic does not mean that T itself is analytic, for of course (vii) is non-analytic. The entire empirical content of T is contained in the postulate (vii). (In what follows 'T' is to be understood in such a way that the postulates (i)–(vi) are *analytic* statements.)

Terms of T such as 'mass', 'elasticity', ' "electrical" charge', and 'gravitational charge' are intended to be analogous to such ordinary observational terms as 'inflammability', 'solidity', 'solubility', etc., in that they are intended as *descriptive* terms, as terms that can be used to ascribe a property to an object, to describe what exists at some instant. Of course a T-term differs from any ordinary observational term in that the meaning of a T-term presupposes the truth of a precise, comprehensive theory, whereas the meaning of a term such as 'inflammability' presupposes the truth of only some extremely limited and imprecise theory. I wish to argue, however, that this difference does not justify one in maintaining that only observational terms, and not also highly theoretical terms such as those of T, can be descriptive, in the above sense.

I must now consider some objections to the thesis that (*a*) a physical theory such as T is conceivable, and (*b*) if such a physical theory is conceivable, then (1) is conceivable, or possibly true.

In the first place it may be argued that a physical theory that ostensibly postulates and describes certain unobservable, theoretical entities cannot be interpreted as *really* postulating and describing these entities, at least in so far as the theory is considered as a theory of *physics*. The job of a physical theory is to predict observable results of experiments, and this becomes possible only when the theoretical terms of a theory have been related to, or interpreted in terms of, observational terms by means of 'correspondence rules'. Thus a physical theory is 'about', not the theoretical entities it ostensibly postulates and describes, but rather the observable results that it predicts. Hence propositions, formulated in terms of the uninterpreted theoretical terms of a phsyical theory, that ostensibly describe initial conditions, cannot be regarded as really describing anything at all. Only propositions formulated in terms of observational terms can be interpreted as describing initial conditions, i.e. something that does actually exist.

There is not space for me here to give a reply to this objection. I shall assume, without discussion, that there is no valid, *general* objection to giving a tentatively realistic interpretation to physical theories.[11] I shall assume that a physical theory such as T, formulated entirely in 'theoretical' terms, unrelated to any 'observational' terms by means of 'bridge' statements, or 'correspondence rules', can legitimately be interpreted as *really* postulating and describing the entities that it *ostensibly* postulates and describes. I assume, in other words, that 'theoretical' terms of physics, in addition to 'observational' terms, can be interpreted as *descriptive* terms, as terms intended to refer to entities or properties conjectured to exist.[12] On this view, 'bridge' statements, connecting 'observational' and 'theoretical' terms, constitute synthetic *identity* statements: they assert that certain observational entities or properties are, as a matter of contingent fact, certain theoretical entities or properties.[13]

Granted that there are no valid, general objections to interpreting a physical theory such as T realistically, it may nevertheless be objected that it is not conceivable that the particles, postulated by T, could have, at any given instant, the kind of properties attributed to them by T. At most, it is conceivable that these particles could have, at any given instant, properties attributed to them by a theory T', where T' is similar to T in every respect except that at least some of the postulates (i)–(vi) are synthetic, not analytic. But propositions, formulated in terms of T', that describe initial conditions, that state what exists at some instant, cannot alone logically imply descriptions of subsequent states of affairs. Hence even if it is granted that it is conceivable that a true, realistically interpreted, deterministic, comprehensive physical theory can be formulated, this does not guarantee that (1) is conceivably true.

My reply to this objection is as follows. If T' is interpreted realistically then it follows *analytically*, from what one means by 'realistic interpreta-

---

[11] Of course in *particular* cases there may well be valid objections to interpreting a physical theory realistically: many valuable physical theories, if interpreted realistically, become incompatible with other accepted physical theories, or internally inconsistent.

[12] One main objection to the thesis that *in general* physical theories cannot be interpreted realistically is that this thesis depends on the possibility of making a *general*, *precise*, *non-arbitrary* distinction between theoretical and observational terms, and no such distinction is, it seems, possible. One main reason why it is *desirable* to interpret physical theories realistically is this: there is an important sense in which only an 'essentialist'—and hence realistic—theory can be an *explanatory theory* (see above, n. 10).

[13] For two recent accounts of 'bridge' statements along these lines, see K. F. Schaffner, 'Approaches to Reduction', *Philosophy of Science*, vol. 34 (June 1967), pp. 137–47; L. Sklar, 'Types of Inter-Theoretic Reduction', *British Journal for the Philosophy of Science*, vol. 18 (1967), pp. 109–24.

tion', that at least some of the postulates of T′ are analytic. For in asserting that T′ is interpreted realistically, one is asserting that T′ postulates the existence of, and ascribes properties to, particles of unstressed radius r. Clearly T′ must attribute some kind of property to the particles if they are to be differentiated from empty space. Let us suppose that T′ attributes elasticity E to the particles. But the assertion that a certain particle has elasticity E (with Young's modulus = Y, Poisson's ratio = σ) must imply that that particle 'obeys' the postulates (ia) and (ib). And this in turn implies that (ia) and (ib) are *analytic* statements, since the meaning of 'elasticity E' presupposes the truth of (ia) and (ib). Furthermore the *meaning* of 'elasticity E' must presuppose the truth of some 'conservation' postulate concerning elasticity, for if the elasticity of a particle varied in an arbitrary manner, it would be meaningless to attribute elasticity E to that particle at some instant.

To this it might be objected that in attributing the dispositional property of elasticity to the particles, one might not mean anything so precise as that the particles 'obey' (ia) and (ib). One might mean simply that when the particles collide, they rebound, momentarily altering their shape.

But what possible justification can there be for maintaining that at any instant an object can only have a somewhat *vague* dispositional property? How could one decide whether a given dispositional property is sufficiently vague to be capable of existing at an instant? Clearly the thesis that 'elasticity E' is too precise a dispositional property to be capable of being possessed by a particle at an instant, must be rejected.

Once it is acknowledged that a particle can have the dispositional property of elasticity at an instant, what justification can there be for denying that the particles can have the dispositional properties of mass, 'electrical' charge and gravitational charge? If a particle can have, at an instant, a property which can only be referred to if (i) constitutes an *analytic* statement, why should not the particles have, at an instant, properties which can only be referred to if (ii)–(vi) are analytic statements?

In short, once it is granted that T can legitimately be interpreted realistically, there can be no more reason for denying that the particles, postulated by T, can have, at any given instant, the dispositional properties of elasticity, mass, 'electrical' charge and gravitational charge, than there can be for denying that petrol can have, at any given instant, the dispositional property of inflammability, or diamond the dispositional property of solidity.

As I have already remarked, the fact that the postulates (i)–(vi) of T are analytic does not mean that T itself is analytic, for of course (vii) is a non-analytic statement. It is true that if T is to be a falsifiable theory, then non-analytic 'bridge' statements must be added to T. But these 'bridge' statements may be regarded as falling within the province of postulate (vii), since they state, when taken together, that all the various observational entities and properties known to exist are in fact certain combinations of entities and properties postulated by T. In other words the 'bridge' statements may be regarded as a partial, but falsifiable, rendering of the statement: The world consists entirely of particles of mass m, charge $\pm q$, unstressed radius r, elasticity E. Clearly T can be a falsifiable theory even though postulates (i)–(vi) are all analytic.

There is a sense in which T, if it were true, would provide an ultimate explanation of phenomena, an explanation whose basic premises could themselves require no further explanation. But, it may be objected, the task of theoretical physics can never be completed in this kind of way, for at any level there must always remain further legitimate theoretical problems to be solved. Hence it would be extremely bad policy for the physicist to formulate any theory analogous to T in the above respect. T, for methodological reasons, must be characterized as a non-scientific, metaphysical theory.[14]

But even if T is true, and does, therefore, provide an ultimate explanation of phenomena, this could never be known for certain. Thus even if T meets with complete empirical success, it will still be desirable for physicists to attempt to refute T, to attempt to devise theories which are not refuted where T perhaps is refuted. One could not be certain, however, that such a programme would meet with success. Just as no one can ever be certain that the 'ultimate', true physical theory has been formulated, so equally no one can be certain that the 'ultimate', true physical theory will never be formulated. I conclude that it would not be methodologically inadvisable for the physicist to formulate a theory analogous to T, supposing such a thing were possible.

A somewhat different objection to the thesis that the truth of T implies the truth of (1) is the following. Suppose a true, comprehensive description, D, of the universe is given in terms of T at some instant. Then D cannot logically imply a description of any subsequent state of affairs, for it is always logically possible, given the truth of D, that entities should suddenly 'pop' into existence and interact with the particles described by D.

---

[14] Popper, for example, has argued that ultimate, or what he calls 'essentialist', explanations ought to be excluded, for methodological reasons, from science; see K. Popper, *Conjectures and Refutations* (Routledge and Kegan Paul, London, 1963), pp. 104–7.

This objection can be met if T is reformulated so that it, in effect, attributes dispositional properties to space, i.e. if T reformulated as a field theory. For if any point of empty space has the property that an entity can exist there only if it is a particle postulated by T, which moves in accordance with the 'laws' of T, then at no point in space can an entity suddenly 'pop' into existence. A comprehensive description of the universe at some instant would not logically permit entities to 'pop' into existence at subsequent instants.

Finally it might be objected that if the argument of this section is accepted, then for any two successive events E_1 and E_2, in any universe whatsoever, (1) will be true, since it must always be possible to formulate propositions P_1 which constitute a description of what exists at the time of occurrence of E_1, and which logically imply propositions P_2 which state that E_2 occurs subsequently. But if (1) is *analytically* true, (1) cannot be interpreted as making an *existential* claim.

My reply to this is as follows. If the propositions P_1 (*a*) are to qualify as constituting no more than a description of what exists at t_1, the time of occurrence of E_1, and (*b*) are to imply logically P_2, then, at some level, P_1 must attribute, to entities at t_1, dispositional properties which cannot, by definition, change. In other words P_1 must incorporate terms which (*a*) ascribe dispositional properties to entities at t_1, (*b*) are such that it follows analytically, form the meaning of these terms, that the dispositional properties in question do not change. (Derivative dispositional properties may of course change. But, at some level, the manner and circumstances in which these dispositions change must not themselves change; and this implies the existence of higher-level unchanging dispositional properties.) Clearly, unchanging dispositional properties cannot be truly ascribed to objects in any universe whatsoever.

IV

Finally, what are the *implications* of rejecting Hume's contention? This question really needs another paper. I can here do little more than indicate what seem to me to be the implications of rejecting Hume's thesis.

When one first reads Hume one is inclined to conclude, considerably shocked, that if Hume's arguments concerning the notion of 'necessary connection' are correct, then:

(7) There can be no rational grounds for the belief that the orderliness, regularity, or *lawfulness* that has been found in the world so far will persist in the future.

(8) Any orderliness, regularity, or lawfulness that does persist must be utterly inexplicable, must be something for which there can be no explanation whatsoever.

Hume's arguments can seem to imply this because one assumes that:

(9) There can only be rational grounds for the belief that past lawfulness will persist in the future if it is rational to believe that that which exists at one instant determines, with logical necessity, what exists subsequently.
(10) There can only be a genuine explanation of observed, persistent regularities if that which exists at one instant determines, with logical necessity, what exists subsequently.

It has often been pointed out, however, that Hume's contention does not entail (7) and (8) above. For if Hume's contention is *true*, then it is *meaningless* to assert 'That which exists at one instant determines, with logical necessity, what exists subsequently'. In other words the stipulations (9) and (10) become *meaningless*. One must therefore revise one's notions of what can constitute necessary conditions for (*a*) rational grounds for the belief that past regularities will persist in the future, (*b*) an explanation of persistent observed regularities.

On the other hand, if Hume's contention is *false*, then the stipulations (9) and (10) are no longer meaningless. Thus the need to revise one's notions of what can constitute necessary conditions for (*a*) and (*b*) above collapses. Both (9) and (10) become legitimate assumptions. And it seems to me that if (9) and (10) *can* be accepted then they certainly *ought* to be accepted.

In short, once one rejects Hume's contention concerning necessary connections, then one must reject also those quasi-Humean theses whose acceptability depends on the *validity* of Hume's contention. It seems to me that quasi-Humean accounts of nomic universality, scientific explanation, and (*a*) and (*b*) above all fall into this category.

NOTES ON THE CONTRIBUTORS

BERTRAND RUSSELL, who died in 1970, was without doubt the most fertile and influential philosopher of the present century.

PAUL EDWARDS, a Professor in the Department of Philosophy of Brooklyn College, in the City University of New York, is perhaps best known as editor-in-chief of *The Encyclopedia of Philosophy* (1967).

WESLEY C. SALMON is a member of the Department of the History and Philosophy of Science at Indiana University. He is the author of *The Foundations of Scientific Inference* (1966).

STEPHEN F. BARKER, a Professor in the Department of Philosophy of Johns Hopkins University, is the author of *Induction and Hypothesis* (1957) and *The Philosophy of Mathematics* (1964).

HENRY E. KYBURG JR. is a Professor in the Department of Philosophy at the University of Rochester. Among other books he is the author of *Probability and the Logic of Rational Belief* (1961) and *Probability and Inductive Logic* (1970).

J. O. URMSON is a Fellow of Corpus Christi College, Oxford. His writings include *Philosophical Analysis* (1956) and *The Emotive Theory of Ethics* (1968).

JOHN W. LENZ is a member of the Department of Philosophy of Brown University.

R. B. BRAITHWAITE was Knightbridge Professor of Moral Philosophy in Cambridge from 1953 until his retirement in 1967. His book *Scientific Explanation* was published in 1953.

MAX BLACK is a Professor at Cornell University. Among his writings are *Problems of Analysis* (1954), *Models and Metaphors* (1962), and *A Companion to Wittgenstein's Tractatus* (1964).

PETER ACHINSTEIN is a colleague of S. F. Barker at Johns Hopkins University. His book *Law and Explanation* was published in 1971.

KEITH CAMPBELL, author of *Body and Mind* (1971), is a member of the Department of Philosophy at the University of Sydney.

NICHOLAS MAXWELL is a member of the Department of the History and Philosophy of Science at University College, London, and a member of the committee of the British Society for Philosophy of Science.

BIBLIOGRAPHY

(not including material in this volume)

For an account of and extensive bibliography on the criteria for the correctness of inductive arguments, which we use in practice, see:

1. Swinburne, Richard *An Introduction to Confirmation Theory* (Methuen, London, 1973).

For Hume's original presentation of the sceptical position, see:

2. Hume, David, *An Enquiry Concerning Human Understanding* (first published 1748) (Clarendon Press, Oxford, 1902), especially sections 4 and 5.

For an elementary modern introduction to the problem, see:

3. Skyrms, Brian, *Choice and Chance* (Dickenson, Belmont, California, 1966), chapters 1 and 2.

For useful extended modern discussions, see:

4. Ayer, A. J., *Probability and Evidence* (Macmillan, London, 1972), especially pp. 3–26.
5. Blackburn, Simon, *Reason and Prediction* (Cambridge University Press, Cambridge, 1973).
6. Salmon, Wesley C., *The Foundations of Scientific Inference* (University of Pittsburgh Press, Pittsburgh, 1967), chapters 1, 2, and 3.

For Popper's scepticism about induction and his attempt to give an account of the activity of the theoretical scientist which does not suppose that he makes inductive inferences, see:

7. Popper, Karl R., *The Logic of Scientific Discovery* (Hutchinson, London, 1959).
8. Popper, Karl R., *Conjectures and Refutations* (Routledge, London, 1963), chapter 10.
9. Popper, Karl R., 'Conjectural Knowledge: My solution of the Problem of Induction', *Revue Internationale de Philosophie* No. 95–6, (1971), pp. 167–97. Republished as chapter I of his *Objective Knowledge* (Clarendon Press, Oxford, 1972).

10. Watkins, J. W. N., 'Hume, Carnap, and Popper' in Lakatos, I. (ed.), *The Problem of Inductive Logic* (North-Holland, Amsterdam, 1968), pp. 271–82.

11. Lakatos, I., 'Changes in the Problem of Inductive Logic' in Lakatos, I. (ed.), *The Problem of Inductive Logic* (North-Holland, Amsterdam, 1968), pp. 315–417.

12. Swinburne, R. G., 'Popper's Account of Acceptability', *Australasian Journal of Philosophy*, vol. 49 (1971), pp. 167–76.

For the analytic justification of induction, in addition to the articles by Edwards and Barker in this volume, see:

13. Black, Max, *Language and Philosophy* (Cornell University Press, Ithaca, 1949), chapter 3.

14. Moore, Asher, 'The Principle of Induction', *Journal of Philosophy*, vol. 49 (1952), pp. 741–7.

This was answered by:

Brodbeck, May, 'An Analytic Principle of Induction', *Journal of Philosophy*, vol. 49 (1952), pp. 747–50,

To which Moore replied in:

Moore, Asher, 'The Principle of Induction (II): A Rejoinder to Miss Brodbeck', *Journal of Philosophy*, vol. 49 (1952), pp. 751–8.

15. Strawson, P. F., *Introduction to Logical Theory* (Methuen, London, 1952), chapter 9 (II).

16. Goodman, Nelson, *Fact, Fiction, and Forecast* (Bobbs-Merrill, Indianapolis, 2nd edn., 1965), pp. 59–66.

For criticism of the analytic justification, in addition to the articles by Urmson, IV, and by Salmon in the Symposium, III, in this volume, see chapter 2 of Skyrms (No. 2 above) and also:

17. Salmon, Wesley C., 'Should we attempt to justify induction?', *Philosophical Studies*, vol. 8 (1957), pp. 33–48.

For the inductive justification of induction, in addition to the articles by Braithwaite and Black in this volume, see:

18. Will, Frederick L., 'Will the future be like the past?', *Mind*, vol. 56 (1947), pp. 332–47.

19. Black, Max, *Problems of Analysis* (Routledge, London, 1954), chapter 11.

For criticisms of Black's approach, in addition to the articles by Achinstein in this volume, see Salmon in No. 15 and

20. Johnsen, Bredo C., 'Black and the Inductive Justification of Induction', *Analysis*, vol. 32 (1972), pp. 110–12

21. Kasher, Asa, 'On the puzzle of self-supporting Inductive Arguments', *Mind*, vol. 81 (1972), 277–9.

For the original formulation of the distinction, often referred to in pragmatic justifications, between justification as validation and justification as vindication, see:

22. Feigl, Herbert, 'De Principiis non disputandum . . .?' in Black, Max (ed.), *Philosophical Analysis* (Cornell University Press, Ithaca, New York, 1950), pp. 119–56.

For Reichenbach's original formulation of the pragmatic justification, see:

23. Reichenbach, Hans, *Experience and Prediction* (University of Chicago Press, Chicago, 1938), chapter 5.
24. Reichenbach, Hans, *The Theory of Probability* (University of California Press, Berkeley and Los Angeles, 1949), chapter 11.

For Salmon's developed version of Reichenbach's solution, see his article, IV, in this volume.

For criticism of the Reichenbach–Salmon pragmatic justification, in addition to the article by Lenz in this volume, see:

25. Black, Max, *Problems of Analysis* (Routledge, London, 1954), chapter 10.
26. Black, Max, *Models and Metaphors* (Cornell University Press, Ithaca, New York, 1962), chapter 11.

For attempted 'vindications' of induction along lines similar to those of Salmon see:

27. Ellis, Brian, 'A Vindication of Scientific Inductive Practices', *American Philosophical Quarterly*, vol. 2 (1965), pp. 296–304.
28. Clendinnen, F. John, 'Induction and Objectivity', *Philosophy of Science*, vol. 33 (1966), pp. 215–29.
This was answered by:
   Jackson, Frank, 'A Reply to "Induction and Objectivity" ', *Philosophy of Science*, vol. 37 (1970), pp. 440–3.
Clendinnen replied in:
   Clendinnen, F. John, 'A Response to Jackson', *Philosophy of Science*, vol. 37 (1970), pp. 444–8.
Jackson replied to this reply in:
   Jackson, Frank, 'Reply to a Response', *Philosophy of Science*, vol. 37 (1970), pp. 449–51.

29. Black, Max, 'The Raison d'être of Inductive Argument', *British Journal for the Philosophy of Science*, vol. 17 (1966), pp. 177–204
30. McGowan, R. S., 'Predictive Policies', *Proceedings of the Aristotelian Society*, *Supplementary Volume* 41 (1967), pp. 57–76

This was answered by:

Sloman, Aaron, 'Predictive Policies', *Proceedings of the Aristotelian Society*, *Supplementary Volume* 41 (1967), pp. 77–94

31. Hunt, G. M. K., 'A Conditional Vindication of the Straight Rule', *British Journal for the Philosophy of Science*, vol. 21 (1970), pp. 198–9.
32. Madden, Edward H., 'Hume and the Fiery Furnace', *Philosophy of Science*, vol. 38 (1971), pp. 64–78.

For description of an imaginary world where inductive inference would not work, see:

33. Black, Max, *Problems of Analysis* (Routledge, London, 1954), chapter 12.

For description of a tribe whose 'criteria of rationality' are very different from ours see:

34. Winch, Peter, 'Understanding a Primitive Society', *American Philosophical Quarterly*, vol. 1 (1964), pp. 307–24.

INDEX OF NAMES

(not including authors mentioned only in the Bibliography)

INDEX OF NAMES

(not including authors mentioned only in the Bibliography)